Lausanne

THEODORE BEZA

THEODORE BEZA

THEODORE BEZA

The Counsellor of the French Reformation

1519–1605

by

HENRY MARTYN BAIRD

AUTHOR OF
'HISTORY OF THE RISE OF THE HUGUENOTS OF FRANCE,'
'THE HUGUENOTS AND HENRY OF NAVARRE,' AND
'HUGUENOTS AND THE REVOCATION OF THE EDICT OF NANTES'

THE BANNER OF TRUTH TRUST

THE BANNER OF TRUTH TRUST

Head Office
3 Murrayfield Road
Edinburgh, EH12 6EL
UK

North America Office
PO Box 621
Carlisle, PA 17013
USA

banneroftruth.org

First published in 1899

First Banner of Truth edition 2022

ISBN
Print: 978 1 80040 302 4
Epub: 978 1 80040 303 1
Kindle: 978 1 80040 304 8

*

Typeset in 11/14 pt Minion Pro at
The Banner of Truth Trust, Edinburgh.

Printed in the USA by
Versa Press, Inc.,
East Peoria, IL

CONTENTS

INTRODUCTION

SOME plants flourish in the shade of mighty trees. If the mighty trees of the Protestant Reformation in Europe were Martin Luther and John Calvin, the likes of Philip Melanchthon, Pierre Viret and Theodore Beza flourished remarkably in their company.

Too often the 'adjutants' have been neglected. However, in recent years, perhaps because of discussions about the Reformation and subsequent reformed scholasticism, interest in the 'Reformers in the wings' has gained momentum. This encourages giving them their due as major actors in the magisterial Reformation. Development of the Reformed faith in France would not have known the surprisingly rapid expansion it did in the 1560s had it not been for the evangelistic efforts of Viret and Beza, functioning as a Genevan 'expeditionary force.'

In the author's preface, written more than a century ago, Henry Martyn Baird comments on the absence of a detailed accessible biography of Beza. This comment holds good today, and justifies the republication of this book.[1]

[1] Shaun D. Wright's *Theodore Beza: The Man and the Myth* (Fearn, Ross-shire: Christian Focus, 2015) has a biographical chapter and presents Beza's main writings.

Baird was one of the great experts on French Protestantism in his day. As a young man he spent eight formative years in Paris and Geneva and then a further two in Italy and Greece, before graduating from Princeton Theological Seminary in 1856.

Baird's historical knowledge and writing on the Huguenots was highly respected. As well as this work on Beza he wrote a *History of the Rise of the Huguenots of France* (2 vols, 1879), *The Huguenots and Henry of Navarre* (2 vols, 1886), and *The Huguenots and the Revocation of the Edict of Nantes* (2 vols, 1895). All of these retain their interest and usefulness.

Beza, ten years Calvin's junior, was born in 1519 at Vézelay in Burgundy. It was a place of pilgrimage—claiming to have relics of Mary Magdalene—and a Benedictine watering hole on the route to Compostela, Spain. Like Calvin, Beza was a jurist and a humanist before his conversion. Called to work with Viret at Lausanne, he subsequently became rector at the University of Geneva and Calvin's right-hand man. He also had close links with the nobility of Navarre and was the mentor of the future king of France, Henry IV, a link he maintained until his death, even after Henry's ('Paris is worth a mass') conversion to Romanism.

Baird traces Beza's ups and downs, successes and failures, joys and sorrows, as he stepped up to the challenge of being the spiritual guide to a growing, persecuted, and then oppressed church. He continued this calling through to the Edict of Nantes in 1598, which granted limited freedom to French believers, and until his death in 1605.

Of particular interest in this biography are Baird's translation of Beza's speech to the French court during the Colloquium at Poissy in 1561, his remarkable work on the French Psalter completing the work of Clément Marot, his moderation at the La Rochelle Synod of the French Reformed Church in 1571, his reaction to the St Bartholomew's Day Massacre a year later, and his literary production (including the Greek New Testament, his Treatises on Secular Power, on Predestination, on the Lord's Supper, his Life of Calvin and the *Icones*—a portrait gallery of Protestant worthies).

Shortly before his death Calvin passed on the *Post tenebras lux*[2] torch to Beza with the injunction 'Hold to true doctrine.' Beza stepped into the shoes of his mentor as the spokesman of French Protestants in the diaspora, and the figurehead of a refugee church. Because those believers were a minority church, faced with error, opposition of the powers that be, and the attacks of the adversary, Beza's work remains a model of faithfulness under duress for believers worldwide in comparable situations today.

PAUL WELLS
March 2022

[2] 'After darkness light.'

AUTHOR'S PREFACE

It is not a little surprising that there seems to be no life of Theodore Beza accessible to the general reader either in English or in French. In German there is, it is true, a satisfactory biography by Heppe, written for the series of the 'Lives and Select Writings of the Fathers and Founders of the Reformed Church,' edited by Hagenbach, besides a masterly work undertaken by that eminent scholar, J. W. Baum, on a much larger scale, but unfortunately left incomplete at his death. Both biographies, however, were published many years ago, and by Baum the last forty years of the activity of Beza are not touched upon at all.

Yet of the heroes of the Reformation Theodore Beza is by no means the least attractive. His course of activity was long and brilliant. He presided over the Reformed Church in the French-speaking countries through a protracted series of years, its recognised counsellor and leader in times of peril both to Church and to State. The friend of Calvin, he was also the friend and adviser of Henry IV until within five years of that monarch's end. Thus his permanent influence can scarcely be exaggerated. Moreover, his career was rich in incidents of dramatic interest. Certainly no more impressive and romantic scene can be found in the history of the period than the appearance of Beza at the Colloquy of Poissy, when for the first time Protestantism secured a hearing before the King and royal family, its advocates not being forced upon their unwilling notice, but, on the contrary, formally invited to set forth the reasons for its existence and for its separation from the Roman Catholic Church.

The history of Protestantism in France could not be written with the part played by Beza omitted. The author has therefore had not a little to say of him in his *History of the Rise of the Huguenots* and in his *Huguenots and Henry of Navarre*.[1] But the protagonist in the drama of the French Reformation merits separate treatment, and a thorough knowledge of the man and of his work requires a development of his life and actions that could find no place in a general history.

For the facts I have gone back to the original sources, most of all to Beza's own autobiographical notes and to his letters. An indefatigable writer, Beza has left us a great mass of correspondence, much of it of historical importance. A portion of that which he judged to be of most permanent value in its bearing upon theological subjects saw the light during his lifetime, first separately and afterwards in his collected theological works, entitled *Tractationes Theologiæ*. I shall have frequent occasion to draw upon these. Of his correspondence more strictly historical in interest, down to and including the Colloquy of Poissy, Professor Baum gathered a large store in the documentary appendices of his biography. Professor Baum had also, many years

[1] New York: Charles Scribner's Sons, 1879, 1886.

since, copied with his own hands, but not utilised, several hundred letters still preserved in the libraries of Geneva, Zurich, Basel, etc. These copies have recently become the property of the French Protestant Historical Society and been added to that society's rich collections in Paris. Most of these letters have never been published. I have been able to secure for my book many interesting facts and illustrations derived from this source.

Besides his letters, I have made great use of Beza's extended treatises contained in the collection already referred to. The original chronicles and memoirs of the time, including the *Histoire Ecclésiastique des Églises Réformées*, erroneously attributed to Beza himself, but undoubtedly composed under his general supervision, have been my guide throughout the narrative. For the titles of most of these works I refer the reader to the appended Bibliography.

As in my earlier histories, so it is now again both a duty and a pleasure to express my gratitude to Baron Fernand de Schickler and Mr N. Weiss, president and secretary respectively of the French Protestant Historical Society, for many acts of kindness and for valuable help in my later researches. I owe to the courtesy of Mr Ferdinand J. Dreer, of Philadelphia, the facsimile of an interesting letter of the Reformer, now in his rare collection of manuscripts.

Henry Martyn Baird
New York University,
September 15, 1899.

THEODORE BEZA

CHAPTER 1

CHILDHOOD AND YOUTH

1519–1539

THE leaders of the great Reformation differed from one another as distinctly in personal traits as in the incidents of their lives and the work which they were called to perform. Theodore Beza, whose career and influence I purpose to trace, did not possess precisely the same remarkable natural endowments that fitted Martin Luther and John Calvin for the accomplishment of their brilliant undertakings, but in a different sphere his task was of scarcely inferior importance, and was accomplished equally well. Like Melanchthon, he belonged to another and not less essential class of men whose great office it is to consolidate and render permanent what has been begun and carried forward to a certain point of development by others. But between Beza and Melanchthon there was a marked contrast of allotted activity. Melanchthon was born fourteen years later than Luther, and survived him by the same number of years. He was, therefore, a younger contemporary of the great German Reformer, and his office was preëminently that of supplementing what seemed naturally lacking in the master whom he loved and revered, moderating that master's inordinate fire, by his prudence restraining the older Reformer's intemperate zeal, by his superior learning and scholarship qualifying himself to become in a peculiarly appropriate sense the teacher of the doctrines which Luther had propounded. Beza was still nearer to Calvin in point of birth, for only the space of ten years separated them. But he outlived Calvin more than four times that number of years, and ended his life at over fourscore, and early in another century. Thus while Melanchthon is naturally to be regarded as a companion of Luther, Beza presents himself to view chiefly as a theological successor of Calvin, in whose doctrinal system he introduced little change and which he merely accentuated, and as an independent leader of the French Reformed Churches during over a third of a century.

More, perhaps, than any of the other prominent leaders of the great religious movement of his time Beza is entitled to be styled the 'courtly Reformer.' Sprung from the ranks of the old French nobility, a man for whom access to the favoured circle of the powerful and opulent was open from earliest youth, with wealthy connections, nurtured in ease and in the prospect of preferment, into whatever department of Church or State he might elect to enter, he manifested in his bearing, his manners, and even in his language the effects of association upon equal terms with the best and most highly educated men of his time. This was an advantage that widened the sphere of his influence, both at the court of Charles IX and at that of Henry IV.

The members of the family from which he sprang wrote their name *De Besze*. Theodore himself so wrote it to the end

CHURCH OF SAINT MARY MAGDALENE, AT VÉZELAY.

of his days, save when he gave it the Latin form of Beza. The family was of old Burgundian stock. Theodore's birthplace was the town of Vézelay, now a decayed and insignificant place of somewhat less than twelve hundred souls. Situated about one hundred and fifty miles southeast of the capital of France, it continues in its obscurity to carry on a limited traffic in wood, grain, and wine, the wood being obtained in the extensive forest of Avallon and being sent down the river Yonne, to supply in part the needs of Paris and its environs. Even in the sixteenth century, Vézelay lived chiefly on memories of its past distinction. In attestation of former greatness, it pointed with pride to a famous abbey church dedicated to Saint Mary Magdalene. The ruins still crown a hill overlooking the town, and even now arouse the curiosity and elicit the admiration of such visitors as, from time to time, turn aside from the beaten ways of travel to more secluded paths. Hard-by is still pointed out the spot where, on Palm Sunday, in the year 1146, the Second Crusade was preached by Bernard, the celebrated Abbot of Clairvaux. The slope of a hill at the gate of the place was occupied on that famous occasion by a throng of lords and knights, of ecclesiastics and persons of every station, too numerous to be contained by any building, all of whom were attracted to Vézelay by the fame of the eloquence and piety of the future saint. Upon the great platform erected at the base of the hill sat Louis VII, King of France, and near him the orator who divided with his Majesty the attention of the vast concourse of spectators. Here it was that, at the close of Bernard's fervid appeal for Palestine, just bereft of the flower of its possessions by the fall of the city of Edessa, not only the lords almost to a man, but Louis VII himself and his wife Eleanor of Guyenne, begged the privilege of attaching the symbol of the holy cross to their garments and of joining the crusade soon to set forth to rescue from the polluting foot of the infidel the land once made holy by the tread of the Son of God.[1]

Nearly four centuries had elapsed from the day on which Vézelay resounded with the cries of '*Deus vult! Deus vult!*' interrupting Bernard's address, when, in 1519, on Saint John Baptist's Day, the 14th of June, Old Style, or the 24th, New Style, was born the future French Reformer. He was a son of Pierre de Bèze, the *bailli* of the place. Vézelay, having lost its importance in other respects, still retained the honour of being the seat of a royal officer bearing this designation. The position was as honourable as it was influential. Pierre de Bèze had married Marie Bourdelot, also of noble descent, by whom he had had six children before the birth of Theodore—two sons and four daughters. Her kinsmen, as well as his, were persons of prominence. Nicholas de Bèze, brother of Pierre, was a counsellor or judge of the Parliament of Paris, the highest judicial body in France. Being wealthy, unmarried, and of an affectionate disposition, Nicholas would gladly have had all the children of Pierre brought to his house in the capital, there to be reared under the most favourable circumstances; nor would he have spared either trouble or expense. Theodore subsequently styled him the 'Mæcenas' of the family. Another brother, having entered the Church, possessed, as Abbot of Froidmont, the means

[1] Michaud, *Histoire des Croisades*, ii, 125 *seq.*; Mills, *History of the Crusades*, 120.

of rendering himself no less serviceable to the promotion of the interests of his nephews. Evidently if Theodore should fail of promotion either in Church or in the judicial career, it would not be from the lack of strong family connections.

There must, it would seem, have been something particularly winning in Theodore, the youngest child in a family of seven children; for he had not emerged from infancy when his uncle, the member of the Parliament of Paris, being on a visit to the *bailli* of Vézelay, conceived so strong an admiration and affection for the child that he begged to be allowed to take him back with him to the capital. The father consented. The mother at first demurred, but afterwards yielded reluctantly in deference to her husband's command. She insisted, however, on accompanying her little son to Paris, where she left him. Nor did she long survive the enforced separation from her child. Theodore, who in after years set it down as a singular mark of the divine goodness that he had been born of such a mother, praises, and apparently not without sufficient reason, both the intellectual and the moral endowments of Marie Bourdelot. To extraordinary nerve and dexterity she added great kindliness of heart. Her attention to the wants of the poor was assiduous. They repaid her untiring solicitude with a sincere love.

It was no ordinary misfortune for Theodore to be separated from, and shortly after deprived altogether of, such a mother and at a so tender age. He was but a puny child, of so weakly a constitution that he barely walked at five years of age. When this dangerous stage was passed, his physical ailments seemed only to increase. At one point in his childhood he became the victim of a malady so painful that he was once, when crossing one of the bridges over the Seine, about to throw himself into the river for the purpose of ending his life and his misery in a single moment.

Such are some of the incidents that have come down to us in regard to Beza's childhood and for which we are indebted to the autobiographical notices inserted in a letter prefaced to his *Confession of the Christian Faith*. The letter was addressed to Melchior Wolmar, a distinguished scholar, to whom, under God, the future Reformer owed, more than to father or mother, that training both of the intellect and of the affections which qualified him for the great part he was to play in the affairs of Church and State.[2]

Melchior Wolmar was born in ancient Suabia, or in what now constitutes the southerly part of the kingdom of Würtemberg, at the little town of Rottweil. Following an uncle, Michael Röttli, to Bern, in Switzerland, he became first pupil, then successor of his kinsman in a Latin school which the latter had founded. Thence Wolmar passed to Fribourg, and a year or two later to Paris. Extreme indigence did not prevent him from gratifying his taste for study, and he gave himself so ardently to the mastery of the Greek language, under the guidance of Nicholas Bérauld and other competent instructors, that of one hundred young men that came up for the degree of licentiate at the University, his name was the first upon the list of the successful candidates. The pleasures or honours of the capital were not so attractive to him as to detain him long on the banks of the Seine, or, more probably, Wolmar's leaning toward Protestant views was too pronounced to make a sojourn

[2] This letter is given in translation in the Appendix.

at Paris either comfortable or safe. Thus it was that, about the year 1527, he established at Orléans a school for youth which soon obtained a considerable degree of popularity. A few boys were received into the family of the founder.[3]

It was perhaps a year after this time that Beza's uncle happened to entertain at his house in Paris a relation residing in Orleans. The guest was a man of high position, being a member of the king's greater council. In the course of the meal, noticing Theodore, who was present, a boy nine years old, he remarked that he had himself a son of about the same age, whom he had placed with a certain Wolmar. So highly did he praise the learning and abilities of this foreigner that, on the instant, Beza's uncle, who had never before heard of Wolmar, declared his intention to take the rare opportunity and to send his nephew to Orléans. He begged that Theodore might be a companion of his guest's son. He would make no account of the opposition which all the rest of the family made to the plan. It is almost needless to say that, when, many years later, Beza reviewed the circumstances from the standpoint of a Protestant and a Protestant leader, he could not but regard the impulse that led his uncle on the spur of the moment to send him away from the University of Paris, long since regarded as the most august educational establishment of the world, to a school newly started in a province by a stranger, as a signal exhibition of the direct interference of God. He styled the day on which he reached Wolmar's house at Orléans—it was the 5th of December, 1528—his second nativity; for it was the point in his life from

[3] See Herminjard, *Correspondence des Réformateurs dans les Pays de Langue Française*, ii., 280, 281, note.

MELIOR (MELCHIOR) WOLMAR
FROM BEZA'S 'ICONES'

which was to be reckoned the beginning of every advantage he received. Never has pupil more enthusiastically admitted the instructor of his boyhood into the company of men whose pictures he affectionately cherishes in his memory, than did Beza insert the portrait of Wolmar in the gallery of worthies which, many years later, he gave to the world with words of high praise. Judging from the profile there sketched, the eminent scholar's appearance indicated the strength of the mind that lay within. The forehead was high and prominent, the nose slightly aquiline, the eyes full of life, the mouth small but firm.[4]

Melchior Wolmar was no longer an obscure man. About 1530 he was invited by the good Princess Margaret of Angoulême, sister of Francis I and grandmother of Henry IV, to be one of that band of eminent scholars with whom she surrounded herself in Bourges, the capital of her duchy of Berry. When Wolmar accepted the call, young Theodore Beza went with him to continue his studies.

If the autobiographical letter which we print in the Appendix fails to supply us with a complete list of the branches the boy pursued under his beloved teacher, his words afford a sketch which the reader's imagination may readily fill out. The teacher was painstaking and gave himself unreservedly to his pupils. He found in Beza a mind fired with a desire to learn. If the natural sciences were few and imperfectly understood at that time, the literature of ancient Rome and Greece was a treasury upon which students might draw without stint. It would have been difficult

[4] See Beza's *Icones*. The book is not paged and the portraits are not numbered.

for a lad of even moderate ability to be constantly under the faithful instruction of any respectable teacher for seven years without acquiring great familiarity with the classical tongues. Under so admirable a humanist as Wolmar, and so unselfishly devoted to his little group of ambitious youth, Beza and his companions gained a command of both Latin and Greek such as few men in our times can claim to possess. To Beza Latin became as familiar as his mother tongue. He used it ever afterwards readily, correctly, and effectively, as one needed to be able to use it who was to speak before kings and the most cultured of audiences. The two languages at once became the key to unlock the treasures of knowledge laid up in past ages. It was no hyperbole in Beza's mouth to say that there was not a branch of learning, even to jurisprudence, into whose mysteries he was not at least partially initiated under the guidance of an instructor who held himself rather a friend and companion in study than a distant and austere pedagogue. Best of all, in Beza's view, Wolmar had not neglected the religious welfare of his pupils, and had imbued them with the knowledge of true religion drawn from the word of God, thereby giving him a claim to their imperishable gratitude.

Yet Theodore Beza was certainly at this time no ardent convert in whom clear convictions of truth had been immediately succeeded by overmastering convictions of duty and by a determination to renounce all selfish plans in favour of a life of voluntary consecration to a Master whose service he henceforth joyfully espoused. This assertion is abundantly proved by his life for the next ten years. Fully as he may have accepted, and doubtless did accept, the word of God as authoritative, and sincerely as he rejected in his heart, and purposed at some future and convenient season to repudiate openly, such doctrines of the Roman Catholic Church as he had learned to be unscriptural, along with the rites which he now viewed as absurd and superstitious, he was by no means ready as yet to make the sacrifices which the frank acceptance of the 'new faith' demanded. If his intellect approved the creed in attestation of which many humble men and women—carders, weavers, and the like—cheerfully suffered martyrdom in France about this time, counting the present life as insignificant and valueless in comparison with the life eternal, Beza was still to wait many a year before reaching such a condition of mind and heart as was theirs. The present life with its pleasures and ambitions occupied both mind and heart pretty fully as yet.

It is interesting at this point to notice that there was another youth destined to be a leader in the Protestant Reformation whose life was equally, possibly even more deeply, affected by contact with Melchior Wolmar. This was the young student from Noyon, Jean Calvin, who also sought to profit by the German instructor's great familiarity with the Greek language. His residence was not a protracted one. He arrived after Wolmar had removed to Bourges, and he was very shortly recalled home by the death of his father. Whether the two pupils, Beza and Calvin, were at this time brought into relations of close intimacy, is not clear. The disparity of their ages may well have kept apart the young man of twenty-two and the boy of twelve, but the elder not less than the younger imbibed the views of their common teacher. It is in fact the statement of one of the most inveterate enemies of the French Reformation, that it was owing to a direct suggestion of Wolmar that the young Calvin abandoned the study of the Code of Justinian to apply himself to the study of theology, and that this was the beginning of that career which was to prove the source of countless damage to the Christian Church. Wolmar, although feigning to be a Catholic, was, says this writer, a means of instilling into Calvin the Lutheran poison, with which Calvin during his own lifetime in turn infected many thousands of souls to their eternal ruin.[5]

Calvin's stay with Wolmar was suddenly brought to an end, as has been stated. That of Beza was terminated, four or five years later, by Wolmar's return to Germany. Recalled to his native land, Wolmar would gladly have taken with him his promising student, but Beza's father resolutely declined to grant his permission, and insisted that Theodore should retrace his steps to the city of Orleans, there to devote himself to the mastery of civil law.

As the son obeyed reluctantly (May, 1535), so he found no great pleasure in his new task. The study of the law pursued without intelligent method, and taught, as it appeared to him, in a barbarous manner, inspired him, not with admiration, but with aversion. Consequently, while not neglecting his legal studies, he began to devote a considerable, possibly the greater, part of his time to polite letters, and found a singular delight in both Greek and Latin authors. It should be remembered that the French tongue was as yet rude. France had thus far produced few writers of genuine literary

[5] Florimond de Ræmond, *Historia de Ortu, Progressu et Ruina Hæreseon hujus Sæculi*, ii, 434, 435 (lib. vii, c. 9).

merit. There was little in contemporaneous literature to divert Beza from the perusal of the masterpieces of ancient Athens and Rome.

Poetry, in particular, attracted him greatly. He appreciated the verses of the poets of a bygone age, and it was no difficult thing for a youth of his tastes and station to imagine himself born to be a poet. Nor indeed was he altogether mistaken. Whatever may be said of the use to which he at first applied his poetical abilities, and however much those abilities, when subsequently employed in the service of religion, have, especially in our age, been studiously underrated,[6] it will be seen in the sequel that while Beza was possessed of no genius calculated by its scintillations to arouse the enthusiastic admiration of the world, his poetical gifts were of no mean rank. It is no accident that the 'battle-psalm' of the Huguenots, so well adapted to be sung at the charge, as it was so often sung during the course of whole centuries, was not from the pen of the facile and timid Clément Marot, but from the pen of Theodore Beza, his resolute and more thoroughly convinced collaborator in the preparation of the Huguenot psalter.

The time for writing the Protestant battle-psalm and such serious compositions, however, was as yet in the distant future, then to be composed under the play of strong and serious views of life. For the present his poetical gifts led Beza to associate himself with a select band of young men of similar tastes, all inclined to unite the study of the law with the more seductive pursuit of the Muses. They

[6] Notably by M. O. Douen in his *Clément Marot et le Psautier Huguenot* (Paris, 1878–79, 2 vols.).

were some of the most cultured and learned members of the University of Orleans, men who, when at a later date Beza was beginning his remarkable career as a Reformer in Switzerland, had already secured high honours in the land upon which Beza's conscientious convictions had compelled him reluctantly but deliberately to turn his back.

What the poems were that Beza wrote at this period, we shall examine a little farther on.

Four years elapsed from the date when Beza parted from Wolmar—four years of a decorous and blameless life spent in the society of honourable and scholarly men—when, in August, 1539, his stay at Orleans came to an end. He had been promoted to the degree of licentiate in law, and he left the university on the banks of the Loire to return to Paris. Let it not be imagined that the training he had received at Orleans even in the matter of law had been insignificant in its bearing upon his subsequent course, nor that he had failed to exhibit that wonderful power of acquisition which characterised his subsequent efforts in every other department of knowledge. Of his great popularity with his fellow-students, there is evidence enough in the circumstance that 'the nation of Germany'—the scholastic division into which, as a native of Burgundy, he was admitted—selected him to be its head under the title of 'procurator.' As such not only did he preside over the internal affairs of the students of his 'nation,' but, with the other nine procurators, had a vote in the university council even in such important matters as the election of the rector of the institution.[7]

[7] Heppe, *Theodor Beza*, 8.

CHAPTER 2

BEZA IN PARIS
1539–1548

THEODORE BEZA had lately entered upon his twenty-first year when, having further literary or professional studies in view, he returned to the French capital. His prospects and his mental attitude deserve notice. He was a man of leisure, well provided with friends, possessed of abundant means of present support, and apparently the master of a secure future. His uncle, the member of the judicial Parliament of Paris, the best friend of his childhood, had indeed been dead for seven years; but his father's other brother, the Abbé de Froidmont, was still alive and was not less attached to him than the judge had been. Theodore was in the enjoyment of the revenues of two rich benefices amounting together to about seven hundred gold crowns. His friends had made this weighty provision for him in his absence and despite the fact that he was not in orders, and, according to his own admission, as ignorant as any other layman could possibly be of all matters of a clerical nature. As if this were not enough, his good uncle had fully made up his mind that Theodore should succeed him in his abbey, worth, at the very least, five thousand gold crowns a year. Besides this, Theodore's eldest brother, so infirm in body that his life was despaired of, held certain other ecclesiastical benefices. There was every reason to believe that these would ultimately go to swell Theodore's income.

In short, the young man was surrounded with every allurement to a life of ease and comfort. Relatives and connections of the family by marriage were alike disposed to further his desires; while other friends, whose favour was conciliated by the reputation he had already gained and by the predictions made of his future distinction, stood ready to applaud and congratulate. Whether he should select the Church or the Bar, his success seemed equally assured.

In his reminiscences of the period of his life now in question, Beza informs us that at this very time he was conscious that all these advantages were but snares laid for his feet by the powers of evil, with the view of preventing him from choosing the path which his inner convictions prompted him to enter upon. He had, that is to say, long since formed the resolution that, so soon as he should find himself master of himself and possessed of a certain competence, he would leave France. He would make his way to Germany, rejoin his old preceptor, and, in society with Wolmar, enjoy the liberty of professing his conscientious convictions, even at the sacrifice of more brilliant worldly prospects.

Meanwhile, however, there was little to show that he had not renounced the hopes kindled within him by the words and example of Wolmar. Without giving a loose rein to dissipation or riot, and while living what was regarded as an exemplary life for a young man of station, wealth, and brilliant expectations, he was quite content to devote the ease conferred upon him by his position to the pursuit of the Muses and to whatever literary studies his fancy might dictate.

Such a life, however, was as far from meeting the legitimate ambition of his father, as it was from satisfying the demands of conscience. Consequently, the next few years were in reality as full of struggle and discontent as they might have been supposed replete with satisfaction and quiet. A brief sketch of Beza's experience at this time is fortunately left us in a letter written by him to an old comrade at Dijon. When he returned from Orléans, Theodore says to his friend, his father looked to his devoting himself at once to the practice of the legal profession. Unfortunately the very thought of such a life inspired him with disgust. The 'palais,' or parliament-house, seemed a house of bondage; to enter its walls was to become a bondman for whom there was no hope of escaping a hateful drudgery.[1] As much as the father insisted, so much the son resisted, urging, not without reason, that his previous training, not to speak of the natural bent of his mind, disqualified him for the lucrative but repulsive profession to which he was urged. Apparently the disputes between father and son were frequent, protracted, and animated. They were ended, or at least adjourned, through the intercession of Beza's elder brother. Unable to oppose the united entreaties of his two sons, the father became less obdurate, and domestic harmony was finally restored by a compact on these terms: that the two brothers should hire for themselves a house at common expense, and that, while the elder should devote himself to the family affairs, the younger should enjoy his liberty to study.

[1] Beza to Pompon, Paris. July 19, s. a. [*sine anno*, without year] Baum, i, 91.

'Accordingly,' says Beza, 'I lived one year and then a second in by far the most blessed manner, since I lacked neither leisure, nor any kind of teachers, nor abundance of means, nor, in fine, the inclination to master those studies which, as you know, have pleased me supremely.'

The untimely, if not altogether unexpected, death of his brother broke rudely in upon Beza's delight. This blow recalled to the father's mind his former purposes regarding his son, and caused him again to insist upon a final renunciation of the scholarly life to which Theodore had hitherto devoted himself.

'I am weighed down,' said Pierre, 'by a great mass of affairs, and have reached an advanced age. It is but just and fair that you, my son, upon whom all my hopes are fixed, should assume the burden. Yield at length and consult your own best interests and the interests of your friends, and give up those empty and profitless studies which you have pursued for so many years.'

Theodore, however, was not convinced that the path urged upon him was that which he ought to take, and resisted with great determination. Conscious of the possession of abilities for which the life of routine in a profession which he detested offered no scope, he felt that to yield would be to make shipwreck of all higher aspirations. In this he was doubtless encouraged by the judgments which his associates had passed upon his literary powers, although not even their most sanguine anticipations could have forecast the particular sphere of his brilliant successes. It is difficult, however, in view of the great part which Beza was destined to play in the religious and political history of the sixteenth century, to close our eyes to the providential guidance of his mind and will in the strenuous opposition which he instituted and maintained to forces that might have made him possibly a counsellor of parliament conspicuous for intelligence and for greater freedom from class prejudice than his fellows, but exercising no appreciable influence upon the great movements of the intellectual and religious thought of his generation.

How long the obstinate contest between father and son might have lasted, and to what lengths the former might have gone in his indignation at the disappointment of his cherished hopes, had it not been for the enlightened views and calm judgment of the Abbé de Froidmont, are questions that we cannot answer. That sagacious kinsman, who had more than once before given useful advice, being now chosen, by mutual consent of the parties, to the honourable office of umpire, gave a decision which if it did not satisfy his nephew's desires, at least seemed to him slightly more equitable than the course hitherto prescribed. 'Inasmuch as Theodore is so averse to the practice of the law,' he said, 'let him indeed continue in the course upon which he has entered; let him, however, become the client of some prince or magnate from whom there may be hope of deriving some fruit of his labours.' Sooth to say, the line of life suggested by his uncle was scarcely less repugnant to the young and ambitious student than that which his father would have had him follow.

'What do you fancy that my feelings were then, my friend Pompon?' he exclaimed. 'Was I to go to the court, I who had learned neither how to dissemble nor how to flatter? Was I to embrace this mode of life subject to so many tumults, I who hoped to live in such honourable leisure?'

Yet yield he must, for fear that worse might befall him. He had chosen, or there had been chosen for him, the Bishop of Coutances as the patron under whose auspices he was to enter upon the life of a courtier; he had in fact just been introduced to the palace and household of this 'magnate,' when circumstances occurred which, as was thought at the time, merely deferred until a future occasion the execution of his uncle's designs, but which in reality, as it turned out, altogether frustrated them. In his contemporaneous correspondence the circumstances in question are somewhat vaguely designated as the 'storms of wars'; but as the letter containing the expression is unfortunately without the date of the year, it is perhaps impossible to ascertain definitely the political or military events particularly referred to. Meanwhile Beza gladly welcomed any respite from the employment to which he had so lately deemed himself condemned.

'Thus has it come to pass,' he gleefully wrote, 'that I have returned to my former manner of life, in which, unless some greater force shall hinder, I shall assuredly grow old. And I feel confident that at length I shall leave to posterity the proof that Beza did not live utterly idle, albeit he lived in the greatest leisure.'[2]

The last words, written in the confidence of friendship, give us the clue to the employments and aspirations of this somewhat obscure period of Beza's life. His was no trifler's existence. If he daily spent some hours in the company

[2] Beza to Pompon. Paris. July 19, s. a. Baum, i, App., 92.

of a select number of wits of his own age, and if he may occasionally have seemed to have no higher aim than by intercourse with them to strive to give a keener edge to his incisive speech, by far the greater part of his time was devoted to more serious efforts. Year by year, partly alone, partly with the help of the numerous excellent teachers whom he had at command, he was making progress in the departments of study upon which he had already entered, and entering fields previously unexplored. All this was to be no less serviceable to him in that future of which he could as yet have had scarcely even a suspicion, than the literary acumen which attrition with men of similar tastes and gifts was conferring upon him. There seem to have been some fruits early in his residence at Paris of the legal studies imposed upon him by his father, or undertaken from a sense of compunction at seeming to pay little or no respect to that father's wishes. A casual reference made in the postscript of one of his letters[3] to a treatise on the Salic Law, that might be expected to issue from the press within a few months, and 'under his auspices,' points apparently to some results of attention given to the theory of law, which was less repugnant to him than its practice. Be that as it may, there is, so far as I know, no evidence that the book or booklet in question ever actually appeared. In the same letter the writer speaks of devoting hours to the reading of Hebrew. Occasionally, too, he varied his work by perfecting his acquaintance with mathematics. To Latin and Greek he undoubtedly still gave great attention. If the foundations of

[3] It is the fourth of the eight letters which Professor Baum was so fortunate as to discover in the Simmler Collection of the Library of Zurich. See Baum, *Theodor Beza*. i, 33.

an accurate knowledge of the latter tongue had been well laid while he was under the instruction of Wolmar, there must have been built up during the years of private study at Paris that superstructure of close and intimate familiarity with the idiom of the language which stood him in good stead both at Lausanne and at Geneva. It was evidently a long course of preliminary reading that qualified him for the discharge of the duties of professor of Greek in the college of Lausanne—a position which he accepted soon after his expatriation, and which he retained for the next nine or ten years—as well as for his work of biblical interpretation.

In the enjoyment of means and of leisure, now at length secured, to gratify to the full his literary and studious tastes, it might have seemed that Beza must possess everything essential to his happiness. It was not so. I have already referred to the unrest of his soul from the moment of his return to Paris, and to the distinct purpose which he had soon formed to break loose in due time from everything detaining him in a land where he could not profess the doctrines with which he had become imbued from association with Wolmar—the purpose to direct his steps to a country in which liberty of conscience reigned, and where, in company with his old preceptor, he might live an ideal existence. This purpose he never renounced. Neither, on the other hand, did the allurements by which he was surrounded lose their force. Between the higher and the lower motives, the struggle in Beza's soul was severe and protracted.[4] I pass on to the events in which the conflict issued.

[4] For a full translation of Beza's confession, whose pathos is scarcely inferior to that of Saint Augustine himself, see his letter in the Appendix.

Of these the first was his secret marriage. Beza had not taken the first step toward becoming a priest. He had never assumed the vows that condemn to a life of celibacy. Yet, in accordance with an abuse against which complaints had certainly been numerous enough, but which no complaints had been potent enough to eradicate, he was enjoying, although a layman, the income of more than one ecclesiastical foundation. He was flattered by the hope of obtaining still greater resources of the same kind in future. There were many other favourites of fortune that found themselves in a similar situation. The world was so used to the sight of laymen fattening upon the church's pastures, that the unthinking were not even greatly startled when the intruder was the most unfit of men for the discharge of sacred functions, possibly as unblushing in the immorality of his life as the libertine Abbé de Brantôme of a later period. They were shocked only when the lay abbot married and shut himself off from the possibility of ever becoming a clergyman.

Desnoz was the name of the young woman upon whom Beza's choice fell. She was of a reputable family, but, as Beza himself admits, of a family inferior in station to his own. In view of the fact that her husband, who was by no means indifferent to matters of the kind, has nothing to say of her gentle birth, we may well dismiss as pure fictions such statements as that she was the daughter of an advocate of Paris, or the sister of a bishop of Grenoble.[5] Be this, however, as it may, the marriage took place apparently at some time in the year 1544, and the witnesses were two of Beza's most intimate and honourable friends, both of

[5] Bayle's *Dictionary*, in the article 'Beza.'

them jurists of distinction, Laurent de Normandie and Jean Crespin. Of the latter I shall have more to say presently. As to the marriage itself, much as the secrecy with which it was entered into must be condemned, the union, duly ratified as it was four years later in a public ceremonial, proved a harmonious and congenial one that lasted until the death of Claudine.

In later times Beza proved himself no irresolute man. At the present time, whether it should be said that the desirability of earthly possessions and ease and leisure to pursue his studies with an assiduity that had won him among his companions the playful appellation of 'the new philosopher,' loomed up before his eyes in exaggerated proportions, or that the far more exceeding value of the favour of God and of a clear conscience void of offence with him and with men had not yet become to him a living reality, he long remained in a pitiable condition of uncertainty, not so much respecting what he ought to do as respecting what he could bring himself to do. Nothing short of a miracle seemed necessary to draw him out of the mire in which, to use his own expression, he found himself caught, unable to come to a definite conclusion; with all his relations prompting him to adopt some certain course of life from which he might acquire wealth and distinction, and his kindly uncle offering him the prospect of still greater property, while, on the other hand, conscience pointed him in a different direction and his wife pressed him again and again to execute his long-deferred purpose to acknowledge her before the world.

That miracle was wrought in his conversion, which dates from the latter part of the year 1548.

Before speaking of this turning-point in his life, it is appropriate that I should speak of the publication, early in the same year, of the collection of his poems which came to be styled his Juvenilia. These celebrated pieces belong altogether to his youth, that is, to the period in which he was in no sense a Reformer, but, instead, a brilliant and ambitious devotee of belles-lettres. Though many of them had circulated freely among the author's friends and admirers, they had never been given to the public through the press.

It was evidently not without some scarcely concealed satisfaction at the neatness of his work, that Beza dedicated these first-fruits of his poetical efforts to his old preceptor Melchior Wolmar. Beza was twenty-eight or twenty-nine years of age. Neither the young man who dedicated, nor the old man who accepted the dedication with obvious delight, saw anything amiss in these poems.

Twelve years more elapsed, and Beza, now become a man of forty, an avowed Protestant and a zealous Reformer, had occasion to dedicate to his former teacher a second volume of an entirely different character, which he entitled a Confession of the Christian Faith. He assigned two motives for so doing. The one was that he might return to Wolmar some harvest from the field which Wolmar had sown; the other, that he might have the opportunity of offering his master a book infinitely better and more holy than the poems which, it seems, Wolmar had urged him to republish. To this statement he appended a few pathetic words:

'As respects those poems, who is there that either has condemned them more than I, their unhappy author, or that detests them more than I do today? Would, therefore, that they might at length be buried in perpetual oblivion! And may the Lord grant that, since it is impossible that what has been done should be undone, the persons who shall read writings of mine far different from those poems may rather congratulate me upon the greatness of God's goodness to me, than accuse him who voluntarily makes confession and deprecates the fault of his youth.'[6]

These are the brave and honest words of a man true to his convictions and more anxious to set himself right at the bar of his own conscience than to forestall the adverse judgment of others. For, in point of fact, learned and cultured men, and none more than the adherents of the other faith, applauded the sprightliness of his verses and never thought of condemning them as wanton, certainly never gave expression to such a thought. Thus the grave and learned President Étienne Pasquier, in his great work on The Researches of France,[7] remarked that 'Beza in his youth composed divers French and Latin poems which were very favourably received throughout all France, and particularly his Latin epigrams, wherein he celebrated his mistress under the name of Candida.' 'In 1548,' he adds, 'when he changed his religion, he made a show of despising them.'

Literary productions upon which their author himself sets a low estimate have in ordinary cases a fair chance of being forgotten by others naturally less interested in preserving them. The odium theologicum of which Beza was the object may safely be credited with being the cause of the survival and celebrity of the Juvenilia. In fact, the

[6] Dedication of *Confessio Fidei, in fine*.

[7] *Les Recherches de la France* (ed. of 1621), 649.

THEODORE BEZA AT THE AGE OF 29.
FROM FIRST EDITION OF BEZA'S 'POEMATA.'

outrageous misrepresentation of enemies, determined to discover in what was most innocent untold depths of depravity, compelled the very author who had vainly sought to consign them to forgetfulness, himself to bring them out again in subsequent editions, so that he might be able to show to the world what were in reality these lighter poems so maligned by men who had a manifest purpose in their inventions. The contrast between the Juvenilia and the sacred drama of Abraham Sacrifiant, or the metrical translation of the Psalms of David, might be unedifying enough; but, at least, the republication was sufficient to cast to the winds those foul calumnies that breed most readily in darkness and ignorance.

What, then, were these much-abused epigrams? Just such poems as a very young man—almost all of them were written before Beza's twentieth year, although they were published some years later—might write, especially if that young man were possessed of a certain skill in composing verses and were much encouraged thereto by the applause that welcomed his first efforts; most of all if, wielding a facile pen, he were uncommonly learned for his age in classical literature, admiring Virgil, adoring Ovid, and conscious of no higher ambition, so far as style was concerned, than to spend his hours of relaxation in imitating and endeavouring to equal or, if possible, excel the wonderful elegance of Catullus. It was the fashion of the age to indulge in a freedom of language which offends a more modern sense of propriety, but by no means proves that the life of the writer was impure. Indeed, the poet indignantly protests against such an inference and confidently appeals to the testimony of those that knew him intimately to establish the contrary.

'There are among my poems,' he wrote, 'a few that are written in somewhat too free a tone, that is, in imitation of Catullus and Ovid; but I had not the slightest fear at that time, nor do I now fear, lest those that knew me as I was should gauge my morals by those playful inventions of my imagination.'[8]

On this score nothing more need be said than that not many of the Juvenilia are open to the charge of indelicacy, while many are above reproach; none more charming and innocent than the celebrated poem addressed to a fictitious Audebert, a companion and equal in years, wherein the rival claims of friendship and love are poetically set forth. It has been the misfortune of Beza, as it is a striking illustration of the perverse imaginations of those who will see evil in everything on which they cast their jaundiced eyes, that this most graceful and delightful of lyrics has been furiously attacked as if it were a shameless avowal of unnatural passion.[9]

In sum, it may be safely said that poems which were read and admired by the cultured throughout France would never have met with censure or provoked controversy, had it not been that their author, subsequently to their publication and many years later than their composition, was converted to other and worthier views of life and its great objects. They belong to a stage of Beza's life with

[8] Dedication of *Confessio Fidei*, page 3.

[9] See the poem 'Theodorus Beza, de sua in Candidam et Audebertum Benevolentia.' Baum, *Theodor Beza*, i, 101, 102, and the edition of the *Juvenilia* by A. Machard (Paris, 1879), 234-236.

which he had completely broken when, under the sway of strong religious convictions, he turned his steps toward Switzerland; and so far from seeking for a life of quiet and self-indulgence, deliberately renounced a future of ease for the prospect of comparative poverty, of conflict, and of peril.

CHAPTER 3

CONVERSION OF BEZA—DEPARTURE FROM FRANCE—CALL TO LAUSANNE—'ABRAHAM'S SACRIFICE'

1548–1550

THE conversion of Theodore Beza occurred a few months after the publication of the *Juvenilia* and in connection with an illness of so serious a nature that his life was for a time in doubt. Never had man greater reason to regard an apparent calamity as a blessing in disguise. He rose from the bed upon which disease had cast him with views and aims totally different from those which he had cherished until then. The same letter that has enabled us to trace to some extent his intellectual development, raises for a moment the veil that hides the innermost spiritual experiences of the man from the scrutiny of his fellow. Hours of enforced idleness, as well as of extreme peril and suffering, were the condition of his gaining the first glimpse of his true character in God's sight. Past and present alike seemed to arise and accuse him, and their testimony could not be silenced or refuted. Turn his eyes which way he would, he found confronting him the judgment throne of an offended Deity. The agony was sharp and protracted. It was mercifully succeeded by a view of the pardon extended to him no less distinct and beyond the realm of doubt. Abhorrence of his sins was followed by petitions for forgiveness, and these by a full consecration of his powers to the service of his Saviour. From extreme darkness verging upon despair, he emerged into a brilliant and enduring light.

Clearness of religious conviction led to decided and instantaneous action. Old objections and obstacles vanished or were brushed aside. Theodore Beza, once thoroughly convinced of duty, was not the man to postpone action, or, in the apostle's words, to be disobedient to the heavenly vision. He did not even wait until he was fully restored to health, but while still far from strong carried into effect the resolution which he had formed of betaking himself to a land where he could freely make profession of his religious belief. He gathered together such of his property as he could carry with him, and, not announcing his purpose to any of his friends or relatives, made his way, accompanied by his wife, and under the assumed name, it is said, of Thibaud de May,[1] to the city of Geneva. He reached it on the 24th of October, 1548.

Such in brief is Beza's account of the decisive step of his life—no precipitate and enforced flight of a villain unwhipped of justice, a flight rendered necessary by flagitious crimes committed, as malignant and mendacious calumniators subsequently and down to our times have dared to assert with unblushing effrontery, but the honourable withdrawal of an honest man from a country with which were bound up all his prospects of preferment and of worldly prosperity, that in a foreign land he might seek and obtain, along possibly with the discomforts of poverty,

[1] Florimond de Ræmond, *Hist. de Ortu, Progressu et Ruina Hæres.* (ed. of 1614), ii, 498.

the freedom to worship God in accordance with the dictates of his conscience. One of his first acts on reaching Geneva was to procure the public and solemn recognition of his marriage with Claudine Desnoz.

His future was all unknown to him. He possessed no handicraft by means of which the emigrant may hope, as soon as he has gained a slight footing in a foreign land, to secure subsistence. Of learned and unpractical scholars there was an abundance both in Switzerland and in Germany. Many of these were penniless and a burden upon their hosts. We have no reason to believe that this was the case with Theodore Beza, who in his quiet removal from his native land may well be supposed to have been able to bring with him all the funds necessary to meet the temporary needs at least of himself and his wife. But his open renunciation of the Roman Catholic Church cut off every channel of supply that had flowed so freely hitherto, save such as came from the paternal estates; and the anger of father, uncle, and other kinsmen might well be expected to interrupt, if not permanently end, all expectations from this quarter. Under these circumstances, Beza's thoughts at first turned to a pursuit which, although not strictly a learned profession, had been taken up by some of the most eminent scholars of the day. I refer to the printing of books, which, in the hands of the Aldi at Venice and the Étiennes or Stephens of his own native land, had attained, or was soon to attain, the distinction of ranking with the fine arts. Jean Crespin, a native of Arras, came to Geneva at the same time with Beza. They were men of about the same age. Both had studied law, and both had been affected by the 'new doctrines,' as they were called. Crespin, in particular, had witnessed in the city of Paris, where he was admitted as an advocate of the court of Parliament, the triumphant death of at least one Protestant martyr. The constancy of Claude Le Peintre, a goldsmith, burnt alive on the Place Maubert, in 1540, seems to have led Crespin to the distinct espousal of the tenets of the Reformed Churches.[2] Similarity of views brought the young men together, and they naturally conceived the idea of establishing at Geneva, on the very frontiers of France, a great printing establishment from which books and publications of various kinds in favour of the Gospel might be issued and circulated far and near throughout the kingdom. The project as a joint enterprise finally fell through; for there was in store for Beza a career of usefulness of quite a different character and better suited to his resplendent abilities. But Jean Crespin did not abandon his purpose. His plans were realised within a few years so successfully that not only did his presses gain a celebrity for the beauty of their products only second to the fame of the presses of the great printers I have named, but became instrumental in giving a great impulse to the doctrines of the Reformation. His own personal activity as an author did good service in his great martyrology, which, in successive editions and under different titles, chronicled the Acts and Monuments of the martyrs who, from Wyclif and Huss until this our age, have steadfastly sealed the truth of the Gospel with their blood in Germany, France, England,

[2] See art. 'Crespin' in Haag, *La France Protestante*, iv, 886. Crespin describes Le Peintre's martyrdom in his great work of which the title is given in the next note (ed. of 1560). fol. 66.

Flanders, Italy, and Spain itself.' It was a great historical and biographical work, not indeed free from occasional errors—errors that may well be excused, in view of the difficulty and dangers encountered in the collection of so great a number of particular facts from widely different sources and even from well-guarded prisons and places of execution—but a work, nevertheless, for the most part, wonderfully exact and trustworthy, with which Crespin is to be congratulated for having linked his name for all time.[3]

But while it may not have been very long before Beza definitely renounced the career to which Crespin would gladly have welcomed him, it did not at once appear to what department of activity a man of such marked abilities should devote himself. For manifold were the advantages he possessed. His personal appearance was striking. He was of good stature and well proportioned. His countenance was very pleasing. Refinement was stamped upon his features. His whole bearing was that of a man accustomed to the best society. His manners at once conciliated the favour of the great and found him friends among the gentle sex. This is the testimony both of the inimical historian of *The Origin,*

[3] The first impression was in French and was entitled 'Le Livre des Martyrs, qui est un recueil de plusieurs Martyrs qui ont enduré la mort pour le nom de nostre Seigneur Jesus Christ, depuis Jean Hus jusques à cette année présente, 1554.' The author's manuscript originally had the title of *Le Livre des Saints*; but the Great Council of Geneva, in authorising its publication, stipulated for obvious reasons that '*Saints*' should be changed to '*Martyrs*.' *La France Protestante*, iv, 890. I quote in the present work the Latin version made by Baduel under Crespin's own eyes, printed at his own presses, and therefore of equal authority with the French, my own copy being of the rare second edition: *Actiones et Monumenta Martyrum*, Geneva, 1560. See Bibliography.

Progress, and Ruin of the Heresies of Our Time, Florimond de Ræmond, and of the Jesuit Maimbourg.[4] The latter writer furthermore volunteers the statement that it was undeniable that Beza's intellect was of a very high order, being keen, ready, acute, sprightly, and bright, for he had taken pains to cultivate it by the study of belles-lettres and particularly of poetry, wherein he excelled both in French and in Latin. To which very handsome tribute the critic somewhat grudgingly adds a concession that Beza knew a little philosophy and jurisprudence, learned in the schools of Orléans. Allowance being made in the last sentence for the strong prejudice of the partisan historian, the portrait may be accepted as sufficiently accurate, as it is unexpectedly favourable.

That Theodore Beza was welcomed with delight by John Calvin need scarcely be said. The great Reformer, now at the height of his renown and usefulness, had never forgotten the promising lad, ten years his junior, who had studied under the same teacher and of whose singular brilliancy that teacher had never tired of making mention. And now that, after a long period of hesitation, Beza, by a single bold step, had broken with the past and, sacrificing rank, ease, and every worldly consideration, had thrown himself in for life or for death with the reformatory movement to which Calvin had devoted his own magnificent powers, the joy and the thankfulness to Heaven with which the latter welcomed the new recruit were mingled with lively curiosity respecting the particular work which Providence had reserved for him to accomplish.

[4] *Hist. de Ortu, Progressu et Ruina Hær.* (ed. 1614), ii., 632. Maimbourg, *Histoire du Calvinisme* (ed. 1682), 217.

As I have said, that work did not at once disclose itself to view. The enfeebled condition of Beza, but lately risen from a very critical illness, did not incline him to great haste in the search. Thus it was that after a few months' stay in Geneva he fulfilled what had for years been a strong wish of his heart, and made a journey to southern Germany to see his old preceptor, Melchior Wolmar, at Tübingen. Pupil and teacher seem not to have met since Wolmar made Beza a brief visit, early in the latter's stay at Paris, when the German was sent on a diplomatic errand by the Duke of Würtemberg to the French court. That was ten years ago; but the intensity of the mutual love of Wolmar and Beza had suffered no abatement. The greetings were as kind and affectionate as could be imagined. Yet Beza made no attempt to carry out his early dream of study and leisure in Wolmar's neighbourhood. It must be supposed that scholarly idleness had lost its charm for a man who had now acquired a new earnestness of purpose; and in the troubled state of Germany at the moment, Beza saw no opportunities beyond the Rhine to further the work to which he had devoted his life.

On his way back to Geneva Beza naturally passed through Lausanne, the most important place in what at the present time constitutes the Canton of Vaud, one of the members of the Helvetic Union. At Lausanne he met Pierre Viret, himself a native of Orbe in this district, who after having played an important part in the reformation of Geneva, had of late been labouring for the same cause in his native region. Viret recognised in Theodore Beza the very man whom he needed as a colleague in the 'Académie,' or

University, recently established at Lausanne, and he begged him to accept a chair in this institution.

The Pays de Vaud, as it was styled, had long been a part of the dominions of the Duke of Savoy. Its conquest by the Bernese was a sequence of the campaign of 1536, in the course of which the great Swiss Canton of Bern sent an army of six thousand men, under the celebrated Naegeli, to the relief of Geneva. Not content with having accomplished the chief object of their undertaking, and encouraged by the absence of the opposition which they had expected to meet, the Bernese proceeded to annex not only the district of Chablais, on the southern side of Lake Léman, but the district of Gex, and the greater part of that of Vaud, on the western and northern shores. At first the rich bishopric of the 'imperial' city of Lausanne was exempted from seizure. But the prize was too tempting. In a second incursion, made only two months later in the same year, the episcopal domain also was incorporated in the possessions of the Canton of Bern. For his misfortune the Bishop of Lausanne, Sébastian de Montfaucon, had only himself to blame. He had been so imprudent as to write from the town of Fribourg, where he had taken refuge, a letter inciting the people of his diocese to take up arms against the Bernese.[5] This was early in 1536. At once the conquerors set about consolidating their power by the abolition of the three special 'estates' of Lausanne, as well as of the 'estates' by which Vaud was governed, and by the substitution of a government administered through eight bailiffs set up at as many places in the district. A solemn

[5] Daguet, *Histoire de la Confédération Suisse*, 332-334.

conference, or colloquy, was called by the Lords of Bern and met, in October, in the cathedral of Lausanne during a number of successive days. Here were discussed ten theses drawn up by the Reformer William Farel.[6] Six commissioners of Bern and of Vaud were present to hear the debate. Four presidents superintended the sessions. Four notaries kept an official record of the proceedings, and read, as the occasion arose, any chapter of Holy Scripture that might be called for. The discussion covered in general the whole field of controversy between Protestantism and Roman Catholicism. It was carried on with vigour, but with more hopefulness by the Reformers—Farel, Viret, Calvin, and others—than by their opponents. As the Roman Catholics entered upon the struggle reluctantly, their first step was to submit a protest on the part of the chapter of the cathedral itself against any disputation. God is not, said they, the author of dissension but of peace, and discussion may be pernicious to the particular church, which even though gathered in Christ's name is liable to fall into error. When this protest and other protests of a like kind were disregarded, the opposition instituted was somewhat wanting in courage, as though the result of the matter were a foregone conclusion. Once, indeed, Jean Michodus, 'the Reverend of Vevey,' grew confident when replying to the Protestant view of the impossibility of justification by works as set forth by Saint Paul, and turned upon one of

[6] It was a disputation after the model of that held at Bern eight years before (January, 1528), in which, in like manner, there had been discussed ten theses, or conclusions, drawn up by Haller and revised by Zwingli. Schaff, *Hist. of the Christian Church*, vii, 104. The particular theses, however, were different in the two cases.

the champions of the other side, Caroli, formerly a Roman Catholic doctor of the Sorbonne, now a professed Protestant, although later he returned to his original faith.

'I have heard many good doctors at Paris,' said he, 'but they did not, like you, explain the third chapter of Romans as referring to the deeds of the law, but only to the ceremonies. And you yourself, Monsieur our master Caroli, I have heard you explain this passage otherwise than as you expound it now.'

To which Caroli could only reply:

'That I expounded this passage as you assert, I confess. I was then of the number of the persons of whom Saint Peter speaks, those ignorant men that wrest the Holy Scriptures, because they do not understand them. So I acted, and could not satisfy my own conscience. Then I set myself to reading the Scriptures and comparing passage with passage, and praying God to grant me a true intelligence. And God has opened my understanding. He has brought me to the true knowledge of his gospel, as you see. Do not therefore marvel if I have changed; but rather do as I have done, forsake every doctrine not taken from the Scriptures, and hold by them alone.'[7]

There was a dramatic episode at one point when the ground of justification was under discussion. Farel called for the reading of the latter part of Romans 3, and exclaimed: 'You see how that it is freely, without desert, without the deeds of the law, that a man is justified!' Hereupon the Roman Catholic disputant, a physician, Dr Blancherose,

[7] The whole discussion is given at great length in the valuable work of L. Vulliemin, entitled, *Le Chroniqueur: Recueil Historique*, 313, foll.

burst out: 'I do not believe that it is so.' At once a Bible was brought and laid before him, not a printed volume of modern times, whose authority might be questioned, but an old manuscript Bible written on parchment, taken from the library of the Franciscan convent, and he was bidden to read the passage for himself. There to his amazement were the words themselves, and, though scarcely believing the evidence of his senses, he cried out: 'It is true! A man is justified by faith as the holy Apostle says! We are not saved by works of righteousness which we have done, but according to his mercy, God saved us!'[8]

The commissioners had no judicial powers. They could only report the proceedings of the colloquy to the Lords of Bern. The answer of the latter was soon forthcoming. The conference ended on Sunday, the 8th of October; on Thursday, the 19th, or only eleven days later, the decree was issued. By virtue of their duty not only to govern their subjects in equity and justice, but 'to employ all diligence and force that these subjects may live according to God in true and lively faith which produces good works,' the Bernese proclaimed their decision 'to cast down all idolatries, papal ceremonies, traditions, and ordinances of men not conformable to the word of God.' In the execution of this purpose, they ordered all their bailiffs and subordinate officers to make a personal visitation, immediately upon the receipt of these letters, and command all priests, deans, canons, and other churchmen so called at once to desist from all 'papistical ceremonies, sacrifices, offices, institutions, and traditions,' as they desired to avoid the displeasure of the government.

[8] *Ibid.*, p. 322.

They especially recommended them without delay to overthrow all images, idols, and altars, whether in church or monastery; doing all this without disorder or tumult. And they bade all these and their other subjects to betake themselves, for the purpose of hearing the word of God, to the nearest places in which preachers had already been appointed or should hereafter be appointed, and to give them a favourable audience. As to the further dispositions respecting the so-called churchmen and church property, the latter gave promise, with God's help, of 'so reasonable and holy a reformation that God and the world shall be well pleased.'[9]

Lausanne had not waited for the receipt of the decision of Bern. No sooner was the conference concluded than the people, anticipating the forthcoming decree, began in an unauthorised fashion the work of destruction and spoliation. The beautiful cathedral of Notre Dame was the first victim of their iconoclastic zeal, and a church whose erection is traced back to the early part of the thirteenth century still bears testimony to the zeal of men who were resolved to remove every trace of a superstitious worship. Here, as elsewhere throughout Vaud, there was no lack of opposition; but the overwhelming influence of the great Canton of Bern everywhere carried the day, and the whole district was ultimately brought over to a profession of the Reformed doctrines.

The immense store of treasures which the cathedral contained was dispersed.[10] A large part found its way to Bern.

[9] See the text in *Le Chroniqueur*, 340, 341.

[10] The list of gold and silver statues, crosses, jewelled reliquaries, and

But fortunately the government of this sagacious republic saw the propriety of applying no inconsiderable portion of the ecclesiastical property that fell into its hands to the promotion of the higher intellectual interests of the region itself. Whether from disinterested motives, or from the desire to attach their new subjects to them by self-interest, the Lords of Bern gave to the communes, or sold to them at an insignificant price, lands heretofore belonging to churches and monastic foundations, and we are told that the proceeds of this property served to form those school and eleemosynary funds which the Vaudois townships still possess at the present day.[11]

A fragment of the treasures, or of the endowment of the cathedral of Lausanne, was applied to the establishment of the 'Académie.' The Bernese, in the capacity of lords paramount, had, in accordance with the prevalent ideas of the rights and duties of the civil government, undertaken to change the religion of the Pays de Vaud. They had taken away a religion that appealed to the senses and to the imagination of the people, and substituted for it a religion which presupposed a knowledge of the word of God; but they had found themselves utterly unable to supply the teachers or preachers of that word whom every place, even to the smallest village, absolutely required in order to prevent the inhabitants from lapsing into a state of still

---

like precious possessions enumerated in detail, in church and chapel, is given in *Le Chroniqueur*; pages 337, 338. It is simply astounding. Not to speak of Persian tapestries, of missals, and of relics of saints of a value difficult to estimate, there were single articles of pure gold weighing fifteen, twenty, eighty, or more pounds apiece.

[11] Daguet, 334, 335.

more abject ignorance than had hitherto prevailed. It was primarily for the purpose of training men for the pastoral office, and not for that of preparing men for professional or public life, that the 'Académie' was founded.[12]

Beza did not at once undertake the duties which he was invited to assume, but returned to Geneva and consulted with his brethren and especially with John Calvin. The call was altogether unexpected,[13] and Beza was at first disposed to decline it. Doubtless, as Professor Baum suggests,[14] the state of his health, not yet altogether restored, was one chief reason for this. But it would appear from the sequel that when he thought of deciding to go to Lausanne the matter of the recent publication of his unfortunate *Juvenilia* weighed much in his mind against such a step. But Viret wrote to Calvin, and the latter with other friends endeavoured to remove Beza's scruples. The authorities of the Canton of Bern, adopting the action of the Academy of Lausanne, extended a formal but flattering invitation. To this Beza felt himself no longer at liberty to turn a deaf ear. It is characteristic of the man, however, and the circumstance throws a bright light upon the sincerity of his character and the thoroughness of his conversion, that before he consented to be inducted into the office of a teacher of sacred as well as secular learning to whom the interests of the young were entrusted, he was foremost in calling the attention of the ecclesiastical council which, as the manner of the Reformed Churches was, met to inquire

[12] *Le Chroniqueur*. 359.

[13] Beza's dedicatory letter to Wolmar. So, too, in his letter to And. Dudithius, below referred to. Baum, i, 131.

[14] Vol. i, 120.

into his past life and into his doctrinal belief, to the great error of his youth.

'Of my own accord,' he writes at a later time, 'I made mention of the Epigrams I had published, lest perchance the matter might be to the damage of the church, because there were among them some of an amatory character and certainly now and then written with too much license, that is, in imitation of the ancient poets. It pleased the assembly of the brethren that nevertheless I should assume that function in the church, in the first place because it seemed plainly unjust that in the case of a person who had passed over to Christ from the Papal religion, just as from paganism, there should be imputed to him the error in question in a life otherwise honourable and blameless, and in the second place, because I voluntarily pledged myself to make it publicly known to all men how greatly that inconsiderate act of mine displeased me.'[15]

On assuming his office, Beza took an oath declaring his hearty approval of all the decrees of the disputation held at Bern in 1528 respecting the Christian religion, and promised, on pain of God's anger, to conform his life and teaching thereto.[16]

Thus began the course of a brilliant and fruitful professorship extending over a period of nine years—1549–1558. The work was congenial. All his past studies had prepared Theodore Beza for a thorough discharge of its duties. Greek was his favourite tongue. Its direct bearing upon

[15] 'Epistola dedicatoria ad And. Dudithium,' May 14, 1569, prefixed to the second edition of the *Juvenilia*, *apud* Baum, i, 131.

[16] The oath in Baum, i, 132.

the preparation for the Christian ministry of the youth that were drawn to his classroom by the reputation of his learning, procured him peculiar gratification. There had been a time when secular learning pursued for its own sake satisfied his highest aspirations; now he could not be happy without the conviction that, in the professor's chair, he was rendering no less important a service to the advancement of religion than he would have rendered in the pulpit devoting his entire time to the work of a popular preacher. Thus it was that his labour became from the very start a labour of love. Apart from the inspiration created by contact with bright minds among his pupils, there was also the friendly intercourse with his eminent colleagues and the growing intimacy with scholars and theologians eminent for their attainments residing in neighbouring cities, men already well known to him by reputation, but now beginning to be familiar to him through personal relations or by correspondence—no small compensation to his mind[17] for the losses he had sustained in forsaking home and native land—men like Bullinger, Musculus, and Haller, not to speak of Calvin himself and Viret.

We should have known, even had not Beza himself expressly told us, that it was this thought and the analogy of the patriarch who, at the bidding of Jehovah, left the land of his nativity not knowing whither he went, that chiefly influenced Beza in the choice of the subject of the first poetical production that he brought out after his conversion. He had not been quite a year at Lausanne when he gave to the world a sacred tragedy, under the title of *Abraham's*

[17] See Heppe, 24.

Sacrifice. In the preface he introduced it with these words (dated Lausanne, the 1st of October, 1550):

'I admit that by nature I have always delighted in poetry, and I cannot yet repent of it; but much do I regret to have employed the slender gifts with which God has endowed me in this regard, upon things of which the mere recollection at present makes me blush. I have therefore given myself to such matters as are more holy, hoping to continue therein hereafter.'[18]

The drama was written originally for the use of the students, and was first performed by them in one of the halls of the former 'officiality,' or seat of the judge representing the late Bishop of Lausanne in the trial of ecclesiastical cases. So favourable was its reception by the public, that it was repeatedly brought on the boards. From Lausanne it passed to other places not only in Switzerland, but in France, where it was played with great applause in many cities. It was also translated into foreign tongues. The famous President Étienne Pasquier, while he is certainly mistaken in the date and occasion to which he ascribes the work, is a witness whose testimony cannot be challenged to the impression it made upon himself: 'Theodore Beza, a fine poet, both Latin and French, composed, on the accession of King Henry [the Second], the *Sacrifice of Abraham* in French verse, so well portrayed to the life, that, as I read it in former days, tears flowed from my eyes.'[19] The most pathetic passage is naturally that which culminates in the last dialogue between the patriarch and his son as the latter is about to be sacrificed. A

[18] Preface to 'Le Sacrifice d'Abraham,' in Baum, i, 74, note.

[19] Étienne Pasquier, *Les Recherches de la France*, 615.

modern French critic of high standing may here be allowed to speak, especially as he institutes a favourable comparison between Beza's work and that of the great Racine himself, which might be esteemed presumptuous if instituted by a foreigner. In analysing the latter part of the drama, A. Sayous, in his *Études Littéraires*, observes upon the passage where Abraham turns to immolate Isaac, that 'here begins a scene that amply justifies Pasquier's tears. It is conducted with singular art. The emotion grows from the beginning to the end—the denouement naturally suspended and the father's anguish prolonged by the young son's questions, the tears of Isaac, his childish prayer, his thought of his mother, and his artless resignation—all this is of a truthfulness that surpasses in pathos the scenes in the French *Iphigénie*, between Agamemnon and his daughter.'

In which bold advocacy of the composition of the French Reformer, the acute critic fortifies himself by citing the German poet Chamisso 'who pushed his admiration so far as to compare the dialogue between Isaac and Abraham to the most divine productions of the Greeks.'[20]

[20] *Études Littéraires*, i, 266. Sayous regards—and he is probably right, from a purely literary point of view—the *Sacrifice of Abraham* as the best of all Beza's French poems, assigning to it a place far in advance of his metrical translations of the Psalms of David. These last were begun during Beza's residence at Lausanne and might be appropriately treated here. I prefer, however, to give them a separate consideration farther on, in a chapter on Theodore Beza and the Huguenot Psalter.

CHAPTER 4

TREATISE ON THE PUNISHMENT OF HERETICS

1554

With little pleasure we turn from the first of the poetical compositions written after Theodore Beza's conversion, to the first of his graver and more important writings in prose.

Abundant attention was given in a previous chapter to the youthful error of Beza into which he fell before he broke with his old thoughts and purposes in life, an error at a later time not merely deplored, but heartily repented of, candidly confessed, and publicly condemned by him to the end of his days. I must now speak of an act of his more mature life which our later age must regard as most reprehensible, an act for which not only did he never express repentance, but which he continued to justify as proper and righteous throughout a full half-century, or to the very time of his death, with an unshaken conviction that he was in the right. I refer to his public advocacy of the tenet, then held by the vast majority of educated and religious men, but now as universally repudiated, that heretics, and especially outrageous blasphemers, may and ought to be punished by the civil authorities, even capitally. In 1554 Beza first published his treatise *Concerning the duty of punishing heretics by the civil magistrate: in answer to the medley of Martin Bellius and the sect of the new Academics* (*De hæreticis a civili magistratu puniendis, adversus Martini Bellii farraginem, et novorum Academicorum sectam*).

The controversy arose from the execution of the Spanish physician Michael Servetus, burnt alive at the stake on the hill of Champel, at Geneva, on the 27th of October, 1553.

The main facts in the case are incontrovertible and are so familiar to all readers of history, that the barest reminder is necessary in this place. Having been apprehended at Vienne, near Lyons, Servetus escaped from the hands of the Roman Catholic judges by a secret flight, and in his absence was condemned, as a heretic and a fugitive, to a death by slow fire. But he had avoided one danger only to fall into another equally appalling. Discovered in the city of Geneva by John Calvin, and by him denounced to the civil authorities, he was again tried, found guilty, and sentenced to the same punishment. Calvin had long since forewarned Servetus of the peril he would incur by coming to Geneva. He now openly advocated his being put to death. It is the great blot upon his name. It is the one great error of his life which has given occasion to his enemies and the adversaries of the Protestant faith to blaspheme. And this is none the less true if we concede, as we must concede, that his fault was the fault of the great majority of his contemporaries, even the most pious and excellent, who with him held the pestilent doctrine that sins against God, transgressions against the first table of the law, may be punished, even capitally, by the civil magistrate. It is not that, according to the popular impression, John Calvin burned Servetus; for, in point of fact, so far from burning him, he opposed this mode of execution as cruel; but that he, with his intellect of the highest order and with a heart which we know otherwise to have been kindly, had not enfranchised himself from old and traditional theories of the province of the secular power, and as a Christian knew not what spirit he was of; indeed, that he seemed to have receded from his own tolerant expressions in the earliest edition of his *Institutes*, wherein he asserted, respecting our treatment of the excommunicated, that we should live with them as with Turks, Saracens, and other enemies of religion, striving, meanwhile, in every possible manner, whether by exhortation and by teaching, or by mildness and gentleness, or by prayers to God, to induce them to turn to the better way and the society of the faithful.

To cruelty in the putting of men out of the world, the men of the sixteenth century were, unfortunately, pretty well used. The *estrapade*, in the neighbouring kingdom of France, had had its host of victims, and the *estrapade*, ingeniously contrived to prolong the tortures of the dying victim, by alternately lowering him into the flames and hoisting him out, in preparation for a new exposure to the fire, was, to say the least, quite as cruel as the ordinary execution at the stake. It was therefore not so much the cruelty of the means used to put Servetus to death, as the inconsistency of the Reformers in resorting to violence to suppress heresy, that shocked many contemporaries, as it shocks us.

Among those that entered a protest against the principle involved in the execution of Servetus, was a writer who signed himself Martin Bellius, but whose true name was suspected by Beza of being Sébastian Chasteillon, or Castalio.[1] It was in answer to his treatise that Beza wrote.

Castalio, if indeed it was he, had given to his small volume, now become extremely rare,[2] a the form of an inquiry into the question, 'Whether heretics ought to be proceeded against, or persecuted, and, in general, how they should be dealt with.' It claimed to be a book 'of the utmost necessity in this most turbulent time,' and was made up of a collection of the sentiments of the learned in ancient and in modern times. To us, as we shall see presently, the chief interest centres in the remarkable dedicatory letter which the author prefixed to it. Castalio was a very erudite man, whose most noteworthy production was a new translation of the Bible into the Latin language, the result of the labours of ten years. In this he strove, while often making a slight sacrifice of the literal form, to give to the Holy Scriptures a clearness and an elegance of expression that would commend them to a wider circle of readers, and enable them to supplant profane writings in the schools. It is no impeachment of his good intentions, or, indeed, of his scholarship, to admit that his Bible won no such place as was anticipated for it by its author. Yet Castalio was no contemptible exegete. If the scholarly reader will take the trouble to run through the pages of the lengthy treatise in which Beza reviews some of the passages translated in his

[1] For a brief discussion of the authorship of this treatise, see Schaff, *Church History*, vii, 794, etc. Prof. Ferdinand Buisson, of Neufchatel, has treated the matter at greater length in his *Sébastien Castellion* (Paris, 2 vols., 1892).

[2] Bonnet, 'Sébastien Castalion, ou La Tolérance au Seizième Siècle,' in *Bulletin*, vol. xvi (1867). See especially p. 539.

own Latin version of the New Testament, and to compare them with the same passages as rendered by Castalio, he will convince himself of this. For if he find Beza's judgment in the great majority of cases to be more sound than that of his opponent, yet will he discover others where the latter shows himself superior. Thus Beza's interpretation of Heb. 5:7, in which he coincides with Calvin, is forced and undoubtedly erroneous, while that of Castalio is endorsed by the latest and best of recent scholars, and is certainly correct.[3] As a teacher and successor of the famous Mathurin Corderius, Castalio had worthily discharged the duties of his office in the college of Geneva, until, in consequence of differences of opinion between himself and his old friend Calvin, he voluntarily retired, and took up his abode first at Lausanne and then at Basel. Here he spent the rest of his days in an honourable but painful struggle against poverty. History has in our own times vindicated his claim to be classed among the first and noblest assertors of the rights of the human conscience. The letter to the Duke of Würtemberg which 'Martin Bellius' prefixed to his book on the treatment of heretics, and in which he fully sets forth his views, has been justly styled 'one of the purest inspirations of the century,' 'one of those beneficent revelations that console for the excesses of another age,' in which 'its author proclaims, with rare eloquence, a truth so novel that it was to scandalise contemporaries—the right of every man to believe freely and to assert his belief, remaining responsible

[3] See 'Responsio ad defensiones et reprehensiones Sebastiani Castellionis, quibus suam Novi Testamenti interpretationem defendere adversus Bezam et ejus versionem vicissim reprehendere conatus est' (published first in 1563). In *Tract. Theol.*, i, 497.

for his errors only before God.'[4] A few sentences describing the state of Christendom may suffice to convey a notion of its spirit: 'Nobody can stand the slightest contradiction, and, although there are today nearly as many opinions as there are men, there is not one sect that does not condemn the others; hence exiles, chains, fires, the gallows, and that lamentable array of punishments for the simple crime of holding views displeasing to the powerful of the earth, on questions in dispute for centuries and still unsettled.' 'I have long been seeking to find out what a heretic is, and here is what I have discovered: he is a man that thinks otherwise than we do respecting religion.' 'I ask you, Who would wish to be a Christian, when he sees men that lay claim to that designation dragged to execution and treated more cruelly than we treat thieves and robbers? Who would not believe that Christ is a Moloch or some pitiless divinity demanding human sacrifices upon his altars?'[5]

It is deplorable to see a man of the intellect of Beza, through the long course of a treatise which, in the edition of his collected theological works, fills not less than eighty-five closely printed folio pages, labouring to overthrow the arguments, for the most part clear and cogent, by means of which Castalio and others, doubtless otherwise his inferiors in dialectic skill, but on this question speaking from the fulness of conviction, had built up a structure which in our eyes at least is impregnable. It is not the only case in which, looking back from a considerable distance of time

[4] Bonnet, *ubi supra*, xvi, 544.

[5] Passages quoted in *Bulletin*, xvi, 542-544, and in Haag, *La France Protestante*, *s. v. Chateillon*, iv, 130, 131.

upon a past conflict of arms, we cannot divest ourselves of the conviction that there has been some frightful mistake, and that, from their character, from their antecedents, from the community of their great aims, the combatants ought to have been fighting, not as enemies, but as friends, in order to conserve and not to tear down, making a common front against common foes. Nor, perhaps, is it an unwarrantable surmise that the strong personal friendship in which he held Calvin, and the ardent desire to vindicate the propriety of Calvin's course, added unconsciously to the virulence with which Theodore Beza treated both the memory of Servetus himself and the man who called in question the justice of the punishment of Servetus. As for that heretic, he is to Beza, I may remark, 'of all men that have hitherto lived the most impious and blasphemous,' while the men who have condemned his trial as iniquitous, are for him the 'emissaries of Satan.'[6]

Castalio and his allies, according to Beza, took three positions, each of which they defended by a variety of arguments. The first was, That heretics ought not to be punished. The second was, That heretics cannot justly be punished by the civil magistrate. The third was, That heretics should not be punished with death. In order to prove that heretics should not be punished, they alleged that the matters in controversy are not as yet necessary to be known, nor can they be known save by the pure in heart, nor, if known, would they make men better; that they cannot be decided by God's written word. They argued from the examples of Judas Maccabeus and of Moses, from the authority

[6] 'De hæreticis a civ. mag. puniendis.' *Tractationes Theologicæ*, i, 85.

of Gamaliel and Paul, from the scriptural description of Charity, from the mildness and gentleness that should characterise all Christians. They asserted that no class of men are less to be feared than are heretics. They brought up instances of Christ's clemency and benignity. They showed that the civil magistrate leaves unpunished much greater offenders—Turks, Jews, the proud, the avaricious, and the like. They boldly claimed that in point of fact no one can be compelled to believe, and therefore the attempt ought not to be made to compel men to believe.

They proved that, if to be punished at all, the punishment of heretics does not belong to the civil magistrate, by our Lord's own assertion that his kingdom is not of this world, and by that of Saint Paul that the weapons of our warfare are not carnal. Theologians, they said, can defend their doctrine, as do the professors of the other sciences, without a recourse to the magistrate. They used Christ and his apostles as examples. They did not forget to notice that the world is incompetent to judge of heresy, and that most princes abuse their authority in this as in other things. They fortified themselves with evidence drawn from the practice of the ancient Church.

As to the third head, they made effective use of the Parable of the Tares and the command to let the tares grow until the harvest. To permit the magistrate to kill the heretic is, said they, to permit him to exercise God's prerogative of killing the soul. If heretics are to be slain, then the greater part of mankind should be put to death. Saint Paul bids us 'avoid,' not 'kill,' the heretic, and enjoins us, 'Judge nothing before the time.' The fear of death makes men hypocrites.

Many are the instances where such punishment has resulted very badly. By the Church under the Emperors the life of even such an arch-heretic as Arius was spared.

Such were, according to Beza, the arguments, often crudely stated, by which the forerunners of that tolerance which has become the law of our higher civilisation undertook to establish principles which for us have become axiomatic truths. As historic evidence of human progress they deserve a place here. Nor would it be altogether uninteresting to note in detail the answers by which Beza attempts to break the force of the arguments of his opponents. But more important is it to examine the grounds on which he undertakes affirmatively to establish his own allegations.

'*Heretics are to be punished.*' By heretics are not meant unbelievers, like Jews and Turks; nor men of blameworthy lives, like thieves and murderers; nor men that err from the truth through sheer simplicity and ignorance; but such persons as lay claim to be called the faithful, and, having been legitimately convicted from God's word, yet, following their own judgment, so pertinaciously and resolutely defend certain false doctrines against the Church, as not to hesitate by their factions to rend the Church's peace and concord. That such men ought to be punished, 'no one—to my knowledge at least,—' says Beza, 'has been found thus far to call in question, with the exception of these new Academics.'[7] They are the greatest pests of the Church, true instruments of the devil for its destruction. The great part of men live far from exemplary lives, and are exposed to

[7] *Ibid.*, i, 143.

the violent assaults of the external foes of the Church; but so long as *Doctrine* remains safe, it appears as a brilliant constellation, a Cynosure by whose rays the pious may hold their course in the midst of the tempests. But when Doctrine itself is so corrupted that the devil lurks beneath it, what remains but that very many will embrace the devil in place of God? What but that very many, abandoning the hope of knowing the truth, will cast from them all religion, and, in fine, there will arise a horrible confusion in the Church of God? The evil is most grave when Satan has transformed himself and attacks the very vitals of the Church. Then the most prompt, the sharpest, of remedies is called for. So far from having no obligation to keep within bounds the spreading cancer, it may be necessary, in order to save the rest of the body, for men to resort to cautery and knife. This is shown by the testimony of God's word. Not to speak of laws against blasphemers and false prophets, or of the acts of Moses, Asa, and Josiah, he that will not hear the Church, we are told, is to be regarded as a Gentile and a publican. If this was said of one who had committed a private wrong, much more ought it to hold good in the case of one who plucks up religious Doctrine itself. Thus did the apostles give over to Satan the heretics Philetus and Hymenæus. The conclusion of the whole matter is, therefore, that 'those who think that heretics ought not to be punished, are attempting to introduce into the Church of God the most pestilent of all opinions, a view that conflicts with the doctrine first given by God the Father, subsequently renewed by Christ, and finally practised by the universal orthodox Church by perpetual consent.' 'So that to me, indeed,' observes Beza, 'such men appear to act more absurdly than if they were to deny that sacrilegious persons or parricides ought to be punished; since heretics are infinitely worse than all such criminals. For which reason I shall not employ more words to prove this part of the question, which I am confident that all who are not altogether unjust judges will concede to me.'[8]

If heretics, then, should be punished, by whom may punishment be inflicted? '*They are to be punished by the civil magistrate*,' Beza replies. The chief end of human society is that God may receive the honour which men are bound to pay him. Now, the civil magistrate is the appointed guardian and governor of human society. He ought therefore in the administration of the affairs of human society to take the greatest account of this its chief end. It is his duty indeed, so far as in him lies, to see that no discord shall intervene in the dealings of the citizens with one another; but since it is not the ultimate and chief end of human society that men should live together in peace, but rather that, living in peace, they should worship God, it is the duty of the magistrate, even at the cost of external peace, if it cannot be done otherwise, to secure the true worship of God throughout the extent of his jurisdiction. So far is it from being his duty to abstain from exercising solicitude for religion. But he cannot conserve religion unless he coerces the pertinacious and factious despisers of religion by the sword (*jure gladii*). It remains, that whoever undertakes to divorce the magistrate from religion either does not know what is the true end of human society, or conceals what he knows

[8] *Ibid., ubi supra.*

perfectly well. The exterior discipline of the Church must be entrusted to one of the two—either to the civil magistrate or to the ministers of the Church—otherwise there is anarchy. It cannot be entrusted to the latter, else there would be a confused mingling of the power of the sword and that of the keys. It must therefore be entrusted to the former. To illustrate: An Anabaptist is denounced. The body of presbyters assembles. He is summoned, but answers that he will have nothing to do with sinners. How does the Church act? If it acts according to God's word, when the unhappy man cannot be corrected in any other way, it delivers him unto Satan, that he may learn not to blaspheme. He, on the other hand, willingly and of his own accord, separates himself from the Church. Other fanatics follow him and so a defection arises. Next some disciple of Servetus or Osiander will come forward. On being summoned, he will present himself, but it will be to *judge* the Church. Being cast out, he too will find disciples, and hence another faction. At length some 'Academic,' an excellent and modest man, forsooth, will make his appearance. When summoned, he will come and will state, by way of preamble, that he is eager to learn, and that he reads and hears everything. If you undertake to teach him, however, he prays that no violence be done to his conscience. If you insist and expose his impudence in corrupting the Scriptures, quite unlike the old philosophers of the Academy, who used to assert that the only thing they knew was that they knew nothing, he will tell you that no one knows anything but himself, and yet he will protest that he condemns nobody. If he can find any means of so doing, he, too, on being ejected from the Church, will set up another conventicle. What shall the Church do in these circumstances? Cry unto the Lord, you say. Yes, and despite Satan's vain opposition, the Church will be saved. But the hungry man cries and does not wait to be fed by an angel as was Elijah. The bread that is given him or that he seeks to obtain by his industry he regards as provided for him by God. Suppose that there be in the Church a Christian magistrate. Must he, who will not tolerate the dissensions of the citizens in profane matters, remain quiet when the great end for which human society was instituted is in question? Or, are those rather to whom the power of the sword is not entrusted, to be permitted to take upon them to exercise coercion? Who does not see that if the ministry thus intrude on the office of the magistrate, as the Roman Antichrist has done, there is the greatest danger of dire confusion as the result of commingling what God himself has made distinct? Then, again, if the pastors, the shepherds of the flock, become transformed into wolves, what is to be done? You will say, Let a Council be convened and let it compel the submission of the unruly. But who shall summon the Council, especially the Universal Council, if not the civil magistrate? For the apostle's prescription remains fixed, Let every soul be subject to the higher powers.[9]

All this, says Beza, is confirmed by the authority of the word of God—and here he cites a multitude of passages of the Old Testament and of the New—and by the opinions of the learned men of more modern times—Luther, Melanchthon, Bucer, and the like.[10]

[9] *Ibid.*, i, 143-145.
[10] *Ibid.*, i, 145-150.

'Heretics are occasionally to be coerced even by capital punishment.' The right of the magistrate to punish heretics being once proven, as Beza believed that he had proved it, he found little difficulty in the matter of the amount or severity of the punishment. The gravity of the crime of heresy is the first and chief ground for the infliction of the penalty of death. Inasmuch as the purpose of the law is to deter men from sin by the example of the punishment meted out to the wrong-doer, it is right that the judge should take great account of humanity. Thus it happens that one and the same offence is visited in the same region, now with a more severe, now with a milder sentence. But there are some crimes which, because of their enormity, are punished, among all races of men above the rank of savages, not indeed by one particular kind of execution, but yet universally by some form of death. Such are parricide, voluntary homicide, sacrilege, blasphemy, impiety, or the violation of the publicly received religion, and other crimes of the sort. The case is clear enough as far as parricide, voluntary homicide, and sacrilege are concerned. It is surprising that anybody should entertain doubts respecting blasphemy and impiety; for nobody can deny that the magnitude of a crime is to be measured by the quality of the person against whom the offence is committed. Blasphemy and impiety, by which God's majesty is attacked, are, therefore, so much the greater crimes as his glory excels the dignity of men. Not that all blasphemers and impious persons indiscriminately are to be punished, but only those that act willingly and knowingly. Those that are without the Church must be left to God, who will judge them or in

his own time enlighten them. But those that are within the Church must be admonished, first, privately, then before a greater number, possibly dealt with more sharply. But if to blasphemy and impiety there be added heresy, that is, a stubborn contempt of the word of God and of Church discipline, and if a mad fury for corrupting others also has taken possession of them, what greater or more flagitious crime can arise among men? If, then, the mode of punishment ought to be regulated according to the greatness of the crime, it would seem that no adequate penalty can be found for this heinous enormity. A man who slays another, or commits any other crime against his neighbour, attacks the commonwealth, yet so as that some estimate can be made of the injury; but he that publicly opens the way for the corruption of God's true worship, starts a conflagration which possibly shall scarcely be extinguished by the everlasting destruction of an infinite number of men. Whether to vindicate the glory of God or to preserve human society, therefore, there are no men whom the magistrate ought to punish more severely than heretical blasphemers.[11]

Such, briefly stated, were Beza's arguments. He found them to be in full accord with the precepts given by the Lord in the Old Testament to slay without pity the introducer of strange gods, the false prophet, the blasphemer, and the profaner of the Sabbath. Such commands, he said, have never been repealed. The Mosaic Law remains in force, with the exception of the ceremonial part. Of the other two divisions, the Decalogue or Moral Law, being an accurate transcript of the Natural Law, in which man's

[11] *Ibid.*, i, 151, foll.

conscience agrees with the unchanging will of God, cannot suffer destruction before nature itself perishes, but abides the certain rule of right and wrong for all nations and for all ages. The third division of the Mosaic Law, the judicial, is also of universal obligation, in so far as its precepts do not relate to one people alone, nor punish the violation of ceremonies now abolished by the Gospel, but embrace that code of general equity which should everywhere prevail.

'In fine,' said Beza, 'I do not hesitate to affirm that those princes do their duty who adopt as examples for their own imitation these laws of God, by establishing, if not the very same kind of penalty, yet certainly the very same measure of penalty, and who, as against factious apostates, enact some form of capital punishment for horrible blasphemy and crime. For the majesty of God should be held to be of such moment among all men, through the everlasting ages, that, whoever scoffs at it, because he scoffs at the very Author of life, most justly deserves to be put to death by violence. This I say, this I cry aloud, relying upon the truth of God and the testimony of conscience. Let my opponents shout until they are hoarse that we are savage, cruel, inhuman, bloodthirsty. Yet shall the truth conquer and show at length that those deserve these epithets who, in their preposterous or insincere zeal for clemency, suffer the wolves to fatten upon the life of the sheep rather than do their duty in vindicating the majesty of God.'[12]

Most deplorable indeed is the error of Beza, both because of the perverted view he presented of the duty of the Christian Church to appeal to the State for aid in its

[12] *Ibid.*, i, 155.

conflict with heresy, and because of the equally disastrous notion he entertained of the duty of the Christian ruler to punish, even with death, the crime of active dissent from the Church's tenets. It is impossible for us, however, to deny the sincerity of the conviction, animating him and his fellow-reformers, that the indiscriminate admission into the Christian State of all shades of religious thought would at no distant period prove the State's ruin. It was this conviction that rendered Beza blind to the consequences that were sure to follow, and that did follow, the approval of the principle enunciated by Saint Augustine that constraint may lawfully be employed to bring the recalcitrant into the Gospel fold. Not to speak of the justification of every form of cruelty found by the apologists for Romanism in the execution of Servetus by Protestants, the enforced conversions of the dragonnades, a hundred years later, seemed to have an anticipated vindication in the theories advanced by those Protestant writers who with strange inconsistency have striven to clear Calvin and Geneva from the imputation of persecution.

Yet Beza was honest in this. He was also honest in his relentless opposition to Castalio, the advocate of toleration—a man whom, in his Life of Calvin, written ten years later, he did not hesitate to style a 'monster,' who 'by advising every man to believe what he chose, opened the door to all heresies and false doctrines.' Meanwhile, no more singular fact could be instanced in this connection than that the Protestant martyrs, commonly known as the 'Five from Geneva,' while daily awaiting death at the hands of the executioner for their religious opinions, set the seal of their unequivocal approval on the sentence meted out to Michael Servetus. One of their number, Antoine Laborie, himself informs us of the fact, in a letter written shortly before his execution. On being reminded by one of his judges 'that God distinctly commanded through Moses, that heretics should be most severely punished,' the future martyr tells us: 'I readily conceded that heretics ought certainly to be punished, and for an example I brought up that impure dog Servetus, upon whom was inflicted the last of punishments at Geneva; but I bade them be very cautious lest they should treat Christians and the sons of God as heretics.'[13]

[13] Crespin, *Actiones et Monimenta Martyrum*, fol. 291. *Rise of the Huguenots*, i, 213, 297.

CHAPTER 5

ACTIVITY AT LAUSANNE
1549–1558

THE life of Beza at Lausanne was far from being uneventful. His health, which we have seen was precarious when he accepted his responsible post in the University of Lausanne, not without fear that it might tax his strength beyond his powers of endurance, was subjected to a severe strain by an attack of one of those strange epidemics which were in the sixteenth century confusedly spoken of as 'the plague.' This occurred in the summer of 1551, when Beza had been professor for less than two years. Within another twelve months Providence laid new burdens upon him.

Five young men, all of them Frenchmen by birth, who had been studying both sacred and profane letters at his feet and at the feet of his colleagues for a longer or shorter space of time, conceived the brave project of suspending their studies that they might visit each his native region in the fatherland and enlighten their own friends and kindred in the truths which they had themselves embraced. It was a particularly hazardous venture to which they felt themselves individually called by God's Holy Spirit; for the French Protestants had fallen on exceptionally perilous times. The cruel Edict of Châteaubriand had lately been enacted. 'A right of appeal to the highest courts has hitherto been granted, and still is granted, to persons guilty of poisoning, forgery, and robbery,' wrote Calvin respecting the new law; 'but this appeal is denied to Christians. They are condemned by the ordinary judges to be dragged straight to the flames, without any liberty of appeal.'[1] To forsake the hospitable halls of Lausanne and enter France, was to rush headlong into a fiery furnace. One of the five, Bernard Seguin by name, a refugee from the region of Limousin, had been an inmate of Beza's house, possibly earning his livelihood in part by service.[2] Another had lived with Viret. But so far from dissuading them, their teachers and patrons applauded their manly and Christian resolve, and gave them letters commendatory of their character addressed to the faithful whom they might meet. However, the immediate issue did not correspond with their expectations. At Lyons, the very first place of importance which they entered, they were arrested, thrown into prison, examined on the capital charge of heresy, and condemned to death. It looked like a sheer waste of valuable lives which with a little more prudence might have been saved. In truth, however, there was no waste. Contrary to all anterior probability, under a law meant to expedite the execution of dissidents from the Church of Rome, they were kept in prison for over a year. During all that time, and long after, the letters that they wrote, containing minutes of the fearless words they uttered in the presence of everything that would naturally have terrified weaker men into silence or submission, thrilled the hearts of multitudes of men and women into

[1] Calvin to Bullinger, Oct. 15, 1551. *Calvini Opera*, xiv, 186-188.
[2] See, at least, Crespin, *Actiones et Monimenta*, fol. 186.

PIERRE VIRET

whose hands they fell. It is safe to say that each of the five 'scholars of Lausanne,' writing from the noisome dungeon of Lyons, made many more converts than he would have, gained had he been permitted to reach his home and preach without hindrance to his friends and neighbours.

The cause of the delay that rendered this activity possible is to be found in the influences which Beza and Viret were able to set in motion. The young men were the protégés and the recipients of the bounty of the powerful Canton of Bern, owner of the Pays de Vaud, and founder of the University of Lausanne. To secure the intercession of the Lords of Bern with the French King, who was in need of Swiss troops, and to direct the efforts of Bern in every quarter that appeared to offer promise of success—this was the incessant study of Beza and his colleagues. They did not hesitate to go in person and plead before the magistracy the cause of their beloved pupils. If all their efforts and all the honest endeavours of the Bernese failed to accomplish the release of the captives, the fault must be laid at the door of Henry II and of Cardinal Tournon, rivals in the ignoble practice of violating assurances and promises solemnly given.[3]

But labours such as this episode of martyr history imposed were far easier to be endured than the trial that awaited Beza two or three years later. I have spoken at

[3] *The Actiones et Monimenta Martyrum* devotes more than half a book, over sixty-four pages (fols. 185-217), to the heroic story of the 'Five Scholars of the Académie of Lausanne'—by no means the least interesting portion of the work. The 'Five Scholars of Lausanne,' who perished at Lyons in 1553, must not be confounded with the 'Five of Geneva,' who were put to death in 1555, at Chambéry, and of whose equally remarkable endurance Crespin tells us, *ibid.*, fols. 283-321.

the beginning of this work of the high position of the Reformer's family, of the ambition of his father and uncles, and of the hopes which both father and uncles based upon the brilliant abilities of the possession of which Theodore had given proof. Even now, although four or five years had elapsed since his withdrawal from France, they could not bring themselves to renounce the dream of seeing him once more at Paris, well started upon a career that would add great lustre and wealth to the already fortunate family. They were encouraged to make the attempt to reclaim him, by false rumours that his success abroad had by no means corresponded with his anticipations, and that they might more easily persuade him because he was a disappointed man. First, therefore, Theodore's elder brother John presented himself unannounced at Lausanne, fully prepared to offer sufficient inducements to bring the exile home. If Theodore was surprised by his unexpected but welcome advent, John was much more astonished to find Theodore occupying a position of honour and influence. Calumny had reported him to be living a dissolute life. He was said to be as much despised by others for his vices as he was himself wanting in self-respect. On the contrary, John found him a prominent citizen of Lausanne, a beloved colleague of scholars of high repute, a teacher enjoying the confidence of his pupils, the pride of a great school of learning. The result of the conference of the two brothers was such as might have been looked for. 'You must before this have heard of the unexpected arrival of my elder brother,' Beza wrote to Calvin. 'He came to institute a struggle with me, in which, thank God! I was so successful that I gained access to the attainment of what I never ventured to hope.' Unfortunately, we have no further information respecting the interview or its ulterior results. We only know that from Theodore Beza's last will and testament it would appear that some of his nephews had been brought up in the principles of a pure Gospel.[4]

The conflict was not over. John Beza at his departure stated to Theodore that, in case his persuasions proved ineffectual, his aged father would come in person to make a supreme effort. Accordingly, some months later, father and son met, on the confines of Franche-Comté. The Reformer looked forward with no little trepidation to an interview of which, if he did not fear the consequences, so far as his own steadfastness was concerned, he dreaded the results in the case of his infirm parent. He therefore wrote to Farel:

'I have received a fresh message respecting my father, which gives me great hope that either he will shortly come in person to us, or that I shall certainly meet him not far from here. Pray for me, I beg you, that I may not be compelled to be the minister of death to him through whom the Lord conferred this life upon me, and, in the next place, that against the impending temptation, the most severe of all, my strength may suffice that I may truly and earnestly ponder what the Lord says: "Every one that hath forsaken father or mother for my name's sake, shall receive an hundredfold and shall inherit everlasting life." For, otherwise, who am I that I should resist these temptations? But I hope to be able to do both this and all things through him who is in truth my Father.'[5]

[4] Baum, *Theodor Beza*, i, 235.

[5] Beza to Farel, April 24 (1554). Baum, *Theod. Beza*, i, doc., 438.

About the same time he wrote to Calvin respecting the same matter:

'A still harder struggle threatens me with my father, whom I am to meet in five days on the borders of the [Franche] Comté. May God give me grace, as I hope in him, not only to withstand courageously his powerful assaults upon my heart, but to win him over, if possible, for my Master. More than all other threats I fear that look, the caressing prayers, the tears of the father, the old man. But I hope that here also, as so often heretofore, my compassionate God will graciously stand by me, that all may redound to his glory.'[6]

This is all that has come down to us respecting the last, painful interview of Beza; but we infer that after a renewed but ineffectual presentation of all the motives which his father could marshal, both parent and child returned to their homes, doubly sorrowful because neither could hide it from himself that their conference had made the gulf of separation between them wider and final.

It is not out of place here to draw attention to a feature of the life of Beza which it had in common with the lives of most, if not indeed of all the rest, of the Reformers, although perhaps to a higher degree than they. The work which they were originally summoned to undertake, and which they accepted under the impression that it was to occupy their undivided attention for the residue of their days, so far from proving to be their sole vocation, was only one, and often by no means the most important, part of their future activities. When, at William Farel's solicitations, reinforced by his

[6] Trans. in Baum, i, 235, 236.

solemn and awful commination, John Calvin renounced his projected studies elsewhere, he supposed himself to be assuming charge of the reformation of the single city of Geneva. He little dreamed of the vast responsibilities, even 'the care of all the churches,' that lay ready to be placed upon his shoulders, whether he wished to bear them or not. In like manner, Theodore Beza, a convalescent, distrustful of his strength to do even this work, accepted the congenial duties of a professorship of the Greek language in the University of Lausanne, little foreseeing, we must suppose, that his chair would introduce him, naturally and by easy stages, to an incomparably wider sphere of usefulness—that, in point of fact, the university class-room was to serve merely as the vestibule of a grander structure—that from a teacher of youth it was to make of him a powerful advocate of the oppressed brethren of his own faith, at a later time the first recognised apologist before kings and princes of the principles for which the martyrs of the Reformed Churches of France had ineffectually striven to secure a hearing, and ultimately the honoured and trusted Counsellor and Leader of French Protestantism.

It was in the years now under consideration that Beza took the first steps in this direction.

We have seen how the circumstance that he had been their teacher induced Beza to assume a prominent part in the efforts put forth to save the lives of beloved pupils, destined victims of religious intolerance. The skill he manifested, and the consciousness to which he awoke, that his mental characteristics, his liberal training, his familiarity from infancy with the best society, his cultivated manners, and his easy and dignified address afforded him special facilities, and therefore conferred special responsibility, for representing the cause of the oppressed at court and in the homes of the powerful, opened his eyes to his advantages and to his duty. As a natural consequence, from this time forward, whenever there were delicate negotiations to be conducted in behalf of the churches of his faith, the eyes of men turned with ever-increasing confidence to Theodore Beza as the most promising man in the Reformed communion to conduct them. On the other hand, Beza himself permitted no considerations of private comfort or ease to deter him from undertaking a work often tedious and burdensome, always making a heavy draft upon his sympathy.

His first attempt in this direction had a political as well as a religious side. The alliance between the powerful and aggrandising Canton of Bern and the far less extensive and independent city of Geneva had been made for a definite number of years and was to terminate on February 8, 1556. It was by no means certain that the ambitious government of the former state would renew a relation from which the weaker city seemed to derive all the benefit. Moreover, Bern had more than once made it clear that there was no lack of persons powerful in its councils who would gladly extend its territory to the outlet of Lake Leman and hold Geneva upon the same tenure on which it already held the Pays de Vaud. If this project should fail, there were men ready to recommend the acceptance of the offers of a close alliance made contemporaneously by Duke Emmanuel Philibert of Savoy. The danger to Protestantism was imminent. Forsaken by Bern, the nearest and most powerful of the cantons in which the Reformation had taken root, the republic of Geneva, the object of the implacable hatred of the Roman Pontiff and of the Roman Catholics throughout Europe, could not have failed to be ground to pieces between the two adjoining countries—France and Savoy—of which the one or the other seemed destined to destroy its independent existence. The danger that menaced Geneva was a danger menacing Protestantism entire, and Beza helped to avert it, by exhibiting, and by inducing others to exhibit, to those in power the consequences that were certain to follow the suicidal policy of disunion. The renewal of the alliance between Bern and Geneva, in 1557, was in great part the result of Beza's intercession at Zurich and with the other Protestant cantons, and constituted in itself a claim to the gratitude of the city which was soon to become his home for the remainder of his life. It formed a new link in the chain already binding him in the closest friendship to John Calvin.

Meanwhile, before this disquieting question had been set at rest, another cause of solicitude arose. The valleys inhabited by the Waldenses, or Vaudois, of Piedmont, constituted a part of the territories taken from the Duke of Savoy by Francis I in 1535. During the score of years which the French occupation had now lasted, the inhabitants, professing to be in full accord with the Protestants, but claiming that they had held their pure faith for centuries before the birth of Luther and even from the time of the apostles, enjoyed a respite from persecution, as grateful as unlooked for. While relentlessly vexing the adherents of the Reformed faith in their own dominions, Francis I and

Henry II had either from policy abstained from similarly maltreating the professors of a kindred faith in the newly acquired domain, or, possibly, had forgotten the very existence of an insignificant body of dissenters who gave them no trouble in a time of general confusion. In consequence of their unwonted exemption from external interference, the Vaudois began to make a freer profession of their faith, to hold more public religious services, and to seek and obtain the services of twenty or more preachers, many of them trained for the sacred ministry in Switzerland, and especially at the school of Lausanne. In the Val d'Angrogna, in particular, they even commenced the erection of houses of worship. Such boldness could not long escape notice. The French Parliament of Turin sent two of its members, the President de Saint Julien and the Counsellor Delia Chiesa, with an ample escort to visit the valleys and put a stop to the progress of heresy. If proclamations could have effected this, the menaces addressed to those that refused to submit, and the rewards offered to those who consented to embrace the Roman Catholic faith, would have sufficed. But the Vaudois either forsook their homes or were deaf alike to threats and to entreaties. This was in 1556. The next year more strenuous measures were instituted. It became evident that nothing short of a determined effort to suppress the Vaudois religion was to be expected. That it would fail miserably in the end, as all similar efforts, before that time and since, have failed, was, it is true, almost a certainty. A Waldensian martyr, put to death for his constancy twenty years before, expressed the truth in a homely fashion, when, just before his execution and being already bound to the stake, he requested a bystander to hand him two stones, and having received them began to rub the one against the other, and then addressed these words to a crowd now curious to learn the significance of his strange actions: 'You imagine that by your persecutions you will abolish our Churches, but that will be no more possible for you than it is possible for me to destroy these stones with my hands or by eating them up.'[7] None the less was the prospect of one of those massacres, that have so often drenched the Waldensian mountain-sides with blood, so terrible that no time was lost in sending forth a cry of distress to summon all friends in Switzerland and elsewhere to the rescue.

Both Geneva and Lausanne heard the news with pity and with horror. Among the destined victims of persecution and death were prominent ministers of whom many formerly studied theology in those cities under Calvin and Beza. There was no opportunity for long consultation. Someone must be promptly despatched to arouse the four great Protestant cantons and the Protestant princes of southern Germany, and induce them to use the privilege of friends or allies with the King of France, by remonstrating against the execution of the proscriptive measures ordered by the court. That man must be courageous, energetic, and quick and fertile in expedients. Above all, he must be sufficiently catholic in his views to be able to conciliate in favour of the proposed intervention the partisans of the different shades of the Reformed faith and the Lutherans, whether broad or narrow in their views. He must, moreover, be a man of conspicuous tact and address, who from his birth

[7] Monastier, *Histoire de l'Église Vaudoise* (Toulouse, 1847), i, 210.

and associations would stand unabashed in the presence of princes and courtiers. Such a man was found in Theodore Beza, and the choice of him was fully justified by the sequel. With him went, as fellow-envoy, the now aged William Farel, the memory of whose masterful ministry of evangelisation in French-speaking Switzerland and in the neighbouring parts was still fresh in men's minds, and whose rash impetuosity, if not altogether extinguished by added years, was well kept in check by the surer judgment of his younger colleague, whom he thoroughly respected and admired. Bern not only gave leave of absence to Beza, but provided him and Farel with strong letters of recommendation to her three confederate cantons of Zurich, Basel, and Schaffhausen. In these places, as everywhere else, Beza was the spokesman. Being unfamiliar with the German language, he spoke in Latin, the universal language of courts and universities, and his ornate periods and graceful eloquence secured him a favourable hearing from all the learned. When it was necessary, the Reformer Bullinger, of Zurich, and others gladly acted as interpreters. With the support of such a man at Zurich, of the leading pastor, Simpert Vogt, at Schaffhausen, and of Simon Sulzer at Basel, it was easy to bring the magistrates to look favourably on the plan of sending a body of envoys from the four evangelical cantons to the French court. The 'instruction' given to them as a guide for the discharge of their commission in a delicate undertaking has come down to us. It was written by Theodore Beza, and is the first and a very favourable example of his papers dealing with political affairs.[8]

[8] Text in Baum, *Theodor Beza,* i, doc., 401-405, April, 1557.

The difficulties increased as Beza and Farel pursued their way, but these were overcome. At Montbéliard—capital of a county now forming part of France—which, many years before, Farel and Toussain had undertaken to evangelise in the midst of great commotions, they found the place altogether won over to Protestantism, but they also found Toussain, who was now at the head of the Church, not only decided in his adhesion to the Lutheran view of the Lord's Supper as opposed to the Zwinglian or to the Calvinistic, but particularly alienated from Geneva and pronounced in his disapproval of the execution of Servetus, and of the apologies written in justification of that lamentable event. This did not, however, in the end, prevent Montbéliard also from endorsing and heartily recommending the mission of the envoys. At Strassburg Beza was welcomed by François Hotman. This eminent scholar, his attached colleague in the University of Lausanne, had, a year or two since, accepted a chair in the University of Strassburg. Here, as elsewhere, the presence of the venerable Farel, who had written nothing to offend Lutheran susceptibilities, proved advantageous. The senate of the city not only paid him and Beza other flattering attentions, but sent Hotman with them, mounted, and with mounted guards of honour, at the city's expense, to carry two letters, the one addressed to Otto Henry, Elector Palatine, and the other to Duke Christopher of Würtemberg. Both these princes received the envoys graciously, the former at Baden, where he was sojourning for his health's sake, the latter at Göppingen. The Elector Palatine, desirous of making the German intercession more effective with the French king by the addition of the influence of Hesse, wrote and despatched by a special messenger of his own a letter to the Landgrave, Philip of Hesse.

An object which Beza had incidentally proposed to himself in his mission, an object of even greater permanent importance to Christendom than the rescue of the Waldenses, was the unification of Protestantism by the reconciliation of the views respecting the Lord's Supper held by the two great subdivisions of the Protestant world. He had conferred at Strassburg with the superintendent and doctor of theology, John Marbach. At Göppingen he met and conversed long with the eminent Jacob Andreæ, his future disputant in a more formal colloquy. There seemed to be some prospect of substantial agreement, and, as the references to Calvin's expressed views were deemed insufficient, Beza was induced to draw up a new and brief confession of faith touching the chief point in controversy. Written with the evident desire to reduce to a minimum the difference between the opinions of Lutherans and Calvinists, the document is a literary and religious curiosity. In some regards it may be compared with those extraordinary articles, with their amazing concessions, which Melanchthon drew up, a quarter of a century earlier, in the vain hope of being able to bring together such discordant views as those of Rome and those of the adherents of the Reformation.[9] Calvin and Beza undoubtedly rejected the opinion of Zwingli, that the elements of bread and wine in the Eucharist are mere signs. It is equally certain that they did not hold with Luther that the body and blood of Christ are really present in, with, and under the bread and

[9] In 1534. See *Rise of the Huguenots*, i, 161, 162.

wine, though these are not miraculously transmuted into very flesh and blood. But it must be confessed that, in the Confession now under consideration, as we shall see, Beza approached as nearly to the Lutheran view as it was possible to do without actually abandoning the Reformed position.

Both the Swiss and the Germans fulfilled their promises and sent envoys to France. Their reception need not detain us long. The Swiss, honest but simple-minded rustics, were kindly but somewhat contemptuously treated, and received no definite answer to their plea in behalf of the Waldenses. They deserve our respect, however, for this, at least, that when at their departure King Henry II, who, through Constable Montmorency, had previously promised them each a gold chain, now sent them a present of two hundred ducats, they proved themselves to be no mercenary boors, by indignantly rejecting the proffered bounty, with the exclamation: 'We seek not gold nor silver, but the safety of brethren who are our members and partakers in the same religion.'[10] The German envoys, who arrived in Paris a full month later than the Swiss, represented seven Protestant princes, all of them entitled to high consideration. They were instructed to impress upon the King of France the injury to his reputation which the report of the cruelties exercised upon his innocent subjects would produce. They were also to urge upon his Majesty the necessity of instituting an impartial investigation, which would surely establish both the purity of the doctrinal tenets and the loyalty of the persecuted. But although a reply was made to the envoys, in the monarch's

[10] See Baum, i, 273, and the extract of a letter from Bullinger to Calvin, given *ibid.*, i, 274, note.

name, it was of no very satisfactory import. For it plainly betrayed the annoyance of the king at what he considered an unnecessary appeal of his conquered subjects to their sovereign's friends, and confined itself to the expression of a hope that the inhabitants of the Val d'Angrogna would henceforth so order their lives, like the rest of his subjects, as not to compel him to exercise severity toward them.[11]

Exactly how much good was effected by the German and Swiss intervention, it is difficult to ascertain. Despite his affected indifference, Henry and his advisers were not insensible to the importance of maintaining a good understanding with their Protestant neighbours and allies. Beside this, however, the king had within a few weeks more engrossing and perplexing matters on hand. On August 10, 1557, his army was defeated with great loss in a pitched battle at Saint Quentin. Constable Montmorency, who commanded it, was taken prisoner. Paris was threatened. It was no time to think about the Vaudois and their proposed annihilation. The project was dropped. Less than two years later, by the treaty of Cateau Cambrésis (on April 3, 1559), the Vaudois valleys, with all the rest of Piedmont, save Turin and two or three other places, passed out of the hands of the French and were restored to their rightful sovereign, the Duke of Savoy.

This was but the first of three successive visits of Beza to Germany in the interest of his oppressed fellow-believers. From the Vaudois or Waldensian valleys of Piedmont the scene of persecution shifted to France and to the city of Paris itself. So precarious was the situation of the Protestants of

[11] Baum, i, 274.

the capital, in view of the sanguinary legislation of Henry II, that although their number was by no means insignificant and was daily growing, they dared meet only by night and with the utmost secrecy. Unhappily a nocturnal gathering held in a house of the Rue Saint Jacques was surprised by their enemies, and, out of a much larger number of worshippers, one hundred and twenty persons, mostly women, with a few men and some children, were apprehended and dragged to prison. Many of them were shortly put to death, and the mob had the gratification of beholding such a sight as a Parisian mob never tired of seeing—the victims of its hatred, some of them young women and respectable matrons, roasted in the flames of the *estrapade*. The political juncture was particularly inauspicious for the 'Lutherans,' as the dissenters from the Roman Catholic Church were still styled. Bigots represented the calamity that had lately befallen the kingdom in the defeat of Saint Quentin as a direct punishment for its sin in tolerating heresy, and stirred up the populace to welcome any new blow aimed at the Protestants. The latter, terrified by what had befallen their brethren, and apprehensive of what might still be in store, anxious above all to save the lives of the prisoners from their impending fate, sent in haste to Geneva to acquaint Calvin with the new disaster and to beg that everything should be done to enlist the interest of neighbouring Protestant States. Again was Beza chosen, in conjunction with the aged Farel and with Budaeus and Carmel, to lay the pitiful case of the French before as many as would listen to their cry of distress. Not once but twice did the Reformer leave Lausanne and exert himself to the utmost to bring both

Swiss cantons and German princes to prompt and decisive intercession. The direct results were not over-encouraging. The Swiss envoys when they reached the court of France allowed themselves to be so completely hoodwinked by the Cardinal of Lorraine, always rich in promises of support, that leaving all to him they found themselves in the end dismissed by the monarch with a message to the effect that he had expected that Zurich, Bern, Basel, and Schaffhausen would be content with his response to them in the matter of the Waldenses of Angrogna, and abstain from sending him ambassadors on a similar occasion, as they had now done. At any rate, he begged his 'very dear and good friends' from this time forth to give themselves no care or solicitude respecting what he might do in his kingdom, since he was resolved to maintain his religion therein as the most Christian kings, his predecessors, had done. In this matter, he said, he had to give an account of his actions to no one but to God.[12] The Elector Palatine wrote a letter which seems to have had some effect in securing a lull in the persecution. Others, especially good Christopher of Würtemberg, did the same. But the German princes were not always moved to prompt and effective action. The old disunion between Lutherans and Reformed had not been suffered to die out by the zeal of the theologians who looked askance at the orthodoxy of their Swiss brethren and were disposed to magnify rather than to attenuate the disastrous differences of Luther and Zwingli, now that Luther and Zwingli had long been in their graves. It seemed to Beza an opportune

[12] The king's answer, November 5, 1557, in *Bull.*, i, 166. *Rise of the Huguenots*, i, 309, 310.

time to labour to conciliate the favour of the Germans, by showing them that the persecuted French Protestants whom they were entreated to help were no heretics, but brethren in substantial agreement with themselves as to the essential truths of the Reformation held in Germany. In common with his colleagues, therefore, he laid before Melanchthon, Brentius, Marbach, Andreæ, and the other most prominent representatives of Lutheran theology, at their gathering at Worms, a written exposition of the tenets of the French Churches, of so irenic a character that the divergences seemed not merely smoothed down, but almost obliterated. In all the Augsburg Confession of 1530, they found but one article which was not in agreement with their own Confession and which they did not accept—namely, the article respecting the Lord's Supper. Even the difficulties in this article they thought could be removed by a conference of learned and pious men. Meanwhile, they declared that 'they had never believed, nor had they taught, that the Lord's Supper is merely a sign of profession, as the Anabaptists believe, or merely a sign of the absent Christ.'[13]

A few months before, while on the embassy to plead the cause of the Waldenses, Beza, speaking for himself and for Farel, expressed himself no less strongly, in a confession of faith which he handed to the Duke of Würtemberg, at Göppingen, as setting forth the doctrine held by the Churches of Switzerland and Savoy, or Piedmont.[14] A sentence or two from this, the first of Beza's utterances

[13] 'Confessio Doct. Eccles. Gallic. Exhibita Theologis August. Confess, in Collog. Wormatiensi.' Baum, doc., i, 409-411. Dated October 8, 1557.

[14] Beza's first 'Apology,' addressed to Claude de Sainctes (1567), in *Tract. Theol.*, ii, 295.

respecting the Lord's Supper, it may be well to quote, in order to show the length to which the Reformer was willing to go in the effort to find a common ground on which to stand with his German brethren:

'We confess that in the Lord's Supper not only all the benefits of Christ, but also the very substance of the Son of man—I say, that true flesh which the everlasting Word took into perpetual unity of person, in which He was born and suffered for us, rose and ascended into the heavens, and that true blood which He shed for us—are not merely signified, or set forth symbolically, figuratively, or typically, as the memorial of an absent person, but are truly and certainly represented, exhibited, and offered to be applied, there being added to the thing itself symbols that are by no means bare symbols, but such that, so far as appertains to God's promise and offer, they always have the thing itself truly and certainly conjoined, whether they be set forth to believers or to unbelievers.'[15]

It is not surprising that, in his attempt to gain over the German Protestants, Beza should have incurred not a little risk of alienating his own friends in Switzerland. His apparent concessions to Lutheran views were highly distasteful to the adherents of the Zwinglian theology, and Bullinger, the Reformer of Zurich, had succeeded not only to the influence but in a great measure to the views of Zwingli. Endeared as he was to Beza by ties of cordial affection and good-will, Bullinger could not but view the utterances of

[15] 'Confessio Fidei Doctrinæque de Cœna Domini Exhibita Illustriss. Princ. Virtemberg., Authoribus Th. Beza et Guilhelmo Farello.' Baum, doc., i, 406, 407. Dated May 14, 1557.

Beza at Göppingen with grave apprehension, as indicative of a danger of schism among Swiss Churches thus far harmonious. Calvin understood his friend better and poured oil on the troubled waters. 'As there is no lurking danger in Beza's confession,' he wrote to Bullinger, August 7, 1557, 'I readily excuse him, because, in consideration of the brethren, with studied moderation he has striven to reconcile fierce men; especially as he previously distinctly explained all his different meanings.'[16] But Bullinger was not fully appeased even by Calvin's intercession, and Beza's efforts to reconcile Lutherans and Reformed by reducing to an apparent minimum the differences that kept them apart, gave rise to an interchange of letters between Lausanne and Zurich, extending over a number of months, which even now may be read with profit. Upon Beza's project of a conference to be held with the view of harmonising discordant views upon the matter under consideration, Bullinger looked with scant favour. He accepted with kindness the explanations of his meaning which Beza, sincerely sorry to have incurred the disapproval of so excellent a friend, made at great length in successive epistles, and he conceded frankly the desirability of mutual love and holy concord between the servants of a common Master.

'Meanwhile,' said he and his colleagues, the pastors and doctors of the Church of Zurich, 'it is not any and every sort of a concord that we long for; but a concord that is religious, moderate, conflicting in nothing with the pure truth hitherto professed, introducing no obscurity or doubt into manifest light and perspicuous doctrine, a concord

[16] Calvin to Bullinger, Aug. 7, 1557. Bonnet, iii, 345.

which on account of its clearness shall be common and welcome to all the pious, abiding and stable, and that shall scatter abroad no new beginnings of fresh dissensions.'[17]

Thus it was that Theodore Beza's attempt to effect a reconciliation between the warring elements within the bosom of Protestantism itself, aroused the suspicion, and drew upon him the animadversion, of many of his own most sincere friends. So had Melanchthon's equally well-meant project of bringing together again the Roman Catholic and Protestant Churches, two- or three-and-twenty years earlier, drawn upon him the displeasure of the greater part of those who learned of it.[18] As, however, Philip Melanchthon comforted himself, when accused of being a deserter to the Protestant cause, not only by the consciousness of his integrity of purpose but by the support and approval of Martin Luther, so did Theodore Beza find ample compensation for the not altogether unreasonable annoyance expressed by others, in the unswerving confidence extended to him by the great Reformer of Geneva. For to Calvin he felt a devotion not inferior to that which characterised the relation of the younger of the Wittenberg theologians to his father in the Lord. Both Beza and Melanchthon, if unsuccessful in accomplishing the desired union, had this consolation, at least, that their labours had been expended in the most honourable and humane of causes, the endeavour to realise the great purpose of the common Lord of all Christian people, that they might be one even as he and

[17] The Pastors and Professors of Theology, Ministers of the Church of Zurich, to Beza at Lausanne, Dec. 15, 1557. Baum, doc., i, 503.

[18] See *Rise of the Huguenots*, i, 186.

his Father were one. And both Melanchthon and Beza were specially inspired by an earnest desire and hope thereby to put an end to the further effusion of blood at the hands of those professing the same Christian faith.

CHAPTER 6

BEZA BECOMES CALVIN'S COADJUTOR AND RECTOR OF THE UNIVERSITY OF GENEVA

1558, 1559

In the year 1558, Beza resigned the professorship which he had held for a little short of nine years, to accept a chair in the new institution which Calvin had long been anxious to found at Geneva, for the promotion of higher learning, but, especially, of theological science.

His course in Lausanne had been brilliant and successful. Of this there could be no question. He had discharged the duties of his office with signal ability and faithfulness, and had been rewarded for his toil not only by the applause of the learned, but by a marked increase in the number of his pupils. From a mere handful of students, the Académie of Lausanne had come to boast an attendance of seven hundred.[1] To this development no instructor, not even François Hotman, the distinguished jurisconsult, during his connection with the University, had contributed so much as Beza. The magnetism of the Reformer's personality, the profound impression made from the very start by his wonderful erudition, his wide acquaintance with classical as well as sacred antiquity, his growing reputation not only as a controversialist, but as a man honoured in the councils

[1] Beza to Farel, April 29, 1558, in Baum, doc., i, 519.

of the leading Protestant powers of Switzerland and Germany and entrusted with the advocacy of the claims of the persecuted both of France and Piedmont,—all enhanced in the eyes of the studious the attraction of the school of learning of which he was a chief ornament.

Why, then, did Beza consent to leave a position so enviable and of such extensive usefulness? The answer to the question is found partly, at least, in the unfortunate condition of discord and embarrassment of the Church of Lausanne. The union of Church and State, always a source, if not of actual, yet certainly of possible trouble, is most productive of mischief in a region which itself is dependent upon another region, its superior by right of conquest or by some other form of proprietorship. The natural and healthy development of the Reformation at Lausanne was hampered by the suzerainty of Bern. It might perhaps have triumphed over the lukewarmness or positive enmity of the irreligious part of the subject city; it was impotent when that element of the population was encouraged by the avowed determination of the paramount authority to tolerate no innovation in the accepted order of things. The Reformer, Pierre Viret, had, many years before, taken an important part in the preparatory work that led to the religious change of Geneva in advance of Calvin's advent, and had subsequently been for a time one of the ministers of that city. He was now and had long been the leading pastor of Lausanne. It was he, as has been seen, that induced Theodore Beza to accept the chair he had held with honour to the city and with credit to himself. A man of solid attainments and of sterling worth, he was at the same time as impetuous and uncompromising as Farel had been in his youth, and had learned none of the prudence that had come to Farel with advancing years. The laxity of morals of a city many of whose inhabitants utterly failed to recognise the external change of religion as affecting their personal and social life, had long weighed upon Viret's heart and conscience. To admit to a participation in the most sacred of Christian rites men and women of whose unfitness there could be no doubt, and who seemed so much the more anxious to present themselves as their coming was opposed by all the good, seemed to him as a pastor to be an unjustifiable act of complicity in a criminal profanation. He resolved to put a stop to it. Having by his ardent zeal brought his colleagues over to his opinions, he gave notice that at the coming Easter the customary celebration of the Lord's Supper would not be observed. He would not desecrate the most sublime and holy ordinance in heaven or on earth. He and his fellow-ministers demanded nothing less than the institution of a system of Church government such as had been successfully established in Geneva and had made of a city noted for the dissoluteness of its denizens the model State and Church of Christendom. Instead of the promiscuous admission to the Lord's Supper of all applicants, whatever their knowledge or ignorance, their consistency or inconsistency of deportment, he demanded the erection of a Church consistory, or session, with power of discipline ranging from the mildest admonition even to formal excommunication. The better and more earnest part of the people, especially the fugitives from persecution in France, welcomed his efforts. But these efforts met with strenuous opposition from such of the inhabitants of Lausanne as looked back with regret to the days when, under the rule of the former bishops of the place, there was little or no inquiry into the life of the laity, or even of the clergy. The resident representatives of Bern gave to Viret's opponents the support of their authority. With a view to the removal of exciting topics from the pulpit, Bern particularly forbade the public discussion of the subject of Predestination. Four clergymen of Thonon, believing it to be their duty, despite the prohibition, to preach on the doctrine in question, were deprived of their places by the government. The classis of Bern replied by demanding freedom of preaching and a form of Church government not unlike that of Geneva, declaring that unless it were granted they could not with a clear conscience continue to exercise their churchly functions. Thereupon the chief magistrate and council of Bern resolved to show the world who was master in the Pays de Vaud, and formally cited by name all the preachers and professors to appear in person before them in the city of Bern, on or before a given date, to receive an answer to the 'articles' in which their demands had been couched. So rough a summons addressed to the clergy and professors of the subject city was itself an indignity; the answer which they received amounted almost to positive insult. For while Viret and his associates were graciously informed that they might preach about Predestination if they had a natural occasion to do so and if they preached in a moderate and edifying manner, they were not encouraged to look for any such improvement in the administration of the Church as they had declared indispensable to the continuance of the discharge of their offices. In fact, the Bernese council demanded a categorical reply, upon the morrow, as to what the pastors and professors intended to do. They, moreover, intimated that, if the latter persisted in the declaration they had made to the effect that in case all their requests were not granted they must ask leave to lay down their offices, they would not only be allowed to do so, but forthwith be banished from the country.

Beza, himself no friend of extreme measures, had originally disapproved Viret's course and maintained a middle ground, entertaining relations of kindly intercourse with both parties. He doubtless hoped that, in the course of time and without resort to an attitude of such pronounced hostility to the ruling power, the desired advantages might be secured through the milder methods of persuasion and greater enlightenment. That he was lukewarm or underrated the importance of the points upon which Viret insisted, is disproved not only by his subsequent attitude when at the head of the Church of Geneva, but by the vigour, zeal, and ability with which in this very year (1558) he maintained in an extended answer to Sebastian Castalio, that the doctrine of the everlasting predestination of God is the sole foundation of man's salvation.[1] He had been induced, reluctantly and against his better judgment, to acquiesce in the course taken by his more radical brethren, lest he might appear to have deserted them at a critical juncture. He thus came to share in the humiliating journey to Bern and the insolent treatment at the hands of the chief

[1] It is the treatise entitled 'Ad Sebastiani Castellionis calumnias,' etc., reprinted in the collected *Tract. Theolog.*, i, 337-424.

magistrate and council. These last circumstances, however, were not needed to complete Beza's disgust with the situation of affairs at Lausanne. Long before their occurrence, he had fully made up his mind to sever his relations with the University and to accept the more congenial work to which Calvin invited him and in the discharge of which he had the alluring prospect of association with the great Reformer whom of all men he honoured and loved most.[2] Viret might be annoyed at the determination of his colleague, and might blame him for abandoning a post which Viret himself had by his ill-judged course contributed to make unendurable for a high-spirited gentleman, indeed, for a man of ordinary self-respect; he could not induce Beza to reconsider his action or consent to prolong his stay in a city where he might look for the repetition of scenes such as he had of late witnessed. The event fully justified his action. Within a few months, Viret and the greater part of his associates in Church and University were themselves reduced to the necessity of following Beza's example. Within that time the decadence of the institution to which Beza's learning had lent a temporary lustre set in. Thus Lausanne lost its great opportunity of permanently possessing the school for the training of the Christian athletes who were to achieve wonders in the cause of French Protestantism

[2] The citation to Bern was dated on the first of August, 1558. See the document in Baum, i, 348. Beza, in a letter to Calvin written on the twenty-fourth of the preceding November, had already betrayed his disapprobation of Viret's methods and his intention to use his own freedom more fully than heretofore (*ibid.*, i, 349). A letter of Calvin, August 29, 1558, informs us that Beza, having sent on his household effects before him, was expected in Geneva within two days. *Calvini Opera*, xvii, 308.

down to the time of the disastrous Revocation of the Edict of Nantes (1685). How, after that event, Lausanne regained a certain prestige in the times of the Church of the Desert, it does not belong to us to relate here.[3]

As for Beza himself, he said nothing, either at the time or subsequently, that might seem to reflect upon Pierre Viret, a man who had in the past deserved well of the Reformation, and was destined still to do good service, both in Geneva and in the Church of Lyons, a man to whom he was attached by strong ties of affection. In his letter to Wolmar, within a year and a half later, he confines himself to the statement, that at the end of his stay at Lausanne, he returned, with the kind consent of the council of Bern, to Geneva, partly because he was desirous of giving himself wholly to theology, partly for other reasons which it was unnecessary to rehearse. And he adds that, not so much of his own choice, as by the advice of men of great eminence, he was induced at Geneva to undertake the office of the sacred ministry.[4]

In Geneva Theodore Beza was at last in the spot where for years, because of his increasing friendship and intimacy with John Calvin, he had found his chief intellectual and moral support and sympathy. Geneva is not distant much over thirty miles in a straight line from Lausanne, and the lake, then as now, afforded an easy and pleasant route. The proximity of the two cities to one another had encouraged the younger man to make frequent visits to his old schoolfellow, now become an associate in the work of the

[3] See the account of the establishment of the theological seminary of Lausanne by Antoine Court, in 1730, in my history, *The Huguenots and the Revocation of the Edict of Nantes*, ii, 462, 463.

[4] See Appendix.

LAUSANNE

Reformation. It was time, however, that two such kindred spirits should no longer be separated even by so trifling a distance. There can be no doubt that irrespective of his plans for making use of Theodore Beza's extraordinary scholarship for the upbuilding of his projected university, Calvin had before this begun to look to Beza as the most suitable man to succeed to the great and multiform duties which Providence had thrown upon him. It is true that Calvin himself was not yet fifty years old, and might, so far as age was concerned, have had the prospect of a long course of activity. But his constitution, never robust, was enfeebled by prodigious study and devotion to the claims of others. At an age when many a scholar is full of strength and vigour, Calvin thought it none too soon to seek for a younger man to be a sharer of his toil and the prospective heir of an inheritance of unremitting solicitude for the welfare of the churches.

The plan of Calvin for the 'Académie' of Geneva contemplated nothing less than the erection of a true university—a daring undertaking in a little commonwealth of a few thousand souls, poor in resources, and threatened by powerful neighbours. The founders were compelled to solve a difficult problem as to the source from which the necessary funds could be obtained. It is a significant circumstance that contemporaneously with the purchase of a site for the school, there was published an order of the magistrates of the little republic, commanding all notaries to exhort those persons who might thereafter employ them to draw up wills, to make bequests for the institution.[5] As Geneva had

[5] 'On the 17th of January [1558],' says an extract from the public records of the republic of Geneva, given by Baum, i, 350, 'a college was established.

hitherto possessed no school for higher learning, a 'College,' or Gymnasium, was also created, for the purpose of affording preparatory training for the Académie, or University proper, thus replacing a more modest school once taught by Mathurin Corderius, of whom I have already spoken, a scholar whose Colloquies were long in vogue, as a manual for the drill of the young in the familiar use of the Latin language. The study of Latin literature was assiduously pursued in the College and found no place in the Académie. In the latter a close acquaintance with the exclusive tongue of the learned was an absolute prerequisite; for who could profit by instruction given in a language which he understood not at all or but imperfectly? Of the departments of a university only the School of Theology was at first instituted, and of this Theodore Beza was the first head or Rector. It was hoped that other schools would soon be added, and indeed the anticipation was partially realised; but the efforts made in this direction were spasmodic and short-lived. A School of Medicine in a small town or village encounters insuperable difficulties through the lack of large hospitals and of clinical instruction. To encourage the study of medicine at Geneva, it is true, a law was passed in 1564, five years after the establishment of the University, which permitted the dissection of the bodies of criminals executed for their offences and even of the corpses of patients that died at the city hospital.[6] But the provision was inadequate even

A college [building] was erected at *Les Hutins de Bolomier*; seven classes were started, and three professors instituted: one in theology, one in philosophy, and one in Greek. Order was given to all notaries to exhort testators to give to the college.'

[6] Article of Professor Cellerier, as below. *Bull.*, iv, 16.

in an age which sent men to the gallows or to the block for a great variety of crimes, and in which the laws of health were very imperfectly known or observed. Three years later (1567), Beza, in asking the prayers of the pastors of Zurich, drew special attention to the new medical department of the University.[7] The study of Law fared better than that of Medicine, but the eminent teachers that were called to lecture were very inadequately compensated for their work or proved restless for other reasons, and made but a short tarry. This was the case with Hotman, after the Massacre of Saint Bartholomew's Day (1572). The School of Theology and its teachers fared better. Yet the narrowness of the provision for their support, which has been estimated as the equivalent of one thousand francs, or two hundred dollars of our present money, was not without its discouraging effect.[8]

The solemn opening of the institution took place on June 5, 1559, in the spacious cathedral of the city, in the presence of the two syndics and of the members of the council of Geneva. The services were impressive. On this occasion Beza, who had at his arrival been merely constituted public professor of Greek literature, but had subsequently been chosen (October 15, 1558) to preach the Gospel and requested to continue his lectures on the Sacred Scriptures, was formally proclaimed Rector, and inducted into office.[9]

A few months later, on November 9, 1559, he subscribed his name to the laws of the Académie, and to the Confession

[7] Inedited letter to Bullinger of March 12, 1567. Copy in Baum collection, Library of French Prot. Hist. Society at Paris.

[8] Article 'L'Académie de Genève,' by Professor J. E. Cellerier, in the *Bull.*, iv (1855), 15—a valuable monograph.

[9] See his address in *Calvini Op.*, xvii, 542-547.

of Faith of the Church of the city. The signature, 'Theodorus Beza Vezelius scholæ rector,' may still be read either in the original *Livre du Recteur*, or in the faithful transcript of the manuscript which has been printed in our own days.[10] The name is followed by the signatures of Antoine Cavallier, of Vire in Normandy, professor of Hebrew; of Jean Tagaut, of Paris, professor of Arts, or Philosophy; and of François Béraud, of Paris, professor of Greek. The last two had been colleagues of Beza at Lausanne and had already followed him to Geneva. Others were yet to come. But with these we have nothing to do here. As to Beza he began at once to devote himself to theology. Calvin had for years been teaching this same subject, and he continued to do so, although he was never formally inscribed as a professor. How they divided the instruction between them is not quite certain; but it must have been as Calvin, the author of the entire scheme, had arranged. The instruction of both was essentially exegetical. Calvin and Beza at first confined themselves to the simple interpretation of the books of the Bible, and successively lectured upon them in alternate weeks. At a later time, while one of the two professors continued to devote himself to exegesis, his colleague treated in his lectures of the 'common places,' or systematic theology.[11]

Self-sacrifice was the law of the school. The salaries, always inadequate to the support of the incumbents of the chairs, were neither regularly nor fully paid. In times of public calamity we shall see Theodore Beza continuing to

[10] *Le Livre du Recteur*. Catalogue des Étudiants de l'Académie de Genève de 1559 à 1859. Geneva, 1860.

[11] Professor Cellerier, *op. cit.*, 15.

teach without compensation, and, indeed, taking upon his shoulders the burden of the entire school, until the return of better days. And in all periods of the history of the Académie of Geneva, from Calvin's time to ours, so high has been the credit of this seat of learning that men eminent in science have, we are told, accepted as a great honour the position of teaching professors. Twice, too, within a space of sixty years, professors raised to the rank of the first magistrate of the republic have continued, despite this high dignity, to instruct their students.[12]

These students, writing their names below the signatures of the professors whom I have named upon the *Livre du Recteur*, at first, like their instructors, subscribed to the doctrines of the Confession of Faith of the Church of Geneva. This practice continued from 1559 to 1576, when, under the presidency of Beza, and no doubt with his full approval, the 'Venerable Company of the Pastors' of the city relieved the young men of the obligation: 'inasmuch,' say the minutes, 'as this [subscription] deprives Papists and Lutherans of the opportunity to come and receive profit from this church, and inasmuch as it does not seem reasonable to press after this fashion a conscience that is resolved not to sign what it does not understand. Moreover the Saxons [Lutherans] have taken advantage of this ordinance to compel our students that go to them to sign the Confession of Augsburg.'[13]

Calvin had well selected his colleague and successor. As unsparing of himself, as indefatigable in labour, as devoted to the interests of the faith which he had embraced as was

[12] Cellerier, 71. The reference is to Professors Lect and Godefroy.

[13] *Ibid.*, 22.

his master, Beza of all men living was best qualified to carry out what Calvin had initiated. Geneva and the world hardly realised the change when the direction of affairs passed, after a comparatively brief interval, from the hands of the one to the other. For Beza, while no blind partisan and no servile imitator, had heartily accepted the system of Calvin, and had become so thoroughly imbued with his spirit, that there was no perceptible break in the influence which emanated from the little city upon the Rhône. Meanwhile, even before Calvin's removal, that influence seemed to be doubled by the accession of Beza as Calvin's coadjutor, and Beza did for France what Calvin himself could not have accomplished.

CHAPTER 7

BEZA AT NÉRAC
1560

THE crisis was fast approaching at which Theodore Beza was to be called to take a more active part in the affairs of Protestantism than was offered by embassies in behalf of persecuted Vaudois. Before long the French court, indeed France entire, was to witness his coming as an advocate of the professors of the doctrines which men still persisted in contemptuously stigmatising as 'new,' and was to hear from his lips the first great plea uttered in defence of those doctrines.

Meanwhile an incident occurred, at first sight of evanescent importance, but destined to exercise a lasting influence both upon Beza's life and upon the course of at least one great personage in France. Toward the close of the brief reign of Francis II, after the conclusion of the famous Assembly of the Notables at Fontainebleau, Antoine of Bourbon, titular King of Navarre, was sojourning in the city of Nérac in the province of Guyenne, of which he was governor by appointment of the King of France. Here he deliberated with his most trusted supporters respecting the position which he should assume in the distracted state of the kingdom. The Huguenots, as the Protestants of the realm had, within a few months, begun to be nicknamed,

ANTOINE DE BOURBON, KING OF NAVARRE

were making such rapid progress that the Papal Church trembled for the consequences. In the late Assembly, Admiral Coligny spoke boldly in favour of a frank concession of religious liberty and advocated a complete cessation of persecution. Others supported his views and did not quail in face of the defiant attitude and threatening words of the Duke of Guise and his partisans. Antoine had held aloof and had not been present at the discussions. Though cowardly and unstable, he had given and still gave men reason to believe that he sympathised with the Reformed and would uphold their cause. When, therefore, Theodore Beza received at Geneva a very pressing invitation from the King and the Queen of Navarre to visit Nérac and give them the benefit of his counsel, it seemed impossible to decline. The 'Venerable Company of the Pastors of Geneva' cheerfully approved his going, while prudently recording upon their minutes a simple statement that, 'on the 20th of July, our brother, Monsieur de Bèze, was sent to Guyenne to the King and Queen of Navarre, for the purpose of instructing them in the word of God.'[1] Nor did Beza, in his efforts to fulfil the part of his mission which in their caution the ministers had refrained from mentioning, neglect the rare opportunity afforded him to work for the more purely religious end which they had put prominently forward. Consternation fell upon the opponents of Protestantism when they learned that Beza had from the pulpit preached publicly before his royal auditors the very doctrines for the profession of which men and women had for so many weary years been subjected to all forms of punishment, even to burning to death.

[1] Baum, ii, 110.

But Beza's activity was not confined to the purely religious sphere. For the first time he had the opportunity to display the abilities of a clear-sighted man of affairs. He was the best adviser of Antoine of Bourbon. His voice rose in protest against the insidious projects of the court. When, at the instigation of the Guises, the King of Navarre was urged to comply with the command given in the name of Francis II to come northward and to bring with him his younger brother Louis of Bourbon, Prince of Condé, in order that the latter might have an opportunity to clear himself of the grave accusations of which he was the object, no one opposed the foolhardy venture more strenuously than Beza. His words were little heeded. Antoine, as credulous as he was inconstant, preferred to listen to the suggestions of Cardinal Bourbon, who came on the unfraternal errand of luring his two brothers to their destruction. Before setting out, indeed, the same king who, a few weeks since, had not dissembled his aversion to the Mass and avowed his preference for the Communion as celebrated by the Protestants under both forms, was seen approving by his presence the Roman ceremonial of the Mass, and compelling the attendance of his little son, the future Henry IV. Deaf to the suggestion of his friends that, if go he must, he should proceed to court under the protection of a powerful escort, he persisted in declining the repeated offers made to him successively, at various points in his journey, of the thousands of men that could be brought to him from Poitou and Gascony, from Provençe and Languedoc, in the south, and from Normandy in the north. He fancied himself safe in trusting the person of Condé and his own person to the most perfidious of personal enemies. Condé, strange to say, for the time partook of his delusion. Neither awoke to the danger until it was too late. That in the end they escaped the fate to which one, if not both, of them seemed likely to be consigned, was due to no foresight of theirs, but to a circumstance beyond the reach of human prescience—the speedy and sudden death of the boy-king, Francis II.[2]

The Cardinal of Lorraine had endeavoured to persuade Antoine to bring to court in his train the Genevese theologian, as well, apparently, as the famous jurisconsult François Hotman, and others of his Protestant advisers. However, neither Beza nor Hotman had any taste for the adventure. Beza accompanied the Bourbon princes only a part of the way, possibly as far as to Limoges, and then struck out, through a country far from safe, in the direction of Geneva. Hotman took some other way. Both had heavy hearts, because both seemed to have laboured in vain.[3] Before Beza there stretched a journey that would have occupied many days under the most auspicious circumstances. He must travel unobserved, and therefore in disguise, and by night.[4] Under the kind protection of Heaven, he escaped every danger, and safely reached Geneva, where his friends, ignorant of his fortunes, had well-nigh despaired of seeing him again.

His short absence of a little over three months was not so barren of permanent advantage as at the time he, and perhaps his friends also, imagined.

[2] See *Rise of the Huguenots*, i, 435-444.

[3] Hotman to Peter Martyr. Nov. 20, 1560, in Baum, ii, 121.

[4] De Thou, ii, 827.

Until now Jeanne d'Albret, Queen of Navarre, had been timid. While her husband seemed to burn with zeal for the Reformation, she was reserved and cold. Sagacious and discerning, she weighed the dangers that invested an espousal of Protestantism. The principality of Béarn and the rest of the kingdom of Navarre on the northern slope of the Pyrenees were after all but a contracted territory in a peculiarly exposed situation. Her ancestors had not been able to protect the greater part of their possessions from Spanish rapacity. How should she, a woman, rescue the small remainder, were she to incur the enmity of the Papal See by a change of faith? What more effective way than this to invite invasion from without and insurrection from within? Yet just in the proportion that Antoine's fervour cooled, did her own ardour rise to a glowing heat. Immediately after Beza's visit to Nérac, and, it would seem, greatly as a consequence of his exposition of the word of God, she came to a decision from which during all the rest of her life she never swerved. The story is best told in the simple narrative of the history of the Reformed Churches of France composed, if not by Beza, at least under his supervision:

'The Queen of Navarre, after the departure of the king her husband, withdrew to Béarn, where she received within a few days tidings of the arrest of the Prince [of Condé] at Orléans, and of the conspiracy against her husband, as well as of certain conferences held in Spain having in view the surprise of her principality of Béarn and the remnant of Navarre. Seeing then that the trust which she had reposed in man was lost, and that all human help failed her, and

JEANNE D'ALBRET, QUEEN OF NAVARRE

being touched to the quick by the love of God, she had recourse to him in all humility, with cries and tears, as her sole refuge, and solemnly declared her purpose to keep his commandments. Thus was it that, in the time of her greatest tribulation, she made public profession of the pure doctrine, being strengthened in her intention by François le Guay, otherwise known as Bois Normand, and N. Henri, faithful ministers of God's word. And committing the issue altogether to the divine mercy, she put on a virile and magnanimous courage, and started to visit and provision for a long siege her stronghold of Navarrenx in Béarn, which, it was rumoured, the Spaniards intended to surprise. There she heard the news of the illness of the king [Francis II] and, soon after, of his death. At Christmas following the receipt of this intelligence, she again made a full and clear confession of her faith and partook of the Lord's Supper. Very soon thereafter she sent to the king [Charles IX] her aforesaid Confession of Faith composed by herself, and written and signed with her own hand; for she was of a singularly fine mind.'[5]

Certainly it was worth all the trouble which Beza took and all the dangers he encountered by the way to know that he had contributed to bring the mother of Henry IV to so resolute a stand. Nor is it strange, in view of all the circumstances, that Beza, when referring to this visit, in the dedication to Henry IV of a treatise published in 1591, should have remarked: 'Moreover, Sire, I am myself one of those that had the grace from the Almighty to be called and

[5] *Histoire Ecclésiastique des Églises Réformées*, ed. Baum and Cunitz (Paris, 1883), i, 370.

received and attentively heard, proclaiming the word of my Master, in your royal house of Nérac, thirty-one years ago.'[6]

As for Theodore Beza, he had shown that he was not only a devoted Protestant, but an able statesman as well. It was through no fault of his that Antoine did not present himself at the French court with a body of men sufficient to enforce the demand for a righteous performance of the promises made at Fontainebleau by a royal council which, while outwardly approving, had no honest intention to execute its engagements.[7]

From this time forth the eyes of the Protestants of France were fixed upon Theodore Beza. When the critical moment arrived that demanded a man both ardent in his religious convictions and eminent in his theological attainments, a man firm and unflinching in the advocacy of the Protestant faith, a man in the constitution of whose character, courage and prudence were singularly well balanced, it was no fortuitous thing that Theodore Beza was summoned to assume an important part with high expectations regarding his success, which, as the sequel proved, were not to be disappointed.

[6] Extract in Baum, ii, 125.

[7] See *Rise of the Huguenots*, i, 434.

CHAPTER 8

RECALL TO FRANCE
1561

THE contingency to which reference was made at the close of the last chapter arose in the year following the incidents therein described. It is important therefore to form some conception of the France to which the Reformer was now officially invited to return after an expatriation of thirteen years, interrupted only by the short visit to Nérac. For his native land had undergone a series of wonderful changes, the most wonderful of them all within the brief compass of the last few months preceding his return.

When Beza withdrew secretly from Paris in 1548, he forsook a country governed with a strong hand, if not in fact by a monarch of mature years, at least, in his name and under his legitimate authority, by the favourites to whom he chose to delegate the entire management of affairs. Francis I had then been in his grave but a year. The reign of the monarch whose chief claim to recognition, whose sole pretence to be called 'great,' was that, as patron of letters and scholars, he aspired to be the representative of the spirit of the Renaissance, had gone out ingloriously in the glare of the burning villages of the Vaudois of Cabrières and Mérindol, and amid the lurid flames of the holocaust of the 'Fourteen' roasted alive on the squares of Meaux.

Proscription of the 'Lutheran heresy' and of all suspected of being tainted with it, was the watchword of the last years of a prince who was at one time believed to favour what were still styled 'the new doctrines,' despite the stout assertions of their advocates that they were but 'the old doctrines' of the Church restated.

If the Reformed doctrines made any progress during the twelve years of Henry II, they made it in defiance of the personal hatred of the king and of a systematic legislation of the most severe and sanguinary character. Yet the advance was both rapid and substantial. Of this the most satisfactory proof is found in the excesses of the inquisitorial tribunal erected by the judges of the Parliament of Paris. That tribunal, from the facility and regularity with which it sent its victims to the flames, came to be familiarly designated as the *Chambre Ardente*. The recent fortunate discovery and publication of the original records of its proceedings[1] gives, in fact, the impression that one half of the atrocities of the famous court had not been told and that popular rumour did injustice to the activity rather than to the humanity of its members.

That Protestantism actually grew, instead of being destroyed root and branch, was patent evidence that it possessed extraordinary vitality. Year by year reports became more frequent of whole provinces 'infected' by the 'poison' of heresy. The capital itself contained its body of believers meeting regularly, but with the utmost secrecy. They had

[1] By Mr N. Weiss, in his *Chambre Ardente: Étude sur la Liberté de Conscience en France sous François Ier et Henry II, 1540–1550* (Paris, 1889). Mr Weiss discovered about five hundred sentences given by the Parliament of Paris from May, 1547, to March, 1550.

indeed been organised as a church, with pastors and other officers. Of this the government was possibly as ignorant as it was ignorant of the fact that, a few months before Henry's death, a representative assembly met within the walls of Paris, composed of delegates from different parts of the kingdom, and adopted a Confession of Faith and settled the Directory for Worship and the Form of Government of the Churches for the time to come. But if Henry was not kept fully informed of these things by his spies, he knew, at any rate, that the judges of his own high Court of Parliament were by no means sound in the faith as judged by the tests of orthodoxy. For did he not, within a month of his death, hear them avow heterodox sentiments in a judicial conference, and did he not openly declare that he would see the guilty burned before his eyes?

The fatal thrust of the misdirected lance of Count Montgomery, in the fatal tourney in honour of the nuptials of Philip II of Spain and Elizabeth of France, rendered futile this threat, by depriving Henry both of eyesight and of life. At his death French Protestantism entered upon a new and more surprising course of growth and development. The princes and nobles that came into power were, indeed, no less determined to suppress the Reformation than Henry had been. But what had appeared possible for a monarch in the flower of his age, was soon seen to be utterly hopeless for a mere stripling, confessedly not ruling by himself, who deliberately handed over the reins of authority to his wife's uncles, the Duke and Cardinal of Guise. For now men who might have continued for an indefinite time to submit to the cruel commands of a lawful king, believed it no sin to oppose the mandates of subjects who had illegally possessed themselves of the machinery of government. The outbreak known as 'The Tumult of Amboise' (1560) was no strange phenomenon. It would rather have been strange had no outbreak occurred. Nor is it surprising that, although the ill-concerted enterprise was speedily put down, the popular ferment was not quieted but rather increased. Now the religious instinct of the masses of the people began more openly to demand satisfaction. Unable to obtain churches for their worship, the crowds resorted to the fields, especially in the provinces most remote from the capital. The services were conducted by ministers, many of them trained in the city of Calvin, and were celebrated, as men said, 'after the manner of Geneva,' that is, with public prayers such as Calvin had drawn up in his liturgy, with the preaching of God's word, and with the administration of the sacraments of Baptism and the Lord's Supper. Mandates of bishops, for the most part non-resident, and proclamations of royal governors and lieutenant-governors might lead to the capture and execution of here and there a minister or of some courageous layman. But these incidents had little or no permanent effect. They did not arrest the advance of a religion which confessedly bore good fruit by promoting morality and good order. At this juncture the government resolved to try the experiment of convening an assembly of the Notables of the realm, for the purpose of obtaining the best advice for allaying the prevalent spirit of discontent.

But the Assembly of Fontainebleau (August, 1560), so far from devising the means of suppressing the Reformation, gave to the advocates of the Reformation their first opportunity to demand liberty of worship. Here it was that Admiral Coligny boldly brought forward two petitions, the one addressed to the monarch, the other to his mother, Queen Catharine de Medici, and both documents presented in the name of 'the faithful' of all parts of France. The documents were unsigned, but the admiral asserted that he could secure, if necessary, fifty thousand signatures in the single province of Normandy. They demanded houses for worship and the clear recognition of the right to assemble in these houses for the service of God. Here too it was that, a day or two later, the same nobleman took the bold step of openly espousing the cause of the Protestant Reformers. At a moment when, under the law, such sentiments as he uttered rendered him liable to the capital charge of heresy, he solemnly declared his belief that, should the houses of worship be accorded and should the royal judges be instructed to maintain his Majesty's authority and the public peace, quiet and universal contentment would at once return. It was a notable circumstance that the occasion upon which Admiral Coligny pledged life and property to the belief that the *people* in nowise wished the crown ill, the occasion upon which he warned the king's advisers that it is a perilous thing to nurture in the king a suspicion of the loyalty of his subjects, was a Saint Bartholomew's Day, just twelve years before that inauspicious Sunday in August on which the grey-haired Huguenot hero laid down his life, a sacrifice attesting the sincerity of his religious convictions.

The next twelvemonth, the last that elapsed before Beza's recall to France, was probably more eventful than any other period of equal duration in the sixteenth century. This was

GASPARD DE COLIGNY

certainly the fact so far as the Protestants were concerned. Francis II died after one of the briefest reigns in French history. The means devised by the enemies of the Protestants for their destruction, including the convocation of the States-General that were to seal the overthrow of their protectors, seemed to have been ordained by Providence for its own ulterior and wiser ends. With the death of their nephew the Guises lost their undisputed ascendancy, and the King of Navarre gained a fresh opportunity to vindicate his right, as first prince of the blood, to the regency of the kingdom. How he was induced to throw away this advantage and other advantages that might have materially affected the progress of the Protestant doctrines, and what were the fruits of his recreancy, I do not purpose to state in detail in this place.[2]

As it was, the day of religious emancipation appeared to have dawned. Many incidents of the early part of the year 1561 might be cited in evidence. One distinguished Roman Catholic prelate made no little stir by openly championing the Protestant movement. Cardinal Odet de Chastillon was the elder brother of Admiral Coligny. He had in his youth entered the Church, having no leaning to the profession of arms. He had recently been making less and less of a secret of his full acceptance of the doctrines of the Reformation. He was count and bishop of the old city of Beauvais, and, as such, one of the twelve ancient peers of the kingdom. Even thus, however, he could scarcely defend himself against the fury of the rabble, when it was noised abroad that, not content with fostering the growth of the 'new doctrines'

[2] See *Rise of the Huguenots*, i, 451, foll., for a full discussion.

in his diocese, he had at Easter absented himself from his cathedral and celebrated the great Christian feast in the chapel of his episcopal palace. There the Gospel had been preached and the Holy Communion administered 'after the manner of Geneva, though something discrepant,'—to use Sir Nicholas Throckmorton's words,—each participant receiving both elements at the hands of the officiating clergyman. Naturally the opposition originated with the clergy.

'Wherewith,' pursues the English ambassador, 'the canons and divers of the popular people, not content, murmured and assembled in great numbers to have wrought their wicked wills upon the Cardinal, who shut himself and his, with divers of the communicants of the town, within his house; yet not so speedily but that some were hurt and killed, and one of the townsmen brought violently before the Cardinal's gate, and there burned out of hand without further proceeding of justice in the matter.'[3]

This was in April. Before the close of the same month about one hundred gentlemen and others gathered in a house of the suburbs of Paris, near the *Pré aux Clercs*, and there held Protestant services. Being discovered, an assault was made upon the house by the populace, but the besieged gentlemen repelled it with harquebuses and such other weapons as they carried. Seven or eight of the assailants were killed before the mob was tardily dispersed by the officers of justice. A few months earlier, the Protestants would certainly have been arrested and tried, and the sequel

[3] Throckmorton to Queen Elizabeth, Paris, April 20, 1561. *Calendar of State Papers* (Stevenson ed.), 82-88.

ODET, CARDINAL OF CHASTILLION

would have been a holocaust of victims offered up on the altar of religious intolerance. Instead of this, the King of Navarre, opportunely coming to the capital in company with Prince La Roche sur Yon, the Duke of Longueville, and many other noblemen, to repress disorders, gave some sound advice to the authors and abettors of all the mischief to which the Parisians were prone. He called before him in the hall of the Louvre, says Throckmorton,

'all the head curates and churchwardens of all the parishes of the town and two of every religious house, with the regents [professors] of the colleges, exhorting them in the king's name to quietness, and charging others for seditious preaching and rather moving the people to tumults and sedition than edifying them.'

He assured them that

'when the same should happen hereafter, the king would make them feel his indignation, and advised them not to molest any man living without open scandal, nor to seek men in their houses, as had been done at the instigation of some there present, whom, he knew and [who] had changed their own weed under colour of scholars.'[4]

Thus wrote the envoy to his royal mistress in May. A few days passed and her Majesty was informed of a still more significant event. The solemn anointing and coronation of young King Charles IX was duly celebrated in the cathedral of Rheims according to immemorial usage, the Cardinal of Lorraine, as archbishop of the city, officiating and saying mass, and the twelve peers of the kingdom assisting. But no inconsiderable number of the nobles, and these among

[4] Throckmorton to Queen Elizabeth, May 4, 1561. *Ibid.*, 96.

the most powerful, absented themselves, and their absence was known to be for no other reason than their unwillingness to countenance a worship which they had come to repudiate as idolatrous. Of the number were the Prince of Condé, Admiral Coligny, the Duke of Longueville, Marshal Montmorency, and his brother Damville. Moreover men noticed that on the part of most of those noblemen who attended there was little or no reverence paid at the solemn moment of the elevation of the host. 'So far forth, thanks be to God, is true religion in this country!' exclaimed the Earl of Hertford, an eye-witness.[5]

At this time, it may be observed, a little frank espousal of the Protestant cause on the part of Queen Elizabeth, a few unmistakable words declaring her firm purpose never to return to the Roman Catholic Church, might possibly have decided the French noblemen that still wavered between the two religions. As it was, the Pope, the Emperor, and the King of Spain received confident assurances from England itself that there would be no difficulty in making the queen change her religion, and Elizabeth's envoy informed her that when a Protestant spoke on the subject to Cardinal Lorraine and Mary of Scots, these 'made their advantage of the cross and candles in your [Queen Elizabeth's] chapel, saying you were not yet fully resolved of what religion you should be.'[6]

Yet, with or without the aid of Elizabeth's example, the Protestants were becoming more and more bold. Old proscriptive laws could no longer be executed. Protestants would assemble for worship. When, a little later, the Queen

[5] Letter to Cecil, Paris, May 20, 1561. *Ibid.*, 116.
[6] Throckmorton to the queen, April 29, 1561. *Ibid.*, 86.

of Navarre journeyed by short stages to court, she had preaching services in her presence wherever she stopped. Then the attendance was marvellous. Fifteen thousand persons joined with her at Orléans in partaking of the Holy Communion. The city had declared itself of the new sect, according to the Venetian Suriano.[7]

Earnest Roman Catholics were startled and discouraged, not least of all the papal nuncio, the Bishop of Viterbo. So sure was he that everything was going to rack and ruin, that he sought and obtained his recall.[8] His successor, Cardinal Santa Cruce, was a man who never lost heart and who came determined to win in spite of all difficulties. Yet it may be noted that, before he had been many months in the country, the correspondence of even this sanguine personage took on almost precisely the same mournful tone as that for which he had criticised his predecessor, and he too was begging to be permitted to return to Rome, in order that he might not witness with his own eyes the funeral obsequies of an unfortunate kingdom.[9]

The one thing that Pope and nuncio, priests and cardinals, united in dreading as the direst of catastrophes was the very thing which Huguenots and patriots with equal unanimity desired as the consummation of all their hopes—that liberty of conscience and of religious worship might at length be conceded. But, at the bare suggestion

[7] Despatch of Michele Suriano, Paris, August 24, 1561. *Despatches*, edited by Sir Henry Layard (*Publications of Huguenot Society of London*, vol. vi.), p. xliv.

[8] Shers to Cecil, Treviso, May 17, 1561. *Calendar of State Papers* (Stevenson ed.), 114, 115.

[9] Letter of January 7, 1562. Aymon, *Tous les Synodes*, i, 21, 22.

that the 'heretics' should be publicly heard in defence of their erroneous views, bigots were beside themselves with anger. The only way to deal with such accursed men was to condemn them offhand and without a hearing, lest their insinuating words should infect others with the poison of heresy. Laymen added their influence to that of clergymen in dissuading the government from making a dangerous experiment. On the eve of the colloquy respecting which we are next to speak, Catharine de Medici, who had, or feigned that she had, the highest respect for the Doge of Venice, while she was suspicious of everybody else, asked advice of Suriano, the Doge's ambassador. The latter gave the customary recommendation—to temporise, to keep things as quiet as possible, to resort now and then, as occasion demanded, to persuasion or admonition, to use a little severity, to gain over by gifts and by promises. But when the queen-mother somewhat shamefacedly admitted that it had been agreed that Theodore Beza should have a hearing in the convocation of the bishops, and that she had hopes of gaining him over in one or another of the ways which the ambassador had just suggested, Suriano demurred:

'In order that she might never be able to assert that this course had ever been counselled or approved by me, I told her that the Canons had expressly forbidden disputing or treating with heretics, and that the bishops would fall under censure. Such a proceeding would be the source of scandal and peril. If it is desired to gain Beza in this way, it were better done privately in a room.' Catharine replying that the bishops were themselves satisfied with the contemplated arrangement, the ambassador stood his ground, and could only reiterate his strong belief that privacy was better than publicity, and that in any case only a few persons should be permitted to be present at the colloquy.[10]

Of assurances that no important changes would be made, indeed, no changes at all affecting the religion professed by the kings of France, predecessors of the present occupant of the throne,—of assurances that the obedience of France to the Pope would be maintained to the utmost and that no attempt would be made to alienate the property of the Church—of such assurances Catharine de Medici was prodigal enough. But whether any reliance could be placed on her word was doubtful. The trouble with her and with her council was that they were as ready to unsay as to say, and that they did not hesitate, when convenient, to deny that they had ever uttered any of their previous assertions.[11]

The queen-mother was, in the estimation of all well-informed men, timid and irresolute. Whether she would favour or oppose the progress of the Reformed religion, was a question which it was at the time impossible to answer with certainty, simply because the decision ultimately reached would not be made according to principles fixed and stable, but must depend upon motives of expediency shifting with the apparent demands of the hour. Of settled convictions upon moral or religious matters she had, or appeared to have, few or none. She was profoundly ignorant respecting doctrine.

'I do not believe,' says Suriano, 'that her Majesty understands what is meant by the word *dogmas*, but I suspect

[10] Suriano's despatch of August 29, 1561. Layard, *ubi supra*, p. xlv.
[11] Despatch of Suriano, September 8, 1561. *Ibid.*, p. xlvi.

FRANÇOIS DE CHASTILLON, LORD OF ANDELOT

that, like others who every day want to dispute concerning religion—all of them, or at least the greater part of them, ignorant people—she confuses dogmas, rites, and abuses, as if they were all one and the same thing. Hence there arises every form of confusion in their disputes and, possibly, also in their opinions.'[12]

But if Catharine de Medici was timid and irresolute, there were others who had fully made up their minds and had the courage inspired by their convictions. The King of Navarre might waver and ultimately throw in his lot with the enemies of the Reformation, but his younger brother, Condé, had no hesitation. Nor was there hesitation on the part of the three brothers Chastillon—the Admiral of Coligny, d'Andelot, and the reforming cardinal, who though he still wore the red robe as a member of the Roman Sacred College, was, as we have seen, not afraid to celebrate the Holy Communion and at a later time to take to himself a wife, and, during his residence at Queen Elizabeth's court, to do efficient work in the interest of the Huguenots and of the other Protestants of the Continent. And, behind these and other important nobles, stood a great body of men, titled and untitled, the majority unknown as yet to the world, though, as the most virtuous and intelligent element of the population, exerting a quiet influence, willing and ready, however, should the occasion come, to suffer loss of property and even death in attestation of their faith.

The times had clearly changed essentially since Beza retired from the kingdom and sought a refuge in hospitable Geneva. True, the battle for religious liberty was not yet

[12] Suriano, *ubi supra.*

won. Legislation was still hostile in the extreme. It was no easy thing for a judge to be both equitable and observant of the law; and between the dictates of the bloodthirsty edicts, as yet unrepealed, and the dictates of natural justice reinforced by a powerful public sentiment in favour of more leniency in dealing with respectable citizens whose only fault was that they did not believe what the greater part of the nation believed or imagined that they believed, the parliaments as well as the lower courts exhibited a singular record of inconsistency verging upon absurdity. Of all the incidents of the year of Beza's return to France, indeed, the most inconsistent and absurd was the publication of a fresh law, known from the time of its issue as the *Edict of July*—little better than an anachronism, inasmuch as at a juncture imperatively calling for the supply of relief, it reënacted severe penalties against all such as should attend conventicles where there was preaching or where the sacraments were administered. The best that could be said for it was that the measure was evidently of a temporary character, a sop thrown to the priests to gain a brief respite from their incessant complaints of the indulgence shown to dissent.[13]

Meanwhile the government had, some months before, so far yielded to the insistence of the friends of progress as to decide definitely that an opportunity should at last be afforded the Protestants of meeting with their opponents and setting forth their views and the grounds of those views. Even the time had been fixed. In an interview which Admiral Coligny held with the ambassador of Queen Eliza-

[13] The edict was enacted July 11, 1561. See *Rise of the Huguenots*, i, 483, foll.

beth by appointment at a place three leagues distant from Fontainebleau, on the 24th of April, he informed him in profound secrecy

'that yesterday it was resolved, in Council, that *in August next* the king would assemble his clergy and keep a National Council in France for religion. And as the Queen of England had dissuaded the king from accepting the Council of Trent and [urged him] to desire one in his own realm, where things might be handled with more sincerity, and it was said that the queen would assist him therein, it is now thought that she will show herself a good friend to the king and to the promotion of true religion, if she will send some of her best learned divines to this assembly, and exhort the Princes Protestant to do the like.'[14]

It is very certain, however, that if such were the hopes of Coligny and other leaders of the Reformed faith, Catharine de Medici never had the idea of inviting either Elizabeth or any German prince to be represented in a French National Council; nor indeed of holding any Council at all in which Protestants should sit as members. As it was, about the same time as the other two orders of the kingdom were in session in the so-called States-General at Pontoise, she summoned all the bishops of France to meet in the neighbouring convent of Poissy,[15] at a convenient distance from the royal castle of Saint Germain en Laye. In justification of her action in calling these representatives of the clergy to consider the present religious situation of France without

[14] Throckmorton to Queen Elizabeth, Paris, April 29, 1561. *Calendar of State Papers*, 83.

[15] On July 20, according to Languet, *Epist. Secret.*, ii, 122.

waiting for the General Council of the Church, which was the great desire of her heart, she excused herself by alleging that she had no intention to make any innovations in ecclesiastical matters, and consequently no intention to do anything at which the Pope could take umbrage.

'But,' said she, 'those who are extremely ill are excusable if they apply all sorts of remedies to alleviate their pain when unendurable, the meantime waiting for the good physician, which I esteem must be a good Council, for so furious and dangerous a disease of which those may speak with more boldness who feel it and are most affected by it.'[16]

Moreover she defended herself for inviting the Protestant ministers, by calling attention to the admirable opportunity that would be offered to convince them of the error of their ways!

'Having been requested by the greater part of the nobles and commons of this kingdom, a few months ago, to grant a hearing to the ministers scattered in various cities of this kingdom, on their Confession of Faith,' she wrote to the French ambassador at the court of the Emperor, 'I was advised to do so by my brother, the King of Navarre, the rest of the princes of the blood, and the members of the council of the king my son. Long and mature deliberation has convinced me that in such great troubles there is no better or more effective means of leading the ministers to abandon their views and of drawing off their adherents than to make their teaching known and discover what errors and heresies it contains.'[17]

[16] Catharine to the Bishop of Rennes, August 23, 1561, in Le Laboureur, *Additions aux Mém. de Castelnau*, i, 725.

[17] Letter to the Bishop of Rennes, Sept. 14, 1561, or five days after Beza spoke at Poissy. *Ibid.*, i, 732.

THE COLLOQU

REDUCED COPY OF THE CONTEMPO

A. The King.
B. The Queen-Mother.
C. Monsieur (Duke of Anjou).
D. Madame (Margaret of Valois).
E. The King of Navarre.
F. The Queen of Navarre.
G. Princes of the Blood, seated the King.
H. Gentlemen of King's Chamber.
I. Table of the Abbess.
K. Cardinal Lorraine.
L. Cardinal Tournon.

EPT. 9, 1561.

J. TORTOREL AND J. PERRISSIN.

M. Cardinal Chastillon.
N. The Chancellor.
O. Bishops and Doctors.
P. Cardinal Armagnac.
Q. Cardinal Bourbon.
R. Cardinal Guise.
S. Theodore Beza, who speaks.
T. Ministers with him.
V. Table of the Nuns.
X. Body-guards of King.
Y. Swiss Guards of King.
Z. Secretaries of State.

It was determined therefore for the first time that the Protestants of France should be heard in defence of their doctrine—a very simple and natural thing, which they had been asking for years with persistence, yet a thing which their enemies had as persistently opposed and denied. They still opposed it, on the present occasion, with one solitary exception. Cardinal Lorraine, strange to say, was quite willing that the Protestants should make a public appearance through their chosen representatives, taking, in fact, so different an attitude from that of his colleagues in the Sacred College as to lay himself open to not a little suspicion. We shall see further on whether this suspicion was well grounded. Undoubtedly, when the Protestants began to look for the man best qualified to represent them at Poissy, their minds turned instinctively to John Calvin, than whom no other was mentally or morally better equipped—a native Frenchman, moreover, who had never lost his interest in the land of his birth, but was more active than any other man alive in promoting by his voice and by his pen the progress of the Reformation in France. Calvin, however, was not to be thought of for an instant. With all their affection for him, the ministers of the Church of Paris distinctly told him so and gave him their reasons. 'We see no means of having you here,' they wrote him, 'without grave peril, in view of the rage which all the enemies of the Gospel have conceived against you, and, the disturbances which your name alone would excite in this country, were you known to be present. In fact, the admiral [Coligny] is by no means in favour of your undertaking the journey, and we have learned with certainty that the queen [Catharine de Medici] would not relish seeing you. She says frankly that she would not pledge herself for your safety, as for that of the rest. On the other hand, the enemies of the Gospel assert that they would be glad to listen to all the other [Reformers], but that, as for you, they could not bring themselves to hear you or to look at you. You see, sir, in what esteem you are held by these venerable prelates. I suspect that you will not be much grieved by it, nor consider yourself dishonoured by being so viewed by such gentry.'[18]

On the contrary, there existed among the adherents of the Roman Catholic party no such inveterate prejudice against Beza. Men had not forgotten that he was once addicted to the lighter forms of literature and was a graceful poet. He would not be out of his native element in the royal court. He might not equal Calvin in his mastery of the science of theology, but he would be a more acceptable disputant. The believers of Paris wrote urging him to come; so did also the Prince of Condé and Admiral Coligny, who, although as yet unknown to him as a correspondent, not only sent him a letter but despatched a trusty agent to lay before him the absolute need of him in which Protestant France stood. As to the King of Navarre, he declared with his usual impetuosity that Beza had no friend at court to whom his appearance would be more grateful than to him, and he promised cheerfully to do everything in his power for the Reformer.[19]

Still Beza delayed his coming. This is not surprising. The Edict of July, to which reference has been made, was poor

[18] La Rivière to Calvin, Paris, July 31, 1561. *Bulletin*, xvi, 603.

[19] See the letters of La Rivière and the others, in Baum, ii (doc.), 34, 35.

evidence of any intention on the part of the court to deal fairly by Protestantism, whose condition, so far as public worship was concerned, it rendered worse rather than better. The Protestants at Paris were nearly in despair. The colloquy of prelates was in session and the time was short. Men began to say that the Protestants would not dare to appear before so goodly a company and stand up for their errors. Should the colloquy finish its business and adjourn without their having presented themselves to maintain the cause of the Gospel, the mouths of the malevolent would be open to decry their pusillanimity and asperse their religion. The princes hitherto favourable would be disgusted. Catharine de Medici never slow to make cutting speeches, was already saying to one and another that she would never be able to persuade herself that the Reformers had any right on their side if they failed to seize the opportunity offered them to manifest and maintain the grounds of their faith. We have an earnest letter in which the Protestants of Paris laid the situation before Beza, imploring him to make no tarrying, and assuring him that the Edict of July—better understood at home than it could be understood at a distance—had been simply made to satisfy King Philip of Spain and the Pope and to extract money from the purses of the reluctant prelates of Poissy—bad motives, doubtless, but containing nothing to discourage the advocates of the truth.[20] Nor was this all. Antoine of Navarre again wrote by a special messenger, this time to 'the magnificent Lords, the Syndics and Council of the Seigniory of Geneva,' praying

[20] La Rivière in the name of the whole Church, Paris, August 10, 1561. Baum, ii (doc.), 37-39.

them in the most affectionate manner to consent to send his 'dear and well-beloved Theodore de Bèze,' than whom he could ask for no person more highly approved, and to despatch him as expeditiously as possible 'to the end that his delay might not hinder the progress of so good a work.'[21]

It was no longer decent or possible to turn a deaf ear to such appeals. Without waiting even for a safe-conduct, Beza set off on the 16th of August for the scene of the coming theological encounter. Six days later he reached Paris.

[21] *Ibid.*, ii (doc.), 39, 40.

CHAPTER 9

RECEPTION AT COURT

1561

THE first tidings that awaited Beza upon his arrival in Paris were by no means encouraging. It is true that he was informed that a number of his colleagues, delegates of Huguenot Churches, some eight pastors in all, had reached the court of France before him, and had been received by the king publicly and with the utmost kindness. Charles was pleased to permit them to present him a petition, and assured them, meanwhile looking upon them 'with a very goodly countenance,' that he would communicate their requests to his council and reply to them by his chancellor. And, inasmuch as these requests were to the effect that their avowed enemies, the ecclesiastics, should not be permitted to act as their judges, but that the king himself should preside at the approaching colloquy, and that the Sacred Scriptures in their Hebrew and Greek originals should form the sole ground for the decision of controverted points, it must be confessed that the Protestants might well be pardoned for entertaining sanguine expectations of the issue.[1] But, on the other hand, there came news of plots on the part of their antagonists, no longer, as was believed, vain rumours, but ascertained facts. A still more tangible

[1] *Hist. Ecclés.*, i, 542, foll.

cause for apprehension was that the very chief of their enemies—the same Duke of Guise who, after the enactment of the intolerant Edict of July, boasted that his sword would never rest in its scabbard when the execution of this law was concerned—expected to reach the royal court on the morrow, at the head of a powerful band of friends and retainers. Well might Beza write to Calvin, when he had been but a few hours in Paris, that he did not know but that he had fallen rather upon a civil war than upon a peaceable conference.[1]

To feelings of discouragement must soon have succeeded more cheerful emotions. The King of France and his court had for some time been at his castle or palace of Saint Germain, or, as it was designated more particularly, in order to distinguish it from the six- or seven-score places bearing the name of one of the most popular worthies in the Roman Catholic calendar, *Saint Germain en Laye*. The very day of Beza's arrival at Paris, a messenger rode in haste to convey to the expectant and delighted Huguenot nobles about his Majesty the welcome intelligence that the man upon whom more than upon any other they depended in the approaching struggle was safe and ready to come to their aid. The distance yet to be traversed by the Genevese Reformer was but fourteen miles. Before nightfall a return messenger was despatched to beg him to come at once to the royal court. Accordingly, the next day (August 23rd), Beza set forth on horseback, accompanied by a cavalcade of friendly Huguenots, reaching in time for the evening meal the abode of the Cardinal of Chastillon at Saint Germain, where he and

[1] Beza to Calvin, August 22, 1561. Baum, ii (doc.), 44, 45.

the delegates of the French Protestant Churches were to be hospitably entertained.[2]

He was not allowed to eat in peace, so anxious were his friends to see him and so pressing were the invitations to come to the castle or palace. A flattering reception awaited him. On entering he was met by the new Chancellor of France, not so famous now as he was destined shortly to become, nor so thoroughly understood to be a lover of country and of toleration, the learned and venerable Michel de l'Hospital. That great man coveted the honour of introducing Beza at the French court, as Beza clearly saw and afterwards wrote down; but the Reformer, not recognising the great heart of L'Hospital, and the great patriotism which that heart contained, was wary and suspicious. There was no time, however, for conference. At the door of the chamber into which he passed, Beza found himself confronted with a number of the grandees of the kingdom. First came the great admiral, Gaspard de Coligny, whom he had barely time to salute before the King of Navarre and his brother, the Prince of Condé, threw themselves upon him, 'with a very great affection, it seemed to me,' as Beza, who by this time was tolerably well acquainted with the shallow and untrustworthy character of the elder Bourbon, noted not without some pardonable misgivings. Meanwhile, two prelates drew near, the cardinals of Bourbon and of Chastillon, both of whom offered him their hands. It were to be wished that Beza had found space to relate, in his letter to Calvin, all that was said, for the little that he did set down is enough to show that in quickness and in tact he was quite ready for

[2] Languet, *Epistolæ Secretæ*, ii, 140.

the occasion. As he grasped the proffered hand of Cardinal Bourbon, he could not deny himself the satisfaction of protesting, doubtless with a mischievous twinkle of the eye, that he, Beza, had undergone no change since—at Nérac, a year ago—the prelate had declined to speak to him, for fear of being excommunicated. The poor cardinal, in his embarrassment, could only answer that he was desirous of understanding matters in truth; to which Beza naturally replied by begging Bourbon to abide by his purpose and by offering his own services to that end. A discussion had almost begun, but both saw that it was no suitable time for controversy, and stopped. To Bourbon's brother, the King of Navarre, Beza playfully, yet earnestly, observed that he greatly feared that his Majesty would soon be less joyful at his arrival, unless he (the king) made up his mind to change his present course of action. To this Antoine replied by an outburst of laughter, and Beza in turn confined himself to assuring him that the words were spoken in all seriousness and that he would do well to think upon the matter.

Such, almost in Beza's own words, were the incidents of the first few minutes of his stay at Saint Germain. New honours awaited him. He was conducted by a company 'far greater than he could have expected,' to pay his respects to the Princess of Condé and to the wife of Admiral Coligny. The next day, which was Sunday, in the lodgings of the Prince of Condé, and in the presence of a large and honourable company that had assembled to hear him, the Genevese Reformer preached a Protestant discourse. At that very moment the prince himself was joining with the Duke of Guise, before the queen-mother and the royal council, in a solemn act of amity and reconciliation. The Duke of Guise solemnly asseverated that he was in nowise the cause or author of the prince's imprisonment at Orléans, and when the prince had declared that he held to be wicked all that had been its cause, the duke positively asserted that he thought so too, and that the matter did not concern him at all. It was a farce, whose insincerity was transparent to all eyes, played with scarcely an attempt, on the part of the actors, to conceal its worthlessness. All that it effected was to permit the prince and the duke to meet in the ordinary intercourse of life with the semblance of having buried all recollection of the unfortunate Tumult of Amboise and of the subsequent counterplot to destroy the Bourbon princes in the last hours of the reign of Francis II.

That day the Protestant deputies received from the king a favourable reply to the petition which has already been referred to. They were assured, although the promise was not as yet in writing and in authentic form, that they should be admitted to an audience and that their opponents should not be suffered to act as their judges.

At about nine o'clock in the evening, Beza was summoned to the chamber of the King of Navarre. Great was his surprise, on entering, to find that, instead of Antoine alone, there were gathered the queen-mother, Catharine de Medici, Prince Condé, the Duke d'Étampes, Cardinals Bourbon and Lorraine, and one or two ladies of the court. Startled though he was and possibly suspecting some snare laid for him, the Reformer did not lose his self-possession and promptly addressed himself to Catharine. In a few words he laid before her the reason of his coming to France.

This was in brief his earnest desire to be of service to his native land. The queen-mother replied courteously and kindly, expressing her very great joy should a conclusion in very deed be reached that might procure peace and quiet to the realm. Thus far there was not a ripple to disturb the interview. Apparently Cardinal Lorraine did not intend that it should end so amicably. After some complimentary words, in which he acknowledged the intellectual ability of the new-comer, he added that he had hitherto known Beza merely by his writings, but now that he had come he exhorted him to study the peace and concord of the kingdom. As Beza had heretofore *afflicted* France, he now had it in his power to assuage her woes. The taunt did not pass unanswered. Again Beza protested the fervency of his desire to serve his king and his country. It stood next only to his desire to serve his God. 'So great a kingdom as France,' he said, 'has nothing to fear in the way of disturbance from my slender abilities. Nay, the idea of such a thing has ever been as alien as possible from my thoughts. My writings have shown this, and a comparison of their contents will make it plain.' 'Have you written anything in French?' asked the queen-mother. To this Beza replied: 'I have written a translation of the Psalms, and a certain Answer to the Confession of the Duke of Northumberland.' Catharine's question, it came out, had been occasioned by the circulation in France of an insulting song, ascribed to Beza as its author, the previous year. Beza positively and at some length denied that the song in question emanated from him.

The mention of defamatory books brought on a theological discussion.

'I have at Poissy,' said the cardinal, 'a book attributed to you, treating of the Sacrament, in which you assert what seems to me an absurdity, that Christ is as much to be sought in the Lord's Supper as before he was born of the Virgin. Moreover, I am told, although this I am not willing to affirm, as I have never seen the book, that you state that Christ is not more *in Cœna* than *in Cœno*'—a play upon words, signifying 'not more in the *Supper* than *in the mire*.' At this the queen-mother and the other listeners were evidently moved, but Beza quietly replied that, when the books were produced, he would not disavow them, if they were his. As to the two propositions which the cardinal had referred to, the sense of the former might be true, although only an inspection of the book would show that; but the latter could not be found either in his books or in those of anyone else possessed of the slightest intelligence in the world. 'Our Confession of Faith,' he added, 'proves in what reverence we hold the Sacraments.'

The discussion drifted into an argument respecting the meaning of the words of our Lord in the institution of his Supper. 'I teach the children of my diocese,' said the cardinal, 'when they are asked the question, "What is the bread in the Supper?" to answer that it is the body of Christ. Do you find fault with this?' 'Why should I not approve the words of Christ?' replied Beza. 'But the question is, "In what way is the bread called the body of Christ?"' Hereupon he proceeded to set forth his own and the Reformed view—namely, that the signs used retain their original nature, the bread continuing to be bread and the wine to be wine; that the thing signified in the Sacrament is the very body of Christ affixed to the cross and his very blood poured out on the cross; that the bread and wine used are not common bread and wine, from which, however, they differ only in that they become visible signs of the body and blood of Christ; that therefore the body and blood of Christ, so far as they are truly given and communicated, are truly present in the use of the Supper, not, as they are esteemed to be, under, or in, or with the bread, or anywhere else than in heaven whither Christ has ascended, that there he may reside, so far as appertains to his human nature, until he shall return to judge the quick and the dead; finally, that, in the Communion, the visible signs are given us to be taken by the hand, to be eaten, to be drunk in a natural manner, but, so far as the thing signified is concerned, that is, the body and blood of Christ, they are offered indeed to all, but they cannot be partaken of save spiritually and by faith, not by the hand, not by the mouth.

Once and again in the course of the conversation, the cardinal expressed his acquiescence in the doctrine propounded. He rejoiced greatly, he said, to hear that these were the sentiments of Beza and his friends, for he had understood that they had thought differently. At one point he expressed a hope that for himself he might retain the doctrine of Transubstantiation; yet he conceded that it might be omitted by the theologians, and he indeed would be unwilling that there should be a schism in the churches because of Transubstantiation. Later on, he protested that he was not urgent in behalf of Transubstantiation and admitted that Christ must be sought for in heaven. In fact he plainly showed to the skilled disputant with whom he had to do that his views were by no means settled, and that he had no true mastery of the subject. His time, he said, had been taken up with other studies. At length he went so far as to say:

'I am unpractised in discussions of this kind, but you have heard what I would say.' 'And you in like manner,' returned Beza, 'have heard from me what should satisfy you. I sum all up thus: The bread is the body of Christ sacramentally, that is, although that body is today in heaven and nowhere else, yet the signs are with us upon the earth. Yet just so truly is that body given to us, and just so truly is it partaken of by us through faith, and that to life eternal because of God's promise, as the sign is naturally extended to our hands.'

Beza's statement contented, or seemed to content, the cardinal. Turning to the queen-mother, who had sat through the long discussion, 'Madam,' he said, 'I believe so too, and this satisfies me.' Whereupon Beza also addressed her and exclaimed: 'Behold then those wretched "*Sacramentarians*" so long vexed and borne down with all sorts of calumnies!'

There was an animated scene for a moment. Catharine de Medici, overjoyed, was not silent. 'Do you hear, my lord cardinal, that the opinion of the Sacramentarians is none other than that which you yourself have approved?' She added a few words about union and conciliation. Cardinal Lorraine himself congratulated the Reformer and said these very words to him: 'Monsieur de Bèze, I have greatly rejoiced to see and hear you. I adjure you, in God's name, to let me understand your reasons and that you also understand mine. And you will not find me so black as some people make me to be.' Beza thanked him and in turn begged him not to desist from pursuing the path of conciliation, professing his own purpose to use for this end every gift God had conferred upon him. Thus the disputants separated and the little gathering broke up. Not, however, before witty Madame de Cursol, one of the auditors, who understood the cardinal well, had taken his hand as she bade him good-night with the significant words: 'Good man for this evening; but tomorrow, what?' With a true intuition she foresaw precisely what came to pass. Scarcely had the next morning come when the cardinal was boasting that he had overcome Beza and brought him over to his opinion.[3]

All these particulars we learn from a letter which Beza despatched to Calvin the following evening. Upon the receipt of it Calvin, not a little amused at Lorraine's pretended friendship, wrote to warn Beza not to trust the prelate's professions. Thirteen years before, he told him, a papal legate, the Cardinal of Ferrara, had imposed upon him (Calvin), lavishing caresses upon him and promising to be the best of friends. And he added playfully his advice that Beza should not display any over-elation because of Cardinal Lorraine's effusive demonstration, nor assume lordly airs toward him, his fellow-Reformer, in view of the circumstance that Calvin could so easily retaliate, particularly inasmuch as a papal *legate* is the superior of any and every simple *cardinal*.[4]

[3] Beza to Calvin, Saint Germain, August 25, 1561, in Baum, *Theodor Beza*, ii (doc.), 45-54. Baum gives both the original French form and the subsequently revised Latin translation. See, also, La Place, *Édition Panthéon*, 155-157; *Histoire Ecclésiastique*, i, 551, 552; *Calvin Opera*, xviii, 630-641.

[4] Calvin to Beza, September 3, 1561. *Calvini Opera*, xviii, 674.

Meanwhile it looked as if the Parisian Protestants might have spared themselves the feverish haste with which they sent for Beza, and that Beza himself might have come by slower stages. The prelates were in no hurry to meet either the representatives of the Protestant Churches or the Reformer from Geneva. They had been in session for three weeks. Instead of any more imposing designation which would, if it approached the notion of a national synod, have excited the ire of the Pope, their coming together had, as we have seen, been styled a *colloquy*, that is, a more or less informal conference. Their time had thus far been spent to little profit; in angry wrangling over such matters as the discipline of the Church, the number of priests, the dignity of the episcopate and of cathedral churches, and the reformation of the monastic rules. They were fully determined, after they had settled all these matters, to adjourn and go home, without giving the slightest attention to the true object for which they had been convened.[5]

Happily, Catharine de Medici was for the time under the influence of good advisers, among whom were prominent the liberal Bishop of Valence and the new chancellor, Michel de l'Hospital. The one or the other of these two men was probably the true author of a letter which Catharine had recently sent to the Pope over her own signature, outlining the radical changes which she regarded as necessary concessions to the spirit of the times. Being ready to give up image worship, the denial of the cup to the laity in the Lord's Supper, the use of the Latin language in public worship, the practice of the celebration of private masses, and

[5] See De Thou, bk. 28 (iii, 63).

other abuses to which the bigots clung tenaciously,[6] she was not likely to listen with patience to the protests of a few bishops who had the effrontery to propose to disperse without giving a moment's consideration to the vital questions that were occupying the serious thoughts of a great part of France and threatened to create a lasting schism. But the delays were interminable, and the air was full of rumours that the Protestants would either fail of obtaining the hearing for which they had been brought to Saint Germain, or, if heard at all, would be heard in such a manner as to defeat the very object in view. The dilatory government was brought to the necessity of instant decision when, on the 8th of September, Beza having been fully sixteen days at Saint Germain, the Protestant ministers, envoys of the churches, presented themselves before Catharine de Medici, and respectfully but firmly demanded that impartial treatment which they had been promised, and assured her that they would immediately leave unless measures were taken to defeat the machinations of their enemies.

Whatever hesitation Catharine had displayed at once disappeared. Before being dismissed from her presence, the ministers had the satisfaction of seeing informal action taken by the members of the royal council that were present, granting essentially all the Protestant requests. The prelates would not be their judges. The minutes of the proceedings would be reduced to writing by one of the secretaries of state, but to this official record the Protestants might add notes or comments of their own. The young king, Charles

[6] Catharine's remarkable letter to Pius IV, of August 4, 1561, in Gerdesius, *Scrinium Antiq.*, v, 339, etc. *Rise of the Huguenots*, i, 500, 501.

IX, would be present, in company with the princes of the blood. To this determination Catharine remained firm. The Sorbonne, or theological faculty of the University of Paris, sent some of their number to wait upon her, entreating her to give no audience to heretics whose teachings the Church had heretofore often condemned, or, at least, if she would hear them herself, not to suffer her young son's orthodoxy to be jeopardised by exposure to such infection. But Catharine was inflexible. The conference was appointed for the morrow, and Charles IX and his suite were to hear what the Reformers had to say for themselves and for their teachings.

CHAPTER 10

SPEECH AT THE COLLOQUY OF POISSY
1561

THE occurrence which is next to be described constitutes one of the critical events in the history of the Reformation in France. Its importance can scarcely be exaggerated.

The adherents of the Reformed Churches had one standing grievance to allege against the established Church and against the government which in the religious domain did little more than carry out the suggestions of that Church. They maintained that the faith they professed was rational and scriptural. Each separate doctrine was based upon some distinct utterance of the word of God. Instead of being newly invented, their belief was the original belief of the Christian Church. Upon every point where it differed from the present creed and the current practice, antiquity was in their favour. Their opponents who cloaked themselves with the pretence of following immemorial usage were themselves innovators, since they upheld a system that came into existence long after the times of the Apostles, so that at best it was fairly entitled only to the designation of inveterate error. These Protestant claims appeared to the multitude and even to the greater part of educated men at first sight strange and paradoxical; for they involved an overturning of all preconceived notions.

But the Reformers did not ask to be believed on their own simple assertion. From the greatest to the least they offered to prove the truth of their statements by the Scriptures of the Old and New Testaments.

Their adversaries stopped their ears. They would not listen to the Protestants when living and still less when dying. If a martyr undertook to vindicate the doctrine for which he was suffering the torture of slow death by fire, his voice was conveniently drowned by the incessant beating of drums, unless, indeed, a gag of wood or iron had already been forced into his mouth to impose silence upon him.

All that the Reformers asked of the ruling powers was to be heard. If they could but gain the ear of the king, they made sure that their arguments were so convincing, the truth so patent, that there could be little fear of the result. If he would listen kindly, candidly, impartially, they cared little for anything else; but they insisted that he and no one else should preside at the audience, and that their enemies should not pronounce upon the truth or falsity of their allegations. If this last was to be the case, that is, if the 'Gospel,' as they confidently styled their doctrine, was to be granted a pretended hearing only to be subjected to the indignity of a prearranged humiliation and defeat—in this case, and in this case alone, they were resolved to refuse to plead. Even personal affront was of little account, so long as it affected them alone. Only let the word have a fair hearing. All else was immaterial.

It will be seen that just this personal affront was to be offered them in the coming encounter. Strange to say, John Calvin had predicted, some ten years before, the very insult which was put upon the Reformers at Poissy, and had then expressed in their name a willingness to endure it. For when, on the 24th of January, 1551, he dedicated to young King Edward VI of England his *Commentary on the Catholic Epistles of the New Testament*, he exclaimed with reference to the attitude of inferiority in which the enemies of the Reformation so persistently sought to place its friends, '*Then let them sit, provided we are heard, declaring the Truth while standing.*'[1]

It was therefore with no slight sense of the importance of the occasion, and with a hearty prayer to Heaven for help to make good use of it, that, about ten o'clock on the morning of Tuesday, September 9, 1561, Theodore Beza set out for Poissy, escorted by a strong detachment of about one hundred horsemen, sent as a body-guard to preclude the possibility of any such treacherous attack as, in the present excited condition of the public mind, would have been nothing less than a national disaster. With him rode, also on horseback, those faithful and courageous men, the ministers and the representatives of the churches to whom had been prayerfully entrusted such a commission as all felt it had never before been the privilege and responsibility of any similar body of men to discharge. It is not probable that, even without Beza, they would have proved unequal to the task of setting forth with clearness and force the Protestant side in the great controversy. In an age much addicted to discussion, these were picked men, whose equals, for

[1] Calvin, Dedication to Edward VI prefixed to *Cath. Epistles.* Dated Geneva, January 24, 1551. *Calvini Opera*, xiv, 34. 'Sedeant illi, modo nos stando quod verum est proferentes audiamur.'

learning as well as natural ability, could scarcely have been found, man for man, throughout the kingdom. Three or four ministers stood forth preëminent. Augustin Marlorat, of Rouen, was the distinguished man who after the siege and capture of the capital of Normandy, not much over a year later, in the first civil war, was judicially murdered for his religion's sake by the provincial Parliament. Nicholas des Gallars was the well-known pastor of the French refugees at London. John Raymond Merlin, a skilful professor of Hebrew at Geneva, was that same chaplain of Admiral Coligny who was as by a miracle saved from the dagger when, in 1572, his patron was assassinated at the Massacre of Saint Bartholomew's Day, and who subsequently, when lying in the garret into which in his flight he had fallen, was as strangely saved from starvation by the hen that daily came and laid an egg for his supply. François de Saint Paul, more famed as a theologian, came from distant Provence, where he was honoured as the founder of more than one church.

The distance from the castle of Saint Germain to the nuns' convent at Poissy is possibly a little over three miles. A straight and broad avenue led from the one place to the other, cutting off the greater part of the extensive forest of Saint Germain on the right from the small portion that lay on the left hand. It required less than half an hour for Beza to reach his destination. The Duke of Guise, to whom this duty had been assigned, received him with as gracious an aspect as he could assume and handed him and his associates over to the conduct of the captain of the royal guard. Following the latter, they were subsequently ushered into the presence of Charles IX.[2]

[2] Beza to Calvin, September 12, 1561. Baum, ii (doc.), 61.

The large refectory of the conventual edifice had been prepared for the unusual meeting, as best it could be, at short notice. A quaint engraving of the time, which Montfaucon has reproduced in his *Monuments de la Monarchie Françoise,*[3] may help us to form an idea of the place in which were assembled all the most distinguished personages of France.

The tables of the nuns ran along the sides of the room, the table of the abbess along the side farthest from the spectator as he entered. In front of this table sat a number of great lords in a row, and before them in turn the princes of the blood royal. In advance of these were six detached seats, places of highest honour. Here sat young King Charles IX, with his younger brother (the future Henry III), and Antoine, King of Navarre, on his right, while the seats to his left were occupied by his mother, Catharine de Medici, his sister, Margaret of Valois, future bride of Henry IV, and Jeanne d'Albret, Queen of Navarre. Chairs had been arranged for the six French cardinals that were in attendance at court, in two rows facing one another and somewhat nearer the door. On the spectator's right were Cardinals Armagnac, Bourbon, and Guise; on his left Cardinals Tournon, Chastillon, and Lorraine, with the High Chancellor of France, Michel de l'Hospital, sitting between the last two. In three rows on benches advancing towards the spectator's left hand were gathered bishops and doctors, while other dignitaries of the same grade occupied a similar position on his right. More toward the centre of the room were a table and seats for the secretaries of state.

[3] Edition of Paris, 1733. tome v, 106.

No seats had been provided for Beza and his companions, the Protestant ministers and delegates, to occupy on their arrival. Swiss guards, in their picturesque costume, and body-guards of the king stood on either side of the entrance; and the lower end of the hall was crowded with men curious to witness and listen to the proceedings.

Charles IX, being a boy of eleven years of age, opened the session with the few simple words which he had been instructed by his mother to utter, and bade the chancellor to set forth the object for which the conference had been appointed. Thus directed, Michel de l'Hospital, seating himself on a stool, 'pretty far forward in the hall toward the right side,' made an appropriate address.

'Both the king's predecessors,' said he, 'and the king himself have tried every means, forcible and mild, to reunite his people so unfortunately divided by a diversity of opinions. Neither force nor mildness has been of much avail. Consequently the division long since begun has been succeeded by a capital enmity between his Majesty's subjects, from which, unless God supplies some prompt and quick remedy, only the entire ruin of the State is to be apprehended. It is for this reason that, following the example of the action of former monarchs in similar straits, the king has called you together, that he may communicate to you his need of counsel and help. Before all things else, he begs you, so far as possible, to devise the means of appeasing God, whose anger is certainly provoked, and of rooting out and removing whatever has offended Him. And should it be found that, through the sloth and avarice of those that are in charge of His service, there have crept in abuses contrary

CHARLES IX

to God's word, contrary to the prescriptions of the Holy Apostles and the ancient constitutions of the Church, his Majesty begs you, so far as your authority extends, to put forth your hands with a resolution that shall take away from your enemies the occasion upon which they have laid hold to speak ill of you and to draw the people away from your obedience. Look also to all that may reform both your lives and the administration of your charges.

'Now, inasmuch as the diversity of opinions is the principal ground of troubles and seditions, the king, following in this the decisions of the two meetings heretofore held, has granted a safe-conduct to the ministers of the new sect, in the hope that a kindly and gracious conference with them may be of great advantage. I therefore beg this entire company to receive them as a father receives his children, and to take pains to teach and instruct them. Then, should the opposite of what was hoped for come to pass, and no means be found to bring them back or to unite us all, it will not, at least, be possible hereafter to say, as has been said in the past, that they have been condemned without having been heard. When this dispute shall have been faithfully reported and published throughout the kingdom, as it really was held, the people will be able to understand that it is for good, just, and certain reasons, and not by force or authority, that this doctrine has been rejected and condemned. Meantime his Majesty promises to be, as all the king's predecessors have always been, in everything and everywhere, the protector and defender of his Church.'[4]

[4] La Place, *Comment. de l'Estat de la Rél. et Rép.*, 158.

Scarcely had the chancellor concluded his temperate speech when Tournon, the oldest of the cardinals present, arose and addressed the king before L'Hospital could carry out his purpose to summon the Protestants. In spite of every rebuff, the bigots had not lost courage and strove at the last moment to prevent the promised conference from taking place. The cardinal was presiding officer of the assembled clergy, both in virtue of seniority and by rank. For he was dean of the college of Roman cardinals and primate of France by reason of his archbishopric of Lyons, to which the primacy was attached. He thanked the king and his mother for their presence, and briefly complimented the chancellor upon a speech which he said was so learned, so wise, and so well constructed that it could not be surpassed. He added that he had come prepared to answer all the chief points in the letters of convocation sent to the prelates, but that now a number of questions of prime importance had just been raised, to which he professed his unwillingness and his inability to reply offhand. He must consult with his colleagues, and he asked for a written copy of the chancellor's propositions. This request L'Hospital denied, saying that everybody had had the opportunity to hear them. Tournon then insisted, on the ground that he needed the paper especially for the benefit of such bishops as had not been present at Poissy and were coming in from day to day. But L'Hospital refused to accord the dilatory motion and ordered the Protestants to present themselves and speak.

At the word, Theodore Beza and the delegates who had chosen him to be their spokesman were brought into the hall by the captain of the king's guard, and came forward until their farther advance was stopped by a rail barring their nearer approach to the king and to the gathered dignitaries of his court and Church. Petty malice had planned the arrangement in order to give to the Protestant ministers the aspect of accused persons who were permitted to clear themselves of crimes laid to their charge, or of culprits about to be sentenced to condign punishment. Of petty malice, sooth to say, this was by no means the only manifestation. 'Here come the Genevese curs!' spitefully exclaimed one of the cardinals, in tones loud enough to be heard distinctly by Beza as he entered in company with another minister from the city of Calvin. To whom the courtly Reformer replied with unruffled composure: 'Faithful dogs are much needed in the Lord's sheepfold to bark at the wolves.'[5]

Beza, like his companions, was simply dressed in the long black Genevan gown, worn in public from the time of the Reformation to the present day by the pastors of the Churches of France and French Switzerland. On reaching the rail he stood for an instant and then addressed the young king in these words:[6]

'Sire, inasmuch as the issue of all enterprises, both great and small, depends upon the help and favour of our God, and chiefly when these enterprises concern the interests of his service and matters that surpass the capacity of our understandings, we hope that your Majesty will not find it amiss or strange if we begin by the invocation of his name, beseeching him after the following manner.'

[5] Contemporary fragment (Tronchin MSS.) in Baum, ii, 238.

[6] Beza's harangue at Poissy is given by La Place, 159, foll.; by the *Hist. Ecclés.*, i, 560-577.

A hush fell upon the entire assembly, as the speaker, ending this exhortation, knelt on the floor and began to repeat the beautiful prayer of Calvin's liturgy. His colleagues on his right hand and on his left also knelt. This example was contagious. The queen-mother fell on her knees. The cardinals and possibly the bishops arose and stood with uncovered heads while Beza reverently uttered the Huguenot confession of sins and supplication for pardon—the very words that had been used and were still to be used by many a martyr suffering the penalty of death for attending conventicles where this prayer was customarily repeated. His words were:

'Lord God! Almighty and everlasting Father, we acknowledge and confess before thy holy Majesty that we are miserable sinners, conceived and born in guilt and corruption, prone to do evil, unfit for any good; who, by reason of our depravity, transgress unceasingly thy holy commandments. Whereby we draw down upon ourselves, by thy just judgment, ruin and perdition. Nevertheless, O Lord, we are sore displeased that we have offended thee, and we condemn ourselves and our evil ways, with a true repentance, beseeching thee that thy grace may succour our distress. Be pleased, therefore, to have pity upon us, O most gracious God! Father of all mercies! for the sake of thy Son Jesus Christ, our Lord and only Redeemer. Blot out our sins and our pollution, and set us free, and grant us the daily increase of the graces of thy Holy Spirit; to the end that, acknowledging from our inmost hearts our unrighteousness, we be touched with a sorrow that shall work in us true repentance, and that this may cause us to die unto all sin and to bring forth the fruits of righteousness and purity that shall be well pleasing to thee, through the same Jesus Christ, our Lord and only Saviour.

'And, inasmuch as it doth please thee this day so far to exhibit thy favour to thy poor and unprofitable servants, as to enable them freely, and in the presence of the king whom thou hast set over them, and of the most noble and illustrious company on earth, to declare that which thou hast given them to know of thy holy truth, may it please thee to continue the course of thy goodness and loving-kindness, O God and Father of lights, and so to illumine our understandings, guide our affections, and form them to all teachableness, and so to order our words, that in all simplicity and truth, after having conceived, according to the measure which it shall please thee to grant unto us, the secret things which thou hast revealed to men for their salvation, we may be able with heart and with mouth to set forth that which may conduce to the glory and honour of thy holy name, and the prosperity and greatness of our king and of all those that belong to him, with the rest and comfort of all Christendom, and especially of this kingdom. O Almighty Lord and Father, we ask thee all these things in the name and for the sake of Jesus Christ, thy Son our Saviour, as he himself hath taught us to seek them, saying, "Our Father, which art in heaven,"' etc.

The solemn confession of sins of the Genevan liturgy, and the equally beautiful prayer of Beza's own composition with which he had associated it, predisposed his hearers to listen to the eloquent and forcible address to his Majesty that followed.

'Sire,' he said, when he had risen from his knees and again stood at the bar, 'it is a great happiness for a loyal and affectionate subject to look upon the face of his prince, since it represents to him, as it were, the visible majesty of God, and he cannot therefore but be greatly moved by the sight to consider the obedience and submission that he owes him. But if it so happen, that not only is he permitted to see his prince, but also be seen of him, and, what is of more importance, heard and finally received and approved, then truly is his a very great and peculiar satisfaction.

Of these four advantages, Sire, it has pleased God in his secret counsels that a part of your very humble and obedient subjects should for a long time have been deprived to their very great regret; until now in his mercy, having heard our continual cries and groans, he has so favoured us as to grant us a blessing rather desired than hoped for—the blessing of seeing your Majesty, Sire, and, better still, of being seen and heard by you in the most noble and illustrious company on earth. Should we therefore never receive any other advantage now or hereafter, yet would the remainder of our lives be insufficient duly to thank our God and render worthy praises to your Majesty.

But when, together with this, we consider that this same day not merely opens the way, but invites us and, after so benignant and gracious a fashion and one so becoming your royal gentleness, constrains us unitedly to testify to our obligation to confess the name of our God, and to declare the obedience we render you, we are compelled to admit, Sire, that our intelligence is incapable of conceiving the magnitude of such a boon, our tongues still less competent to express what affection enjoins. So great a favour surpassing all human eloquence, we prefer to confess our own impotence by a modest silence, rather than belittle such a benefit by the defect of our words.'

Having thus given utterance in graceful periods, if in an exaggerated style quite foreign to the taste of our later times, to those sentiments of submission which the men of the sixteenth century found none too strong for their unbounded loyalty, the orator proceeded to point out the single blessing which he and his friends still lacked. They had been permitted to see their king, to be seen by him, to be received by him with kindness. There yet remained the fourth point, that their service be accepted as agreeable by his Majesty.

'This also we hope to obtain,' said Beza, 'and God grant that our coming may put an end not so much to our past wretchedness and calamities, the memory of which is as it were extinguished by this happy day, as to what has ever seemed to us more grievous than death itself, namely, to the troubles and disorders that have come upon this kingdom by reason of religion, with the ruin of a great number of your poor subjects. Now several things have hitherto prevented us from enjoying so great a benefit, and these would still cause us to despair, were it not that, on the other hand, there are a number of things that tend to strengthen and assure us.

'There is, in the first place, a persuasion rooted in the hearts of many persons by a certain misfortune and perverseness of the times, that we are turbulent and ambitious men, obstinate in our opinions, enemies of all concord and tranquillity. It may also be that there are other people whose notion of us is, that, although we are not altogether enemies of peace, yet we demand it under conditions so rough and harsh as to be in nowise admissible; as if we were undertaking to turn the whole world upside down, in order to create another after our own fashion, and even to despoil some of their property in order to possess ourselves of it. There are several other hindrances of like magnitude or even greater, Sire; but we much prefer that their memory be buried rather than that we should reopen ancient sores by rehearsing them now that we are on the point, not of making lamentations and complaints, but of seeking the most prompt and suitable remedies.

'And what then gives us such assurance in the midst of so many hindrances? Sire, it is no reliance upon anything in us, seeing that we are, in every way, of the smallest and most contemptible in the world. Neither is it, thank God! a vain presumption or arrogance, for our vesture and lowly condition do not comport therewith. It is rather, Sire, our good conscience, which assures us of the excellence and justice of our cause, of which, therefore, we hope that our God, by means of your Majesty, will be the defender and protector. It is also the gentleness already to be recognised in your face, your speech, and your countenance. It is the equity which we see and have learned by experience to be impressed upon your heart, Madam,'—here he turned to Catharine de Medici. 'It is the uprightness of you, Sire, and the illustrious Princes of the Blood,'—this he said, bowing to the King of Navarre, the Prince of Condé, and those that sat with them. 'It is also the evident grounds we have to cherish the hope that you, our highly honoured lords of the Council, conforming yourselves to one and the same resolution, will not be less inclined to grant us so holy and necessary a concord than we are to receive it. And what more shall we say? There is still another consideration that encourages us. It is that we presume, according to the rule of charity, that you, gentlemen, with whom we are to confer'—and he turned to the cardinals and bishops on his right and on his left—'will exert yourselves in conjunction with us, according to our small measure, rather to clear up the truth than to obscure it; to instruct rather than to debate; to weigh arguments rather than to gainsay; in short, to prevent the malady from making farther progress rather than to render it altogether incurable and fatal. Such, gentlemen, is the opinion we have conceived of you, and we pray you, in the name of that great God who has gathered us here and who will be the Judge of our thoughts and of our words, that notwithstanding everything that has been said, written, or done during the space of forty years or thereabouts, you will with us lay aside all the passions and prejudices that might hinder the fruits of so holy and praiseworthy an undertaking, and that you will expect of us, if you please, what, with the help of God's grace, you will find in us, namely, a mind tractable and ready to receive everything that shall be proved by the pure word of God.

'Do not think that we are come to maintain any error, but to discover and correct every defect that shall be found, either on your side or on ours. Do not regard us as possessed of such overweening conceit as to undertake to ruin the Church of our God which we know to be eternal. Do not imagine that we are seeking the means of making you like unto ourselves in our poor and humble condition, wherein nevertheless, thank God, we find singular contentment. Our desire is that the ruins of Jerusalem may be rebuilt; that this spiritual temple may rise again; that the house of God built of living stones may be restored in its integrity; that the flocks so scattered and dispersed by a just vengeance of God and by the carelessness of men, may be rallied and gathered again in the sheepfold of the supreme and only Shepherd.

'Such is our purpose, such all our desire and our intention, gentlemen. If you have not believed it heretofore, we hope that you will believe it when we shall have conferred, in all patience and mildness, respecting what God has given us. Would to God that, without going farther, instead of entering upon opposing arguments, we might all raise a hymn to the Lord and join hands with one another, as has sometimes happened between the armies even of unbelievers and infidels drawn up in battle array. It were a great shame for us if we profess to preach the doctrine of peace and good will and meantime are the most easily estranged and the most difficult to reconcile. What then? These things men can and ought to desire; but it belongs to God to grant them, as also he will do when it shall please him to cover our sins by his goodness and dissipate our darkness by his light.

'And while on this topic, Sire, in order that it may be understood that we intend to proceed with a good conscience, simply, clearly, and frankly, we shall declare, if it please your Majesty to grant us permission, what in sum are the principal points of this conference; yet in such a manner that, with God's help, no one shall have any just occasion of offence. There are some who think and would gladly persuade others that we differ only respecting things of slight consequence, or respecting matters that are indifferent rather than essential points in our faith. There are others who, quite on the contrary, through lack of being well informed respecting our belief, suppose that we are agreed as to nothing whatever, any more than Jews or Mohammedans. The intention of the former is as praiseworthy as the opinion of the latter is to be rejected. This will, we hope, appear in the sequel. But certainly neither those who hold the one nor those that hold the other view open the way to a true and solid agreement. For if the latter are to be believed, the one of the two parties can exist only by ruining the other, a thing too inhuman to be thought of and most horrible in the execution. If again the opinion of the former is to be received, it will be necessary that many matters remain undecided. From this there will result discord more dangerous and damaging than ever.

'Thus, then, we admit (and we can scarcely make the admission without tears) that just as we agree respecting some of the principal points of our Christian faith, so also we disagree as to a part of them. We confess that there is one only God, in one and the same infinite and incomprehensible essence, distinct in three persons, consubstantial and equal in everything and everywhere, that is to say: the Father unbegotten, the Son eternally begotten of the Father, and the Holy Ghost proceeding from the Father and the Son. We acknowledge one only Jesus Christ, true God and true man, without confusion or separation of the two natures or of the properties of the same. We acknowledge that in so far as he is man, he is not the son of Joseph, but was conceived by the secret power of the Holy Ghost in the womb of the Blessed Virgin Mary, virgin, I say, both before and after his birth. We acknowledge his nativity, his life, his death, his burial, his descent into hell, his resurrection, and his ascension, as they are contained in the Holy Gospel. We believe that he is on high in the skies, seated on the right hand of God, where he will remain until he comes to judge the quick and the dead. We believe in the Holy Ghost, who enlightens, comforts, and sustains us. We believe that there is a holy Catholic, that is, universal Church, which is the assembly and communion of saints, outside of which there is no salvation. We are assured of the free remission of our sins through the blood of Jesus Christ, in virtue of which, after that these same bodies being raised again shall have been reunited to our souls, we shall enjoy blessed and eternal life with God.

'"How then?" someone will say. "Are not these the articles of our faith? Wherein then are we discordant?" First, in the interpretation of a part of them; secondly, in that it seems to us (and, if we are mistaken in this particular, we shall be very glad to know it), that men have not been satisfied with the aforesaid articles, but for a long time have not ceased adding articles to articles; as if the Christian religion were a structure that is never completed. Moreover, we say that what has been newly built, so far as we are able to learn, has not always been built upon the old foundations. Consequently it rather disfigures the structure than serves to deck it out and adorn it. Nevertheless more attention has often been given to these accessories than to what is essential. But to the end that our intention may be still better understood, we shall bring out these points in detail.

'We assert, therefore, and we hope to establish our assertion in all sobriety by the testimony of the Holy Scriptures, that the true God, in whom we are to believe, is robbed of his perfect righteousness, if we undertake to set up, in opposition to his anger and just judgment any other satisfaction or cleansing, in this world or in the next, than that entire and complete obedience which can be found in no other than in one only Jesus Christ. And, in like manner, if we say that he frees us from only one part of our debts, inasmuch as we pay the other, he is despoiled of his perfect mercy. Hence it follows, so far as we can judge, that when we would learn on what ground we obtain paradise we must take our stand upon the death and passion of one only Jesus Christ, our Saviour and Redeemer, or else, instead of the true God, we should adore a strange God, who would be neither perfectly just nor perfectly merciful.

'From this also depends another point of very great importance touching the office of Jesus Christ. For if he alone is not entirely our salvation, that so precious name of Jesus, that is to say, Saviour, announced by the angel Gabriel, would not be his proper name. In like manner, if he is not our only prophet, having fully made known to us the will of God his Father for our salvation, first, by the mouth of the prophets, afterwards in person in the fulness of times, and later by his faithful apostles; if he is not also the sole head and spiritual king of our consciences; if he is not also our only eternal priest, after the order of Melchisedec, having, by one offering of himself, made once and never repeated, reconciled men to God, and become now sole intercessor for us in heaven until the end of the world; in short, if we are not altogether complete in him alone, then the name and title of Messiah or Christ, that is to say, anointed of God and devoted to this end, will not belong to him.

'If, therefore, men will not be satisfied with Christ's own word alone, faithfully preached and subsequently reduced to writing by the prophets and apostles, Christ is dispossessed of his office of prophet. He is also degraded from his position as head and spiritual king of his Church, if new laws are made for men's consciences, and from his place as priest forever, by those who undertake to offer him up anew for the remission of sins and who are not satisfied to have him as sole advocate and intercessor in heaven between God and men.

'In the third place, we are not agreed either as to the definition, or as to the origin, or as to the effects of the faith which, following Saint Paul, we call "justifying faith," and through which alone we believe that Jesus Christ with all his benefits is applied to us. As to good works, if there are some persons who regard us as despising them, they are very ill informed; for we do not separate faith from charity any more than we can separate light and heat. And we say with Saint John, in his first epistle, that whoever says that he knows God and does not keep his commandments makes himself a liar by his own conscience and in his entire life. However, we frankly confess that we disagree in this matter on three principal points. The first is touching the origin and first source from which good works proceed; the second, what they are; the third, for what they are good. As to the first, we find no other free will in man save that which is made free by the sole grace of our Lord Jesus Christ; and we say that our nature, in the state into which it is fallen, needs before all things to be, not helped and sustained, but rather slain and mortified by the power of God's Spirit, inasmuch as grace finds it not only wounded and weakened, but altogether destitute of strength and opposed to everything that is good, yes, even dead and decayed in sin and corruption. And we render this honour to God, that we do not claim to share in this matter with him. For we ascribe the beginning, and the middle, and the end of our good works to his sole grace and mercy working in us. As to the second point, we accept no other rule of righteousness and obedience before God than his commandments, as they are written and recorded in his Holy Word. To these commandments we do not regard it lawful for any creature to add, nor to subtract from them, so as to bind the conscience. Respecting the third point, namely, for what purpose they are good, we confess that so far as they proceed from the Spirit of God working in us, since they proceed from so good a source, they ought to be called good, although if God were to examine them strictly, he would find only too much to find fault with.

'We say also that they are good for another purpose, inasmuch as by them our God is glorified, men are drawn to the knowledge of him, and we are assured that, the Spirit of God dwelling in us (a fact which is known by its fruits), we are of the number of his elect and predestinated to salvation. But when we seek to discover on what grounds we have eternal life, we say with Saint Paul that it is a free gift of God, and not a reward due to our merits. For Jesus Christ, in this respect, justifies us by his sole righteousness, which is imputed to us, sanctifies us by his holiness, which is imparted to us, and has redeemed us by his one sacrifice of himself, which is granted to us, through a true and living faith, by the mere grace and free gift of our God. All these treasures are communicated by the power of the Holy Ghost, making use to this end of the preaching of God's word and the administration of his Holy Sacraments. Not that these are necessary, seeing that he is Almighty God, but forasmuch as it pleases him to make use of these ordinary means to create and nurture in us that precious gift of faith which is as it were the only hand to lay hold on, and as it were the only vessel to receive Jesus Christ for salvation with all his treasures.'

From this exposition of the Protestant view of good works the speaker naturally proceeded to consider the word of God and the Sacraments to which he had just referred.

'We receive as the word of God only the teachings recorded in the books of the prophets and apostles, called the Old and New Testaments. For by whom shall we be certified of our salvation if not by those who are witnesses above reproach? As to the writings of the ancient Doctors and the Councils, before receiving them without dispute, we should have first to make them accord altogether with the Scriptures, and next among themselves; seeing that the Spirit of God never contradicts himself. This, gentlemen, we think you will never undertake to do. Should you undertake to do it, you will please pardon us if we say that we shall never believe it possible until we see it actually accomplished. What then? Are we of the race of that wretched Ham, son of Noah, who uncovered his father's nakedness? Do we esteem ourselves more learned than so many ancient Greek and Latin Fathers? Are we so conceited as to think that we are the first that have discovered the truth and to condemn for ignorance the whole world? God forbid, gentlemen, that we should be such. But methinks you will allow that there have been Councils and Councils, Doctors and Doctors, seeing that it is not in our days alone that there have been false prophets in the Church of God, as the apostles warn us in a number of places and, particularly, in the fourth chapter of the first epistle to Timothy, and in the twentieth chapter of the Acts of the Apostles. In the second place, as to the Councils and Doctors that are received, since all the truth that can be found in them must necessarily have been drawn from the Scriptures, what more certain means shall we find of deriving benefit from their intelligence than by testing everything by that touchstone, and considering the testimony and the reasons given by the Scriptures, on which they will be found to have based their interpretation?'

The conclusion drawn by Beza is:

'We therefore receive the Holy Scriptures as a complete declaration of everything needful for our salvation. As to what may be found in Councils or in the books of the Doctors, we cannot and ought not to prevent you, or ourselves, from deriving help from them, provided it be founded on the express testimony of Scripture. But, for the honour of

God, do not bring up to us their bare authority, without trying everything by this touchstone. For we say with Saint Augustine (in the second book of Christian Doctrine, chapter sixth): "If there be any difficulty in the interpretation of a passage, the Holy Ghost hath so tempered the Holy Scriptures, that what is obscurely stated in one place, is very clearly stated elsewhere." I have spoken at some length on this point, in order that everyone may understand that we are not enemies either of the Councils or of the old Fathers, by whom God has been pleased to instruct his Church.'

Beza had reserved to the last the consideration of two subjects—the Sacraments and the government of the Church. He excused himself on the ground of lack of time from the fuller treatment of the former which its importance would justify, and confined himself to a summary statement of the belief of the Protestant Churches.

'We are in agreement [with the Roman Catholics] as we think,' said he, 'in the description of this word "sacrament," namely, that the sacraments are visible signs by means of which our union with our Lord Jesus Christ is not simply signified or represented to us, but also is truly offered on the Lord's side, and consequently ratified, sealed, and as it were engraven by the virtue of the Holy Ghost upon those who by a true faith apprehend him who is thus signified and presented to them. I use this word "signified," gentlemen, not to enervate or annihilate the sacraments, but to distinguish the sign from the thing it signifies in all virtue and efficacy. Consequently, we grant that in the sacraments there must of necessity intervene a heavenly and supernatural mutation. For we do not assert that the water of the Holy

Baptism is simply water, but that it is a true sacrament of our regeneration and of the cleansing of our souls in the blood of Jesus Christ. In like manner, we do not assert that in the Holy Supper of our Lord the bread is simply bread, but the sacrament of the precious body of our Lord Jesus Christ which was given for us; nor that the wine is simply wine, but the sacrament of the precious blood that was shed for us. However, we do not say that this change is effected in the substance of the signs, but in the use and the end for which they are ordained. Nor again do we say that it is effected by virtue of certain words pronounced, nor by the intention of him who pronounces them; but by the sole power and will of him who has ordained this action so divine and heavenly, of which therefore the institution ought to be repeated aloud and clearly, in a tongue that is understood, and distinctly set forth, in order that it may be understood and received by all that are present. So much for the external signs. Let us come to what is testified and exhibited by the Lord through these signs.

We do not say, what some, in consequence of having failed to understand us well, have thought that we teach; namely, that in the Holy Supper there is a simple commemoration of the death of our Lord Jesus. Therefore we do not say that in it we are made partakers merely of the fruit of his death and passion; but we join the inheritance with the fruits proceeding therefrom, saying with Saint Paul in the tenth chapter of First Corinthians, that the bread which we break according to his institution is the communion of the true body of Jesus Christ which was given for us, and that the cup of which we drink is the communion of the true blood which was shed for us; even in that same substance which he assumed in the womb of the Virgin and which he took from among us to heaven. And I pray you, gentlemen, in God's name, what can you therefore seek or find in this holy sacrament which we also do not seek and find there?'

The statement was certainly far removed from the view of the Reformer Zwingli and of the Sacramentarians so called. But Beza did not hide from himself the fact that it would satisfy neither the Roman Catholics nor the Lutherans.

'I understand very well that a reply is quite ready on this point. The one party will ask us to acknowledge that the bread and wine are transmuted, I do not say into sacraments of the body and blood of our Lord Jesus Christ (for this we have already admitted), but into the very body and blood of Jesus Christ. The other party, perhaps, will not press us so far as this, but will require us to grant that the body and blood are really and corporeally either in, or with, or under the bread. But on this matter, gentlemen, for the honour of God, hear us patiently without being scandalised, and put off for a time all the opinion you have conceived of us. When either one of these opinions shall have been proved to us by Holy Scripture, we are ready to embrace it and to hold it until death. But it seems to us, according to the small measure of knowledge that we have received of God, that this transubstantiation is inconsistent with the analogy and propriety of our faith, insomuch as it is directly contrary to the nature of the sacraments, in which the substantial signs must of necessity continue to be true signs of the substance of the body and blood of Jesus Christ; and it likewise overthrows the truth of his human nature and his ascension. I say the like of the second opinion, that of consubstantiation, which, in addition to all that has been said, has no foundation in the words of Jesus Christ, and is in nowise necessary to our being partakers of the fruit of the sacraments.

'If hereupon someone asks us whether we make Jesus Christ to be absent from his Holy Supper, we reply that we do not. But if we look to the distance of the places (as we must when the question respects his corporeal presence and his humanity distinctively considered), we say that his body is as far removed from the bread and wine as the highest heaven is removed from the earth, in view of the fact that, so far as we are concerned, we are on the earth and the sacraments also, and that as to him, his flesh is in heaven, glorified in such wise that, as says Saint Augustine, glory has not taken away from him the nature of a true body, but its infirmity. If then anyone would conclude from this that we make Jesus Christ absent from his Holy Supper, we answer that this is an erroneous conclusion; for we render this honour to God, that we believe, according to his word, that, although the body of Jesus Christ is now in heaven and not elsewhere, and we are on the earth and not elsewhere, we are nevertheless made partakers of his body and blood in a spiritual manner and by means of faith, as veritably as we see the sacraments with the eye, touch them with the hand, put them into our mouth, and live of their substance in this bodily life.

'This, gentlemen, is in sum our faith on this point. As it seems to us (and if we are mistaken we shall be very glad to be informed) it does no violence to the words of Jesus Christ or of Saint Paul. It does not destroy the human nature of Jesus Christ, nor the article of his ascension, nor the institution of the sacraments. It does not open the door to any curious and inexplicable questions and distinctions. It does not at all detract from our union with Jesus Christ, which is the chief end for which the sacraments were instituted, and not to be either adored, or kept, or carried, or offered to God. And lastly, if we are not deceived, it does much more honour to the power and to the word of the Son of God than if we imagine that his body must be really joined to the signs in order that we should become partakers of them.

'We do not touch on what remains concerning the administration of Holy Baptism; for we believe that no one of you, gentlemen, would place us in the ranks of the anabaptists, who have no stouter enemies than we are. And as to some other particular questions on this score, we hope, with God's help, that, the chief points being settled in this mild and friendly conference, the rest will be concluded of itself.

'As to the other five so-called sacraments, true it is that we cannot give them this name until we have been better instructed in the Holy Scriptures. Meanwhile, however, we think that we have reëstablished true *confirmation*, which consists in catechising and instructing those that have been baptised in infancy, and in general all persons before admitting them to the Lord's Supper. We teach true *penitence* also, which consists in a true acknowledgment of one's faults and satisfaction to the offended parties, be it public or private, in the absolution which we have in the blood of Jesus Christ, and in amendment of life. We approve of *marriage*, following the injunction of Saint

Paul, in the case of all those who have not the gift of continence, and consequently do not think it lawful to bind anyone thereto by a vow or perpetual profession, and we condemn all wantonness and lust in word, gesture, or act. We receive the degrees of ecclesiastical charges according as God has ordained them in his house by his Holy Word. We approve of the *visitation of the sick* as a principal part of the sacred ministry of the Gospel. We teach with Saint Paul to judge no man in a distinction of days and meats, knowing that the kingdom of God does not consist in such corruptible things. Meanwhile, however, we condemn all dissoluteness, exhorting men continually to all sobriety, to the mortification of the flesh according to every man's need, and to assiduous prayer.

'There still remains the last point—concerning the external order and government of the Church. Respecting this, we are of the opinion that we may be permitted, gentlemen, to say, with your consent, that everything therein is so perverted, that everything is in such confusion and ruin, that, whether one consider the order as now established, or have a regard to life and manners, scarcely can the best architects in the world recognise the marks and vestiges of that ancient edifice so well adjusted by the apostles with compass and rule. Of this you yourselves are good witnesses, as you have busied yourselves about it of late. In short, we shall pass over these matters, which are sufficiently well understood, and which it were better to cover in silence than to utter.

'To conclude, we declare before God and his angels, before your Majesty, Sire, and all the illustrious company that is about you, that our only purpose and desire is that the form of the Church may be brought back to the simple purity and beauty which it had in the times of the apostles of our Lord Jesus Christ; and, as to those things that have since been added, that such as shall be found superstitious, or manifestly contrary to the word of God, may be altogether abolished; that those which are superfluous may be cut off, that those which experience has taught us lead to superstition may be removed. If there be found others useful and proper for edification, after a mature consideration of the ancient canons and authorities of the Fathers, let them be retained and observed in God's name, according to what may be suited to the times, places, and persons, to the end that with one accord God shall be worshipped in spirit and in truth, under your obedience and protection, Sire, and the protection of the persons established by God under your Majesty for the government of this realm. For if there be any that still think that the doctrines which we profess turn men away from the subjection which they owe to their kings and superiors, we have, Sire, wherewith to answer them with a good conscience.

'It is true that we teach that our first and principal obedience is due to our God, who is the King of kings and Lord of lords. But if our writings do not suffice to clear us from such a crime laid to our charge [as disloyalty to our sovereign], we shall bring up, Sire, the example of very many lordships and principalities, and even kingdoms, which have been reformed according to this same doctrine. These will suffice us as good and sufficient testimony for our acquittal. In short, we take our stand respecting this matter on what Saint Paul says in the thirteenth chapter of Romans, where, speaking of temporal government, he expressly enjoins that every soul be subject unto the higher powers. “Nay,” Saint John Chrysostom says on this passage: “even were you an apostle or an evangelist, for that such subjection does not derogate from the service of God.” But if it has happened, or if it should hereafter happen, that some, covering themselves with the mantle of our doctrine, should be found guilty of rebellion against the least of your officers, Sire, we protest before God and your Majesty, that they are not of us, and that they could not have more bitter enemies than we are, according as our poor condition permits.

‘In fine, Sire, the desire we have to advance the glory of our God, the obedience and very humble service due to your Majesty, our affection for our native land and specially for the Church of God—these have brought us to this place in which we hope that our good God and Father, continuing the course of his loving-kindness and mercies, will confer upon you, Sire, grace such as that which he conferred on the young King Josiah, two thousand two hundred and two years ago; and that under your happy government, Madam [Catharine de Medici], assisted by you, Sire [the King of Navarre], and the other and excellent princes of the blood and lords of your council, the ancient memory shall be revived of that renowned Queen Clotilde, who served of old as the instrument of our God to give the knowledge of himself to this realm. Such is our hope. For this we are ready, Sire, to employ our own lives, to the end that, rendering to you very humble service in a matter so holy and praiseworthy, we may behold the true golden age in which our Lord and Saviour Jesus Christ shall be worshipped by all with one accord, as to him belong all honour and glory for ever. Amen.'

Here Beza and his company kneeled for a moment. Then rising he continued, at the same time presenting to the king the Confession of Faith of the French Churches:

'Sire, your Majesty will be pleased to give no thought to our language, rough and unpolished as it is, but rather to the affection that is wholly given to you. And, inasmuch as the points of our doctrine are contained clearly and more fully in this Confession of Faith which we have already presented to you, and on which the present conference will turn, we very humbly beseech your Majesty to do us again this favour of receiving it from our hands, hoping by God's grace that, after having conferred on it in all sobriety and reverence for his holy name, we shall find ourselves in agreement as to it. And if, on the contrary, our iniquities prevent such a blessed consummation, we doubt not that your Majesty, with your good council, will know how to provide for everything, without prejudice to either of the two parties, according to God and to reason.'

Such was the first plea of the Reformation that reached the ear of a king of France. It was confessedly not unworthy of the orator from whose mouth it came, of the rare occasion, of the subject, of the presence in which it was delivered.

One dramatic incident that interrupted the quiet course of Beza's speech has been purposely omitted, in order that the reader may have before him the unbroken argument. I must go back to narrate it.

The dignified bearing and the well-chosen words of Beza, uttered with force and grace, and breathing the spirit of profound conviction, had commanded the close and respectful attention of his hearers, even when he uttered unpalatable sentiments, from the beginning of his discourse until he was well on in the discussion of the nature of the sacraments. It was otherwise when the Reformer came, after a formal rejection both of the Roman Catholic and of the Lutheran doctrines, to speak of the relative places of the body of Jesus Christ and of the consecrated elements in the Lord's Supper. At the words, '*We say that his body is as far removed from the bread and wine as the highest heaven is removed from the earth*,' a number of the prelates who had long been inwardly chafing with anger and indignation could contain themselves no longer. Cardinals, bishops, doctors of the Sorbonne, began to express their dissent in loud and violent tones. Amid the din that instantly arose, Beza's voice was quite drowned for the time, and the only intelligible words that could be made out were exclamations of 'He has blasphemed! He has blasphemed God!' coming from one and another of the ecclesiastics. The bystanders looked for nothing else than that they should accompany their cries with a symbolic rending of their clothes. Cardinal Tournon, who had risen to his feet, turned to the young king, and prayed him either to command Beza to desist from speaking, or to suffer him with his brethren, the Roman Catholic prelates, to retire from the place. The queen-mother, however, thought that there had been quite enough of this, and commanded silence. Cardinal Lorraine, less ardent or more politic than some of his colleagues, joined with her in the attempt to restore order. Beza, who meanwhile had stood unmoved the sudden outbreak of this unexpected storm, continued his speech and finished it according to his original design.

At the close of Beza's address there was a second demonstration. No sooner had he stopped than Cardinal Tournon, 'all trembling with wrath,' rose and, as primate and presiding officer of the assembly of prelates, addressed the king. It was, he said, by his Majesty's express command that the cardinals and bishops, in order to obey him, had consented (not, however, without conscientious scruples) to listen to these new evangelists. For they foresaw that the latter might, as they had done, utter things unworthy of the ear of a Most Christian King, things that might well have offended many people who were about his Majesty. The assembly of the prelates, suspecting that this might occur, had, continued the cardinal, instructed him in this case to beseech the monarch very humbly not to believe or give credit either to the meaning or to the words uttered by the person who had spoken in behalf of the adherents of the new religion, and to beg him to suspend the judgment he might form on the matter until he should have heard the remonstrances which the assembly intended to make to him. By this means the prelate hoped that his Majesty and all the honourable company by which the king was supported would be able to learn the difference there exists between truth and falsehood. He begged that a day might be assigned the prelates for this purpose, and he added that, but for the respect they entertained for his Majesty, they would have arisen on hearing the blasphemous and abominable words that had been uttered, and would not have suffered the conference to proceed. What they had done, they had done in order to obey his Majesty's command; and they prayed him very humbly to persevere in the faith of his fathers, and invoked the Virgin Mary and the blessed saints in paradise, both male and female, that this might be.

The cardinal was about to say more, but Catharine cut his speech short. She assured him that nothing had been done in the affair save by the decision of the royal council and with the concurrence of the Parliament of Paris. The end in view, said she, was not to make innovations or commotions, but, on the contrary, to appease the troubles proceeding from the diversity of religious opinions, and to bring back those that had strayed from the right way. The truth was to be established by means of the simple word of God, which must be the sole rule. 'We are here to hear both sides,' said she. 'Reply, therefore, to the speech of Monsieur de Bèze to which you have just listened.' Cardinal Tournon declined to accept the challenge on the ground that the speech had been a long one, and could not be answered offhand; but he promised that if a written copy were afforded to the prelates, they would prepare a suitable rejoinder. The point was conceded, and herewith the proceedings of the day came to an end.

CHAPTER 11

FURTHER DISCUSSIONS—THE EDICT OF JANUARY—MASSACRE OF VASSY

1561, 1562

In the last chapter I have given a translation of Beza's speech of September 9, 1561, before the King of France, the chief noblemen of his court, and the assembled cardinals and bishops of the realm. Of this memorable address I have inserted nearly the whole, and almost always in a close rendering. Two reasons have moved me to do this. The speech possesses a peculiar historical importance, irrespective of the person who was the mouthpiece of the Protestants, now for the first time officially summoned for their defence to the bar of public opinion. As such, it may be regarded in the light of a great State paper, wherein every sentence is of weight, while every position that is taken has a more or less direct bearing on the subsequent course of the French reformatory movement. This is the more general consideration. The more special and personal has reference to Theodore Beza himself. As a work of art, the address at the Colloquy of Poissy exhibits, better, perhaps, than any of his other productions, the striking oratorical abilities of the man whose name it instantly made famous. At the same time, its importance as an exposition of the theological views of Beza, and, we may add, of Calvin, should not be overlooked in a biographical work like the present. The doctrinal contrast between the Reformation and the Roman Catholic system, on the one hand, and between the position of Beza and the positions of the Reformers of Wittenberg and Zurich, on the other, is so clearly marked in this document, that the most superficial of readers can have little difficulty in forming a distinct conception of the individuality of Beza as a theologian.

That his effort had proved a great success cannot be denied. Friends and foes were agreed on this point at least. Hubert Languet, the distinguished Protestant negotiator, who chanced to be in Paris at the time, expressed himself scarcely more strongly respecting the brilliancy of the oration than did Claude Haton, the curate of Provins. But whereas the Protestants gave it their unqualified approval, the Roman Catholics condemned with great bitterness those utterances respecting the sacraments which had raised the passionate protests of Cardinal Tournon and his associates. There is no doubt that Catharine de Medici and others who shared her politic views regarded Beza's frank statement as a needless and offensive expression of opinion, and deplored what they stigmatised as a blunder that came near wrecking the conference. But whoever will look with calmness at the entire situation must come to a different conclusion. A suppression of the candid views of the Reformers on so critical a point might indeed have prevented an explosion of priestly indignation at this particular juncture. But it could only have postponed what must have come sooner or later. And such difficulties are for the most part best met when met most promptly. A conference broken off because of a clear and unmistakable expression of opinion on an important theological subject—had indeed such a result ensued—would have wrought far less damage to the Protestant cause than might have resulted from an insincere and dishonest treatment of a distinctive dogma, or from a politic silence, by which the whole tone of the discussion would have been lowered and the self-respect of its professors would have been sacrificed. Calvin saw this, and, so far from condemning, he applauded Beza's boldness in unqualified terms.

'Your speech is now before us,' he wrote to Beza on receiving the text of the oration, 'wherein God wonderfully directed your mind and your tongue. The testimony that stirred up the wrath of the holy fathers could not but be given, unless you had consented basely to practise evasion and expose yourself to their derision.'[1]

Beza had nothing to retract and no apology to make. Hearing, however, that the queen-mother was, or pretended to be, displeased with what he had said on the matter of the Lord's Supper, he wrote to her, the next day, to explain both what he had said, which, on account of the uproar created by the prelates, she had possibly not heard distinctly, and the object for which he had said it. The letter is a model of manly frankness. Far from modifying his speech in any particular, he repeated for Catharine's benefit the very words that had given offence. He declared that what had moved him to use them was a desire to defend his co-religionists from the charge of sacrilegiously making Jesus Christ to be absent from his Holy Supper.

[1] Letter of September 24, 1561. Bonnet, iv, 229.

'But,' said he, 'there is a great difference between making him present insomuch as that he there truly gives us his body and blood, and saying that his body and blood are united with the bread and wine. I acknowledged the former, which is also the chief thing; I denied the latter.'

Beza begged as a favour that he might be permitted to set forth his views more fully before her and any other persons who might give him instruction in case he was wrong. He closed his letter with passages from Saint Augustine and Vigilius, Bishop of Trent, who had expressed themselves quite as strongly as he had done respecting the matter in hand.[2]

It is perhaps needless to say that no such opportunity as Beza asked for was vouchsafed to him. The prelates, averse from the beginning to anything like free and fair discussion with the Protestants, were still more disinclined to treat with them since they had heard the magnificent exposition of the Reformed doctrines by one who was at the same time forcible and gentle, courteous and self-possessed. But a promise had been given that Beza should be answered, and that promise the Cardinal of Lorraine undertook to redeem just one week after Beza had spoken. The place was the same; the assembled dignitaries were the same; the Protestants were the same except that their numbers were increased by the arrival of the distinguished Peter Martyr. In one respect, however, there was a notable difference. The cardinal, instead of speaking, like Beza, from behind a bar, was provided with a pulpit from which he

[2] The letter is given in La Place, 168, 169, and in the *Hist. Ecclés.*, i, 580-584.

might deliver his discourse as one having authority, and thus appear to be either a learned preacher instructing the ignorant, or a judge pronouncing the final sentence of the law upon offenders.

And how did he attempt to answer the full, clear, and candid exposition of the Reformed faith made by Beza? Chiefly by an assumption of a lordly superiority, with a slight admixture of patronising condescension and unsolicited compassion. He began by lauding at great length both the temporal authority of kings and the spiritual authority of ecclesiastics. He concluded with an appeal to Charles IX to adhere to the religion of his predecessors, all of them loyal to the holy Catholic faith, from whom he had inherited the distinction of being styled not only 'Most Christian' but 'First Son of the Church,' and with a corresponding appeal to Catharine de Medici, promising for himself and all his associates of the Gallican Church that they would not spare their very life-blood in the maintenance of the true Catholic doctrine, nor fail to do their full duty in the service of the king and the support of his crown. On only two points of the Reformed confession did the cardinal even pretend to enter into argument. He maintained that the Church is no mere aggregation of the elect, but includes the tares along with the wheat. He argued that the presence of the Lord in the Eucharist is not spiritual alone, but real and corporeal as well. As for the rest, he treated the Protestants as wayward but misguided children for whom he had no reproaches to utter, but only pity; the more so that they had shown some disposition to receive instruction and to return to a Church that was ready to welcome them so soon as they consented to submit to her authority. But if they would not return, and if their ministers would accord in doctrine neither with the Latin nor with the Greek Church, and indeed remained at variance with their fellow-Reformers, the Lutherans of Germany, he suggested that the French Protestants ought to withdraw to some remote region where they would cease to disturb flocks over which they had no legitimate authority, to a solitude where at least they might remain until their new-fangled opinions should grow as old and venerable as the creed of the established Church.[3]

When the Cardinal of Lorraine was through, the prelates at once made a dramatic demonstration of their approval, starting to their feet in a body, and, with Cardinal Tournon at their head, pressing about Charles IX. They begged the young prince to remain constant to the teachings of the Church, and particularly to require that Beza and his associates should accept and sign what they had just been taught, before being permitted to receive any additional instruction. The Genevese Reformer rose in his turn and claimed the privilege of answering Cardinal Lorraine on the spot—a request which, for reasons of her own, Catharine de Medici thought fit to deny, promising that he should have an opportunity at a later time.[4]

With this incident the Colloquy of Poissy assumed so different a shape as scarcely to be the same. The clergy could with difficulty be persuaded to consent to meet the Protestants a third time, and when they yielded to pressure, the small room of the prioress was large enough to contain all

[3] La Place, 170-177; *Rise of the Huguenots*, i, 528, 529.

[4] La Place, 177.

that presented themselves—a dozen bishops and cardinals with about as many attendant theologians bearing ponderous tomes, the works of the Church Fathers of the first five centuries, from which Cardinal Lorraine was to refute the Reformed doctrine. On the other side, the twelve Protestant ministers were again admitted, but not the laymen. Charles IX was absent. In his place came Catharine de Medici and the King and Queen of Navarre, with sundry members of the royal council. The conference was undignified and disorderly. Its regular course was interrupted by the intemperate speech of a Dominican friar, Claude de Sainctes, and by the absurd demand sprung upon the French Protestants by Cardinal Lorraine that they should answer categorically the question, whether or no they would consent to subscribe to the Augsburg Confession which was received by the Protestants of Germany. Evidently no good could be expected to come from a conference which bade fair to degenerate into an unseemly wrangle. Yet, two days later, in a meeting at which Beza was permitted to reply to the prelate's unreasonable proposal, the Reformer maintained his dignified composure. He reminded the queen-mother, with manly frankness, of the issues dependent upon the conference. It was of supreme importance that this should be conducted in a fair and friendly manner. He retorted with quiet but effective irony to an ill-timed speech made at the last session by a Roman Catholic theologian, Claude d'Espense, who endeavoured to show that the Protestant ministers were intruders who had assumed their office without a proper 'call.' What, asked Beza, if a bishop were to ask a Reformed pastor his authority for undertaking to preach and administer the sacraments, and were to be met with the counter-questions: 'Were you elected to the episcopate by the elders of your church? Did the people seek for you? Were inquiries instituted regarding your conduct, your life, and your belief?' or, 'Who ordained you, and how much money did you pay to be ordained?' Many a bishop's cheek would blush were he compelled to reply to such an interrogatory. Nor was Beza less happy when he drew attention to the circumstance that Cardinal Lorraine, instead of undertaking to prove by the Church Fathers of the first centuries the falsity of the Protestant position and thus affording his antagonists the opportunity to meet him on the field of honest discussion, demanded of them that they subscribe to an article said to be extracted from the Augsburg Confession and treating of the doctrine of the Lord's Supper, as the condition of future conference.

Beza was ably reinforced by the Florentine, Peter Martyr Vermigli. This famous Italian exile, now over sixty years of age, respecting whom an opponent (D'Espense) frankly admitted that there was no other man of his time that had written so amply and with so much erudition on the subject of the Lord's Supper,[5] had come to France upon the pressing invitation of Catharine de Medici, and provided with a special safe-conduct from Charles IX. He was a striking personage. Beza, in his collection of lives of worthies and their portraits, written long after,[6] felicitously styles him a phoenix born from the ashes of Savonarola. From a monk and visitor general of the Augustinian order,

[5] La Place, 197.

[6] Beza, *Icones*, *s. v.*

Martyr had become a Reformer, and had fled beyond the Alps. He was a professor at Strassburg with Bucer. In King Edward's reign he laboured in England with zeal and acquired a distinguished place among those who strove to make the services of the Established Church free from the taint of Roman Catholicism. He was appointed to lecture on the Scriptures at Oxford. After her accession, Queen Elizabeth, as Bishop Jewel tells us, was altogether desirous that he should be invited back to England, that, 'as he had formerly *tilled*, as it were, the University by his lectures, so he might again *water* it by the same.'[7] He had now been five or six years at Zurich, a coadjutor of Bullinger, at the head of the Church and exercising a powerful influence across the Channel, especially by his letters. His great reputation and the dignity of his presence added force to his admirable address. In French he could not have spoken with freedom. He would therefore naturally have used Latin, the common language of the learned world; but he preferred to fall back upon his native tongue, in order that Catharine de Medici, like himself a Florentine, might understand him the more readily. A little while later on the same day, when Lainez, the second general of the Jesuit order, and as such the successor of Ignatius Loyola, obtained permission to speak and uttered a coarse tirade against the Reformers, likewise employing the Italian tongue, no objection was made to his procedure. But Peter Martyr was rudely interrupted by the Cardinal of Lorraine, who petulantly exclaimed that he did not want to listen to a foreign tongue.[8]

[7] Jewel to Martyr, Nov. 5, 1559. *Zurich Letters* (Parker Society), p. 68.
[8] La Place, *ubi supra*.

PETER MARTYR VERMIGLI

There was little more of the colloquy which had begun so pompously, and it adjourned never to meet again. In its train followed a few private conferences in which five Roman Catholics chosen for their supposed moderation of sentiment met an equal number of Protestant ministers in one of the rooms of the mansion occupied at Saint Germain by the King of Navarre, and deliberated upon some of the points at issue. Beza was one of the company. His colleagues were Peter Martyr Vermigli, Augustin Marlorat, Jean de l'Espine, and Nicholas des Gallars. The party was compelled by the demand of the bishops at Poissy to take up first the question of the presence of Christ in the Lord's Supper. Although this was the very point of difficulty between Reformed and Roman Catholics, less trouble was found in coming to an agreement than anyone not familiar with the constitution of the joint commission on the Roman Catholic side would have apprehended. Peter Martyr, loyal successor of Zwingli and Zwingli's views, put the matter plainly from the Protestant position when he told his associates that, for his part, he believed that the body of Christ is truly and as to its substance nowhere else than in heaven; while he did not deny that the true body and true blood of Christ, given on the cross for the salvation of men, are, by faith and spiritually, received by believers in the Holy Supper. Twice did the conferees laboriously draw up an article which should express the thought of Martyr, yet in such language as to satisfy both parties. The first result of their efforts was instantly rejected by the bishops. When the supposed objection had been obviated by important changes of phraseology and a second article had been prepared, which the Roman Catholic members felt confident would prove fully acceptable, their work was scornfully repudiated and the bearers were dismissed with the accusation of having betrayed their cause to the Protestants. The Protestants were no better pleased with the article than were the Roman Catholics, and by mutual consent all further attempts were abandoned to reconcile what was really irreconcilable; or, rather, to gloss over substantial disagreement by means of terms that could be, and would be, interpreted diversely by different persons. All that could be said to the credit of the recent effort was that it had been honestly made with the earnest purpose to postpone, or, if possible, avert altogether, the outbreak of civil war which all intelligent men saw to be imminent.

With the discharge of Beza's commission to plead the Protestant cause in the Colloquy of Poissy, the object of his coming to France was fulfilled. He was anxious to resume his duties at Geneva. When, however, he applied for leave to start on his homeward way, he was so far from obtaining it that Catharine de Medici sent for him and strongly urged that he should remain at least for a time. Her request might have been disregarded, high as was the advantageous estimate of his character and services which it implied. It was otherwise when Prince Condé, Gaspard de Coligny, and the most prominent members of the Huguenot party added their vehement solicitations, begging that he should not desert them at a time when it was given out that the settlement of the religious status of the adherents of the Reformed faith was about to be settled by an Assembly of Notables. In the circumstances, Beza had no choice but to

LOUIS OF BOURBON, PRINCE OF CONDÉ

subordinate his personal preferences to the general good of the cause. He was the less anxious to be at home, perhaps, that he heard from Geneva that the theological school was suffering no detriment by reason of the absence of one of its two theological professors, since his colleague was teaching immense numbers of students. Just at this moment an enthusiastic correspondent of Farel wrote: 'It is a marvel to see the number of persons that listen to Monsieur Calvin's lectures. I estimate them at more than a thousand daily.'[9] Meanwhile, still more phenomenal was the continual increase of avowed Protestants in almost all quarters of France. Everybody heard of the unprecedented gatherings of worshippers that took place in certain cities and towns; but everybody did not know, as Catharine de Medici learned by instituting a special inquiry, that the Huguenots had over two thousand churches in France—more precisely, two thousand one hundred and fifty and over, varying in size from a single church comprising almost all the inhabitants of some considerable town and ministered to by two or more pastors, down to a church of a few members in the midst of an overwhelmingly superior Roman Catholic population.[10] As for Beza, his most pressing desire for the moment was that the Protestants, conscious of growing numbers, might restrain their natural impetuosity for at least two months; so sanguine were his hopes that the coming Assembly of Notables would materially better their condition.[11] The queen-mother was evidently glad to give

[9] De Beaulieu to Farel, Geneva, October 3, 1561. Baum, ii (doc.), 92.
[10] *Hist. Ecclés.*, i., 743-745.
[11] Beza to Calvin, November 4, 1561, Baum, i (doc.), 121.

audience to the Genevese Reformer in France, and reckoned upon his cooperation in the maintenance of peace. Nor were his services unimportant.

On January 17, 1562, the results of the deliberations of the Assembly of Notables were published in the form of a royal edict—known in history as the *Edict of January*. For the first time in French history the Protestants were accorded official recognition, and gained a part, at least, of their natural rights. Not only were they suffered to reside in the kingdom, but they were permitted to worship God in gatherings of unarmed men and women, anywhere outside of the walls of the cities. If they were commanded to surrender all the edifices of which they had taken possession situated within the city walls, the loss was of small consequence in view of the importance of the cardinal concession, especially as the law guaranteed them safety and protection on the way to and from their places of worship.[12]

After the enactment of the Edict of January, there remained much to occupy Beza's attention. First of all, there was the task of allaying the dissatisfaction of his fellow-believers, who had not unreasonably hoped for a law that should accord complete religious equality both of worship and of profession, and who were impatient that their anticipations remained unfulfilled. Here Beza's ability and wide influence were of great service to the queen, who, there can be no doubt, was sincerely desirous of ending the present state of uncertainty and consequent danger, by the

[12] See the text of the Edict of January in the original French in many works, *e.g.*, Du Mont, *Corps Diplomatique*, v, 89-91; *Mémoires de Condé*, iii, 8-15; *Hist. Ecclés.*, i, 752-758.

cordial acceptance of the edict by both religious parties. I may instance, in particular, a letter which he drew up in the name of the ministers and deputies of the Churches while these still remained at Saint Germain, and which was sent to all the Protestant congregations throughout France, counselling them to accept loyally the king's edict, and encouraging them to hope that the new law would prove only the harbinger of better things to come. The letter was accompanied by a paper taking up all the fourteen articles of the new law, examining each in turn, and explaining how it should be observed.[13] I cannot speak further of these able documents, the circulation of which had the desired effect of securing the submission of the Huguenots. Nor shall I detain the reader long with a fresh conference between Protestant and Roman Catholic theologians, in which Beza played a conspicuous part, and as a consequence of which he attained yet greater prominence. Catharine de Medici still clung to the hope that by discussion a common ground might be reached. Under her auspices a larger company than the last convened in the grand council hall of the castle of Saint Germain. Iconoclasm had become a common feature of the reformatory movement of late, much against the will of the leading Reformers, despite, indeed, their vehement protests; but it was difficult to restrain the people, and the statues and paintings of saints, whether adorning the interior or the exterior of churches, fared ill at the hands of mobs intent on the forcible removal of the insignia of popery. It may have been this circumstance that led Catharine to propose Images and Image Worship as

[13] In *Mémoires de Condé*, iii, 93-98, *Hist. Ecclés.*, i, 760-766.

the special topic for the consideration of the learned men she brought together. But nothing came of their debates, unless it be that they showed not only that the views of the Roman Catholics and of the Protestants were irreconcilable, but that the former were not agreed among themselves. It was the Roman Catholic Bishop of Valence, Montluc, that brought out the startling fact that one zealous controversialist, Artus Désiré, had had the effrontery to compose a metrical substitute for the second Commandment, as versified by the Protestants, wherein the Almighty was made *to order*, instead of *to forbid*, the making of graven images of anything in heaven, on the earth, or under the earth, and to be *greatly pleased* with, instead of condemning, whatever honour or worship was paid to it.[14] Beza's long speech was a masterly discussion of the entire theme, and received the strong commendation of his brethren, however little it may have convinced his opponents.[15] The profitless conference lasted about a fortnight, from the 28th of January to the 11th of February, 1562.

Twenty days later came the Massacre of Vassy, the spark which kindled a conflagration that was to rage in France for most of the rest of the century.

The Edict of January, with its equitable, but limited, concessions to the Protestants, was supremely distasteful to the Roman Catholic Church and to the bigoted adherents

[14] The stupid parody ran:

'Tailler tu te fera image
De quelque chose que se soit.
Si honneur lui fais et hommage,
Ton Dieu grand plaisir en reçoit.'

[15] *Hist. Ecclés,* i, 781-798.

THE MASSACRE OF VASSY, MARCH 1, 1562

A. Barn where preaching was held at which about 1,200 persons were present. B. Duke of Guise, who commanded. C. The Minister in the pulpit praying to God. D. The Minister, attempting to escape is wounded in several places and would have been killed, had not the sword

broken in two. E. Cardinal of Guise leaning on a wall of the parish cemetery. F. Roof broken by the worshippers to make their escape. G. Several persons leaping the city wall escape to the fields. H. Some attempting to escape by the roof are shot. I. The box for the poor carried off. K. The trumpets sound twice.

of that Church who would have toleration for none but themselves. It was, consequently, an object of special abhorrence to the family of Guise, a family which aspired to represent the most extreme tendencies in Church and State and thereby to strengthen its already exorbitant influence. The enactment of the Edict of January was a virtual repeal of the intolerant Edict of July of the previous summer, respecting which Duke Francis of Guise, more blunt of speech and less politic than his brother, Cardinal Lorraine, had openly boasted that his sword would never rest in its scabbard when the execution of the ordinance was in question. He was in a state of irritation which any fortuitous incident might easily convert into insane fury. On Sunday morning, March 1, 1562, while on his return from a conference at Saverne, near the banks of the Rhine, with Duke Christopher of Würtemberg, he chanced to enter a small town of Champagne named Vassy, at this time a fief whose revenues were enjoyed by his kinswoman Mary, Queen of Scots. A congregation of Huguenots were worshipping in a rude barn which they had transformed into a sanctuary. Their services were interrupted by the duke's followers. It is needless here to decide precisely how the assault was brought on, whether by the nobleman's express orders, or by the forward zeal of his attendants and without his previous participation. The main facts are indisputable. A band of peaceable Protestants were broken in upon, in the midst of their prayers and hymns, under the eyes of one of the first noblemen of the kingdom, and men, women, and children, who had come to worship the Prince of Peace, were slaughtered like sheep, and without distinction of age or sex. Many fell within the rude but sacred enclosure, fugitives were picked off by the arquebusiers and slain before they could reach a place of safety. Fifty or sixty persons dead and about twice that number of badly wounded were the fruits of that Sunday morning's work.

Say what they would, the friends of Guise could never prove that the massacre was not in glaring violation of the edict signed only six weeks previously, forbidding judges, magistrates, and all other persons, of whatever station, quality, or condition they might be, from hindering, disquieting, molesting, or in any wise attacking 'those of the new religion' in or when going to or from their places of assembly outside of the walls of the cities.

When the news reached the French court and the capital, the Protestants loudly protested against the daring infringement of the law, and demanded the punishment of the law-breaker, whom they denounced as a murderer. Beza was still in France. The Churches begged him to represent them and to use his recently acquired influence in securing from the queen-mother and her advisers a prompt condemnation of this first blow struck at the Edict of January. Francour accompanied him as a representative of the Protestant nobles. The two envoys found Charles IX and Catharine de Medici at Monceaux. In an audience at which were present Antoine of Bourbon, King of Navarre, the recently arrived papal legate, Cardinal Ferrara, and others, Beza clearly and forcibly set forth the attack that had been made upon the solemn decree of the king by one of his subjects, on his own personal responsibility, and the evident plots laid to ruin the Huguenots of France. He frankly and temperately laid before his Majesty the disasters that must certainly flow from such flagrant acts of injustice if permitted to pass unpunished. Catharine returned a gracious reply, promising that the matter should be thoroughly investigated, and that, if the Protestants exercised self-restraint, ample provision should be made to satisfy them. The Duke of Guise would not, she hoped, pursue his journey to Paris. She had written to him and requested him not to do so.

There was one person who had listened to Beza's remarks and to the queen's conciliatory response with ill-concealed anger, and who could contain himself no longer. This was Antoine of Bourbon, formerly, as we have seen, and so long as it served his purpose, an ardent friend of the Reformation, but of late a pronounced ally of the Guises, since the promise of the restoration of his old kingdom had been held forth to allure him. He now broke out with reproaches against the Protestants for going, as he said, armed to their preaching services.

'Arms in the hands of the wise,' replied Beza, 'are bearers of peace. The occurrence at Vassy shows how necessary they are to the Church, unless safety be otherwise provided, and this provision, Sire, I most humbly beg you, in the name of the Church which until now has cherished such hope in you, to make.'

The legate, a troublesome priest, whose sole mission to France was in the interest of the maintenance of proscription laws against the Huguenots, here attempted to support Navarre's allegations by descanting upon the misdeeds of the Protestants which recently had caused riot and bloodshed at their place of assembly near the church of Saint Medard. Beza, having been present on the occasion referred to, was able to refute the prelate's calumny on the spot, after which he repeated the demand for the punishment of the Duke of Guise, who was known to be coming armed as in a time of war—a procedure from which nothing but mischief could ensue. Hereupon Antoine of Bourbon threw off all disguise, and avowed himself the duke's friend and partisan. 'Whoever,' said he, 'shall touch my brother the Duke of Guise with the tip of his finger, will touch my whole body.'

It was a critical juncture in the history of French Protestantism, and the champion of French Protestantism realised the full responsibility that devolved upon him. First he begged Antoine to hear him patiently as one whom he had long known and whom he had, not many months ago, requested to come to France to help in giving peace to the realm. Next he reminded him that the way of justice is God's way, and that justice is a debt which kings owe to their poor subjects. To ask for justice is to wrong nobody. Antoine had attempted to excuse the massacre at Vassy by alleging that the Protestant worshippers had thrown stones at Guise and his followers, and that thereupon the former had been unable to restrain the fury of his men, and bloodshed followed. Princes, said he, are not to be expected to submit to being stoned. 'If that be so,' the Reformer quietly responded, 'the Duke of Guise will be exculpated on producing the persons who committed the fault.' And then it was that, rising to the height of that commanding eloquence which few of his contemporaries knew so well how to attain, he closed his address to the insincere King of Navarre with words which the Churches of France never forgot, but which, through the ages of persecution that were to follow, they cherished as a motto to sustain their courage. 'Sire,' he gravely said, 'it belongs in truth to the Church of God, in whose name I speak, to endure blows and not to inflict them. But it will also please your Majesty to remember that she is an anvil that has worn out many hammers.'

Thus the incident closed, and Beza took his leave. 'It was God's will,' says the author of the history of the origins of the Protestant Churches, 'that these words should be spoken to the King of Navarre, and that, notwithstanding, Beza should return safe and sound, having discharged a sufficiently hazardous commission.'[16]

Within a few weeks there broke out the first of those unfortunate civil wars in which the Huguenots became involved. Condé took the field at their head. Catharine de Medici, who had implored his assistance in letters still extant, the authenticity of which cannot rationally be doubted,[17] ended a period of vacillation, and not so much consented, as was forced, to put herself into the power of his opponents. Beza could not in conscience desert the Huguenots at a moment when his services were imperatively needed. His return to his pulpit and to his lecture-room at Geneva was of necessity long deferred.

[16] *Hist. Ecclés.*, ii, 3-6.

[17] See the text of letters in *Mémoires de Condé*, iii, 213. *Rise of the Huguenots*, ii, 32.

CHAPTER 12

COUNSELLOR OF CONDÉ AND THE HUGUENOTS IN THE FIRST CIVIL WAR

1562, 1563

IT was not without an effort that the French Protestants had succeeded in obtaining from the little republic of Geneva, ever jealous of its rights, the 'loan' of Theodore Beza until this hour. The earnest letters of the excellent and highly respected Jeanne d'Albret, Queen of Navarre, supported as they were by the entreaties of Admiral Coligny and other Huguenot noblemen, however, prevailed over the reluctance of the Genevese, and on December 22, 1561, the Great Council prolonged Beza's leave of absence for three or four months.[1] We shall see that this was not the last time that the request was repeated, and that the patience of the government of Geneva was sorely tried. In the sixteenth century there was such a thing as having a pastor and professor who was too much in demand. For there was one thing upon which friends and foes were in full agreement: both assigned to Theodore Beza, with signal unanimity, the foremost place among Protestants for eloquence. Claude Haton, the prejudiced but discriminating curate whose memoirs are among the most readable papers of the century and well reflect public sentiment on nearly

[1] Haag, *La France Prot.*, ii, 513.

every point, proclaimed him the most highly esteemed of all the preachers of France for his fair words, more than for his learning.[1] To have conceded the superiority in learning also, would have seemed to the ecclesiastic a species of endorsement of Beza's success at Poissy.

The people, making no such distinction, flocked to the Huguenot services to hear him. On the very day and at almost the precise hour that the Duke of Guise entered Paris, despite the queen-mother's prohibition, Prince Condé was accompanying the Huguenot minister, with a body-guard of four or five hundred horsemen (others said more), to a preaching place beyond the Porte Saint Jacques, where he discoursed to a crowded gathering. The papal nuncio, Cardinal Santa Croce, writing to the Pope's minister, Cardinal Borromeo, the next day, found in this and similar occurrences presages of evil to come.[2] For, as the nuncio never tired of reiterating at the French court, unless the *preachers* were driven from the kingdom, all other precautions would be of little avail for the rescue of the Roman Catholic cause.[3]

The duties now devolving upon Beza were of the most varied and complex character, and the literary training which had qualified him for dealing with very different subjects was called into constant requisition. As a Christian minister, who was also the most highly trusted friend of Condé, he was at one moment occupied in consulting for the best interests of religion and morality in the Huguenot

[1] *Mém. de Claude Haton*, i, 253.

[2] Santa Croce to Borromeo, March 19, 1562. Aymon, i, 99.

[3] The same to the same, March 22, 1562. *Ibid.*, i, 105.

camp, at another in justifying to friends and foes the course of the prince and his associates. The tergiversation of Antoine of Navarre had made the position of his queen, brave Jeanne d'Albret, a difficult one at court; it had also made the attitude of the Huguenots to the wife of their new opponent by no means simple. It was soon reported to the Queen of Navarre that the Protestant soldiers in their camp had dropped all references to her husband from the petitions which, as dutiful subjects, they were wont to utter in behalf of the King of France and the princes of royal blood. We have a noble letter in which Theodore Beza, replying to a communication from Jeanne, who complained of this omission, as well as of the iconoclasm of the Huguenot troops, espouses the cause of his brethren with manly frankness and firmness, yet also with respect and true affection. A few sentences alone can here be given of a paper that deserves to be reproduced entire. The Reformer does not conceal his aversion to the prevalent image worship, but neither does he permit this aversion to prevail over his love of law and order.

'As to the first point, Madam, respecting which you were pleased to write me,' wrote Beza, 'I can say nothing about this overthrowing of images, except what I have always felt and preached: that is to say, that this mode of action does not please me at all, inasmuch as it seems to me to have no foundation in the word of God, and as it is to be feared that it proceeds rather from impetuosity than from zeal. Nevertheless, because the deed itself is in accordance with the will of God, who condemns idols and idolatry, and because it seems as if, in so widespread a movement, there were some secret counsel of God, who, it may be, intends by this means to put to shame the greatest by means of the smallest, I content myself with reprehending in general what is deserving of reprehension, and with moderating such impetuous procedures as much as it lies in my power. But that destruction of the monuments of the dead is entirely inexcusable, and I can assure you, Madam, that the prince is fully resolved not only to make the most thorough investigation, but also to inflict such punishment as may serve as an example to others.

'As to the last point in your letter, … I shall tell you frankly what I think and what attitude all the Churches of these regions take. So long as the king your husband gave evidence of the fear of God, he was named with you in the public prayers, because of the hope that was entertained that he would improve little by little, as so often he professed his purpose to do. Subsequently, when it was seen that he was banding together with the enemies of God, still we did not cease to make supplications for him by name in the prayers of the Church; and this with so much the more ardour as we foresaw the danger of ruin to be greater and more evident. This lasted until, to our great regret, he so burst all bounds as not only to scandalise the Church, but, what is worse, to proclaim himself head and protector of those whose hands are reeking with the blood of the children of God, of those who have always professed themselves the persecutors and desperate enemies of the latter. You may believe, Madam, that it was not without deep anguish that we heard and witnessed this piteous change, and that we were brought to this point. For how could we pray against the enemies of God and his Church, and, at the same time, name one of the chief enemies among those persons whom we hold in highest esteem? Yet would I not come to the point of pronouncing a final sentence of rejection, for there are those who have drawn very near to that point who yet have received grace and mercy. As for myself, although I see in him at present more evidence of rejection than of salvation, yet am I unwilling to determine what God has counselled for the future, according to the riches of his great mercies, and I am content to be ignorant of what God has concealed, rather than too rashly condemn the sinner with his sin. I have not therefore removed him from the prayers, as though cutting him off for ever from the Church, but his name has merely been omitted from the place where he was mentioned for the aforegoing reasons. Yet nothing prevents his being comprehended under the general designation of "the princes of the blood," whom we conjoin with the king in special respect. Otherwise you would have far greater occasion to complain than he; for it has seemed indecorous to name you without him, and I see that the greater number [of worshippers], in order to cover the matter in some fashion, omit mention of you also. And yet I am as certain as that I shall die, that your memory, Madam, is as precious and dear to all the Churches of God as that of any person in this world.'

These words would seem to have been penned shortly after a narrow escape of Beza from falling into the hands of his enemies, to which he alludes near the close of his letter.

'I came near being surprised on my return from Angers,' he writes, 'and, from what I learn, the king your husband,

Madam, must have written expressly on the subject with threats little befitting the service which all my life long I have desired to render him. Praised be God, who delivered me from this danger, showing me in very deed that it is better to serve him than to serve men. But I protest before my God, that this has not changed my affection, and that I would not bemoan my death today, were it to conduce to his salvation.'[4]

Very different in style was the document which Beza was perhaps at this very moment preparing for publication in the name of the Prince of Condé, and which was given to the world a week later.

The three leading Roman Catholic noblemen, having fully determined to precipitate a civil war, ostensibly for the purpose of hindering the further progress of Protestantism, but in reality so as to secure for themselves the undisputed mastery, had just presented to the crown their exorbitant demands in the form of two petitions, of one and the same date, and constituting in effect a single document. The contents were sufficiently radical to satisfy the most bigoted friend of the old order of things. Ignoring altogether the recent tolerant edict of the king, the subscribers stipulated that the exercise of any other religion than the Roman Catholic and Apostolic religion be interdicted in France by a perpetual and irrevocable law, and that all royal officers, of whatever kind, be compelled to conform to that religion or else leave the realm. Churches that had been seized and damaged must be restored and repaired, the sacrilegious must be punished, all that had taken up

[4] Beza to the Queen of Navarre, May 13, 1562. *Mém. de Condé*, ii, 359-363.

arms without authority from the King of Navarre must lay them down or be pronounced rebels. If all this were done, they professed themselves ready to retire from the kingdom, in fact, to go to the ends of the earth. They would not even require as a condition that Condé should participate in their exile, nay, they would prefer to have him return to the royal court, where, doubtless, he would deport himself in a manner worthy of a prince of the blood royal.[5] In other words, should the prince dismiss all the Protestant troops that were flocking to his standard, he was welcome to make a fresh trial of the perils that await the credulous man who risks his neck upon the good faith and promises of inveterate enemies. Only the opportune decease of Francis II had saved Condé's life at Orléans, a little over two years since; he was now invited to find out by a new experience whether Heaven would a second time interfere as signally in his behalf.

We can scarcely suspect the Duke of Guise, Constable Montmorency, and Marshal Saint André of such simplicity as to imagine that they could impose upon the Prince of Condé; but they had hopes of imposing upon the people by their cheap display of magnanimity. It required a skilful hand to defeat their purpose, and certain it is that Condé had at his command no more skilful hand than that of Theodore Beza. The reply which went out to the world in the name of Louis de Bourbon was so keen that ordinarily well-informed contemporaries such as the historian De Thou, at a loss to ascertain who could have composed it, were driven to the absurdity of conjecturing that it might have emanated from the pen of the shrewd and versatile

[5] *Mém. de Condé*, iii, 392.

Bishop Montluc, author of some of the ablest State papers of the period.

The writer branded the pretended petition or petitions of the Roman Catholic leaders as an arrogant assumption of authority that in no sense belonged to them. What they had put forth was in point of fact not a petition but a decree, made by the duke, the constable, and the marshal, with the coöperation of the legate, the nuncio, and the Spanish ambassador. The league they had formed was more full of danger and more sanguinary than that of Sulla, or that of Cæsar, or that of the Triumvirate of Rome. Its authors had refused to obey the queen's commands and retire to their governments. They had come to Paris in arms, contrary to her express commands; and no prayer of hers or of the young king could induce them to leave the capital. They had forcibly brought Catharine and Charles from Fontainebleau to Melun, and from Melun to Paris. Such was the reverence and humility of which they prated; while the love they pretended to bear to their country did not prevent them from calling in foreign arms to plunder it and, if God did not prevent, to subdue and ruin it.

'And then,' wrote Beza in Condé's name, 'they demand a perpetual edict to settle matters of religion; and when we ask for the maintenance of the edict that has been made until the king's majority, they tell us that this is an uncivil and unreasonable demand; that it is the prerogative of the king, when it seems good to him, to change, limit, amplify, and restrict his edicts; and that when we ask of him that what has already been ordained by him and his council be kept and maintained during his minority, we wish to keep his Majesty in prison and captivity. Meanwhile they want the edict which they three have framed to be perpetual and irrevocable. If the reason alleged by them against us is to be received, for that same reason we shall conclude that they themselves wish to detain the king a prisoner both in his minority and in his majority, nay, we are warranted in saying that they think that they can lord it over not merely the person of the king, but over the whole realm, since in a matter of so great importance and involving such consequences, they dare present an ordinance authorised by but three persons. What more did ever Augustus, Mark Antony, and Lepidus, when by their wicked and infamous Triumvirate they overturned the laws and the Roman commonwealth? Had they been moved by honest zeal, as they assert, by a peaceable and not a seditious zeal, by a zeal for religion and not for ambition, they would not have begun by active measures. They would have come unarmed, they would have presented themselves with humility and reverence; they would have set forth the causes that moved them to disapprove of the Edict of January; they would very humbly have begged the king and queen to examine, in conjunction with their council, with the advice of the parliaments, and the other estates, whether by some other means a remedy might be found for the troubles, to the preservation of the honour of God, and of the security and greatness of the king and kingdom. Had they thus spoken, they would have shown that they were inspired by no other passion than the zeal of their consciences. As it is, their course of action sufficiently reveals the fact that religion serves them only as a means to secure a following and to introduce division among the king's subjects. With one portion and in conjunction with foreigners, they purpose to make themselves masters and lords of everything. To them I am constrained to say that the princes of the blood, whose enemies they have always been and whom they have ever driven into the background, so far as they were able, will not suffer foreigners and persons not called to the government, to take it upon themselves to make edicts and ordinances in this kingdom. Yet they want and demand that the Romish religion, which they call Catholic and Apostolic, alone be established and recognised in France, and that preaching and the sacraments be forbidden to the adherents of the Reformed religion. It is a Duke of Guise, a foreign prince, a Sieur de Montmorency, and a Sieur de Saint André, who enact an ordinance contrary to the Edict of January, accorded by the king and the queen his mother, the King of Navarre, the princes of the blood, with the king's council and forty of the greatest and most notable personages of all the parliaments. It is these three that draw up a law against the petition presented by the States, that is to say, the nobles and Third Estate at Orléans and, later, at Saint Germain; both of which estates petitioned the king to be pleased to grant places of worship to the adherents of the Reformed religion. These three make an ordinance that cannot be executed without a civil war, without putting the kingdom in danger of evident ruin. This they themselves see and admit. And this is the way the kingdom stands indebted to them, and this is the fruit born of their wisdom and good zeal, or, to speak more properly, of their intrigues, underhand practices, and ambition to rule.'

With such words did Beza make the Prince of Condé to characterise the new Triumvirs, while defending the cause which these Triumvirs had conspired to overthrow. Again, as in his letter over his own signature to the Queen of Navarre, being compelled to touch upon the iconoclasm out of which the enemies of the Protestants made so great an accusation, he dwelt upon the efforts that had been conscientiously put forth to check and punish the practice, and again he contrasted the fault, as fault it undeniably was, of destroying lifeless statues in stone, with the far more heinous crime of ruthlessly destroying the persons of men and women made in the likeness of God.

'If the breaking of images merits punishment, as I fully believe it does—inasmuch as the act is committed contrary to the king's ordinance,—what punishment do those expect who cloak themselves so readily with the king's name, for the murders that have been committed by themselves and, following their example and at their solicitation, at Vassy, at Sens, at Castelnaudary, and at Angers—where it is well known that five hundred men and women have been slain for no other reason than their religion? He that dictated the "petition" should have examined his own conscience and have recognised the fact that it is not found that the lifeless image has ever cried for vengeance; but the blood of man, who is the living image of God, cries for it to Heaven, and calls it down, and brings it, even though it tarry long.'

To the suggestion that Condé and those who were in arms with him ought to be declared rebels, the prince was made to respond that this was an article that called for a reply in another way than in writing. He hoped, he said, within a few days, to go in search of those that made the assertion, and settle by arms the question, whether it belonged to a foreigner and two insignificant persons such as they were, to judge a prince of the blood and two thirds of the noblemen of the kingdom, and pronounce them to be rebels and enemies of the kingdom.

Finally, in a passage of great beauty and oratorical force, the prince was made by Beza to institute a startling contrast between the demand of the new Triumvirs and that which he himself made:

'I ask for the maintenance of the Edict of January, and they wish of their own authority to annul and abolish it. They ask for the destruction of an infinite number of houses, as well of the nobles as of the common people; I ask and desire that all the king's subjects, of whatever quality they may be, shall be upheld, protected in their estates and property, and preserved from all insult and violence. They wish to exterminate all the adherents of the Reformed religion; and I desire that we may be reserved to the time when the king shall reach his majority (at which time we will obey what he shall be pleased to command us), and that meanwhile the adherents of the Romish Church shall not be disturbed, molested, or constrained in their property or in the exercise of their charges. They demand an armed force to execute what they have undertaken, and do not consider that they will compel an infinite number of worthy people to defend themselves. They do not take into consideration the scarcity of the means at their disposal, nor regard the troubles and the ruin that civil war brings. What is worse, they have engaged in writing to introduce foreign arms, which means, in plain talk, to give the kingdom to be the prey of its enemies. On the contrary, I do not ask to retain my arms, I do not make use of the king's money, I do not call foreigners to enter the kingdom, and have declined those offered to me. God is my witness that I have begged them not to come and to prevent others from coming, either for or against us … They demand that we be declared rebels; they demand our lives, our honour, and our consciences. We demand nothing whatever of their lives, their honour, their property, or their consciences, nor wish them any other ill save that to which we are willing to bind ourselves—which is, that they and we withdraw to our houses, and this according to the conditions more fully set forth in our Declarations and Protestations heretofore made and sent to the king and queen.'

Such was the tenor and such were a few points of the noble document wherein the brilliant Genevese Reformer supplied the young Prince of Condé with a defence clear and convincing to every dispassionate reader, if, in those exciting times, any dispassionate readers were still to be found.[6]

A recital of the incidents of this eventful war do not belong here. The reader must look elsewhere for the massacres on the one side and the reprisals on the other, for the wearisome tale of acts of unnecessary cruelty and brutality, for the blunders almost surpassing belief committed by men who esteemed themselves and were regarded by others as wise and prudent. Contrary to his expectations, Beza was detained with the army at Orléans, where he took a part

[6] In the *Mém. de Condé* iii, 395-416.

in drawing up that remarkable set of articles regulating the discipline and morals of the army, which was intended to make Huguenot warfare a model for all future generations, but which in reality lasted barely a couple of months. The daily prayers and the frequent preaching in the prince's presence devolved upon him, but was the smallest part of his duties. It was not forgotten that he was no novice in diplomacy, and when Admiral Coligny's youngest brother, Andelot, was despatched to levy troops in Germany as auxiliaries to the depleted army of the prince at Orleans, it was natural that Beza should be thought of as of all men the most likely to succeed in securing the favour of the German princes with whom he had treated when pleading the cause of the persecuted Waldenses of Piedmont and the victims of calumny and judicial murder in Paris. His visit to the banks of the Rhine and to Switzerland afforded him an opportunity to go to Geneva and confer with Calvin. It did not permit him to resume his cherished duties at the University and in the church of Saint Pierre. His allotted place was evidently still in France and with his brethren who were there fighting against almost overwhelming odds and never more in need of a clear-headed, far-sighted counsellor, a faithful, energetic, and untiring man of affairs. Beza's leave of absence, even with the renewal which had been granted, had long since run out. But when Calvin added his solicitations to Beza's exposition of the critical condition of Protestantism in France, the syndics and council of the republic were forced to see that the interests of the Reformation everywhere were involved in their decision, and preferred the general good to the convenience of Geneva. In doing so, they recognised the fact that new responsibilities had been thrown upon Beza, and that, in view of his great administrative abilities, he had been compelled to assume an office scarcely less important than that of a military commander, since it had to do with the supply and control of the sinews of war. The minute of their action, which is still extant, is as honourable to their disinterestedness as to Beza's tried integrity of character.

'Monsieur de Bèze,' the record states, 'being called to France not only as a minister, but also as treasurer, the Council and the ministers have found themselves in great embarrassment, reflecting, on the one side, upon the great need we have of so great a man and upon the dangers which he may run, and, on the other, upon the desolation of the Church and the comfort he will administer to her, and upon the unseemliness of discouraging, by a refusal to let him go, those who are with so much valour and firmness defending the cause of the Gospel, and of incurring notable reproaches at their hands. Finally, we have judged that we ought not to have our own particular interest so much at heart, as the advancement of God's kingdom and glory; and the said Beza has been permitted to act as he shall deem fit.'[7]

After his return to France, Beza was present at the battle of Dreux, and witnessed the defeat and capture of the Prince of Condé, singularly enough offset in the same battle by the capture of Marshal Montmorency, the commanding general of the Roman Catholics, and the death of Marshal Saint André, a second of the so-called 'Triumvirs.' That inveterate calumniator, Claude de Sainctes, who will be

[7] State Records of Geneva, September 21, 1562, in Baum, ii, 699.

remembered as one of the disputants at the Colloquy of Poissy, accused the Reformer, some years later, of having *fought* in that engagement; an assertion which Beza denied.

'I was certainly present at the battle, both at the beginning and the end (why should I not, having been duly called there?), and, indeed, which you may wonder at more, dressed in my cloak and not armed, nor may anyone cast in my teeth either the slaying of anybody or flight.'[8]

The first civil war lasted two or three months more. Its conclusion was hastened by a tragic event. Duke Francis of Guise, while inspecting the works by means of which he seemed about to capture the city of Orléans, then held by the Huguenots, was treacherously shot by a miscreant named Poltrot, and died within six days. By whom the assassin had been instigated to the deed is even now uncertain. After at first glorying in his act, he broke down through fear of death and accused Admiral Coligny, Beza, M. de Soubise, and others. Subsequently he retracted his statements and declared them to be false; but while suffering his horrible sentence and being torn asunder by four horses, he again returned to his improbable story. Admiral Coligny and all those whom he had accused denied with the greatest solemnity that they had prompted the assassin to commit his dastardly action. With others we have nothing to do. Theodore Beza said that, so far from having counselled the man, he had never, to the best of his knowledge, laid eyes upon him.[9] All fair-minded men cleared him, and most

[8] 'Ad F. Claudii de Xaintes Responsionem Altera Th. Bezæ Apologia' (reprinted in *Tract. Theol.*, ii, 362), a pamphlet first published in Geneva, in 1567.

[9] *Ibid., ubi supra.*

FRANÇOIS, DUC DE GUISE

men held the crackbrained assailant of Guise to be a wild enthusiast whom fancied personal wrongs or the wrongs of his party had led to seek vengeance for himself.

At the expiration of hostilities Beza returned to Geneva and resumed the functions he had been compelled to intermit for about a year and a half. To the admiration which he had aroused in friends and foes alike, he had added the strong affection and confidence of all the French Huguenots won by his arduous and disinterested services in their behalf.

Of dangers incurred there had been no lack. For just in proportion as his friends had come to love and rely upon him, so had the enemies of Protestantism, within and without the kingdom, come to hate him as the most redoubtable opponents. That they invented falsehoods respecting him was nothing strange; it was Beza's experience to the very end of his days. On the present occasion the fabrication was a rumour that obtained wide currency to the effect that Beza and Calvin had had so a violent quarrel that the former did not dare to return to Geneva! In the full belief that the story was true, the Duchess of Parma, Spanish Regent of the Low Countries, thinking it likely that Beza might wend his way to Holland or Germany, secretly ordered the frontiers to be watched and offered a reward of one thousand florins for Beza's capture, dead or alive. The Reformer was portrayed as a man of medium stature, with a high and broad face, and a beard that was half grey.[10]

[10] *Rise of the Huguenots*, i, 388.

CHAPTER 13

SUCCEEDS CALVIN—EDITS THE GREEK NEW TESTAMENT
1563–1565

THE public records of Geneva bear witness to the general joy and thanksgiving to God that were felt and expressed at the safe return of Theodore Beza after his long and eventful absence. He reached his home on May 5, 1563. It was therefore over twenty months since he had set out upon his important mission, full of courage, but not blind to the dangers of the enterprise. Within two days of his arrival, a minute appears on the registers of the Council, to the effect that 'great thanks, and offers of every kind of service, have been received from all the French Protestant lords, for the great and important services which Monsieur de Bèze has rendered to them, as well as to all the churches of the kingdom.' And a strong light is shed upon the esteem in which the Reformer was held in his adopted city, and upon the reputation he had gained through the unselfishness of his past life, by a statement in the same documents, six days later (May 13, 1563), that a resolution had been passed voting to grant all that he may need to Beza—'le Spectable de Bèze,' in the curious phraseology of the times—'who has expended much money in his travels and who would say nothing about it, even were he in great straits.'[1]

[1] Minutes in Baum, ii, 730.

By no one was he more cordially welcomed than by Calvin himself, not an old man—for he was not yet fifty-four years of age—but evidently fast nearing his end. The relation between the two men had long been of the closest and most affectionate character. Although the difference of age was only ten years, Beza had, from the first moment that he set foot in Geneva, assumed to the older Reformer the relation of a child to his parent. Intense admiration for the wonderful intellectual endowments of Calvin ripened into a love such as can exist only between strong characters that think the same great thoughts. Calvin saw in Beza not the slavish copy of himself, but a scholar of greater polish and wider knowledge of polite society, better capable of dealing with courts, with a stronger physical constitution, and therefore having the promise of being able to accomplish much that was denied to his own enfeebled health. The mutual discovery of their respective qualifications to carry on different parts of the great work committed to them, supplementing each other, yet acting in complete harmony, came early. It came on Calvin's part long before Beza's stay at Lausanne approached its end. For when, in 1551, Beza, having occupied his chair in the Académie of that city for only two years, was ill of the pestilence that proved mortal to so many, and was reported to be dying, Calvin tells us that he was prostrated with anxiety; and this not for himself alone, but also and chiefly for the Church to which he felt him to be so essential. 'I should not be a man,' he wrote at this time, 'if I did not love him who loves me with more than a brother's love and honours me as a father.[1] Beza's life was mercifully spared on that occasion,

[1] Letter of June 30, 1551. *Calvini Op.*, xiv, 144, 145.

and, now that twelve years of the most confiding friendship and interchange of views on every important point that could interest intelligent men had passed over their heads, the love was still more intense.

But a return to the precise relations subsisting between the two men before Beza went to France was now impossible, so rapidly had Calvin's health failed. He must assume the heavier of Calvin's burdens, while waiting for the dreaded moment when, with Calvin's death, he must attempt to bear them alone.

It is a notable circumstance connected with the period of the world's history of which we are treating, that it gave birth to a horde of writers not merely lovers of scandal but authors of impudent calumny against whose envenomed pen the reputation of no prominent champion of the so-called 'new doctrines' was safe, either as to great matters or as to small. Beza's antagonist at Poissy, the monk Claude de Sainctes, was of this type. Among his many inventions, he was not ashamed to assert that, so far from having been selected by Calvin to be his successor, Beza, in his inordinate ambition and rapacity, scarcely waited for Calvin's removal from the earth to foist himself upon the Church and State of Geneva. Beza's reply to this fabrication is, as usual, dignified and crushing

'There was no one in this city at that time,' he writes, 'who did not know that when, at length, I had returned home from your slaughter-house, that is, from the first civil war, and when illness precluded Calvin's presence at our gatherings and especially at the meetings of the presbyters, I was designated, by the request of all my colleagues and of

Calvin himself, who urged me to accept when I declined to do so, to sustain a portion of his load. And this also does everybody know, and the whole Council first of all, that, when Calvin died, it was only unwillingly and with reluctance that I took upon my shoulders this load; that in this matter I was moved by no consideration more than by Calvin's own will, expressed while he was yet alive; and that I accepted it on no other condition but that at the end of the year someone else should be elected. I call God and all my brethren now to bear witness that each successive year I begged of my colleagues that this should be done, but never obtained my request.'[2]

The records of the 'Venerable Company' prove the truth of Beza's solemn assertion. They tell us, moreover, that the pastors took the precaution to reserve for themselves the right of examining and, if necessary, censuring even before the end of the year whatever might seem deserving of reprobation in the conduct of him whom they continued to regard as only the equal of his brethren.

'The moderator,' so the minutes read, 'shall always recall Monsieur Calvin, who, so severe against the vicious and the impious, never made use of an inordinate authority in his relations with his brethren; but, on the contrary, adapting himself so far as possible to all, managed to lighten the task of each.'

And so the custom remained until 1580, when a more frequent renewal of the election came into vogue. Even then it was Beza himself, with the support of Trembley,

[2] 'Ad F. Claudii de Xaintes Responsionem Altera Th. Bezæ Apologia,' *Tract. Theol.*, ii, 360.

that urged a change by which each member was in turn called upon to preside at the meetings for a single week. The innovation could not, in the very nature of the case, make any diminution in some of Beza's other engrossing cares, especially such as arose from his vastly extended correspondence with the churches of all parts of Protestant Christendom.[3]

It fell to Beza's lot, as the friend upon whom the mantle of the master fell, to tell the story of Calvin's life and death to the world, and to tell it promptly.

Of Calvin's works, the last to be finished was his *Commentary on Joshua*. It remained unpublished at the time of his death. Beza brought the work out with a biography of the author prefixed, in lieu of the customary preface from the author's own pen. It opened with a few touching and appropriate words.

'Had it pleased God to preserve to us longer His faithful servant, Mr John Calvin, or, rather, had not the perversity of the world moved the Lord to take him to himself so soon, the present would not be the last of the works in which he has so faithfully and happily busied himself for the advancement of God's glory and for the edification of the Church. Nor would this commentary issue without being crowned as it were by some excellent preface, like the rest. But it has happened to it as to poor orphans who are less highly favoured than their brethren, in that their father has left them too early. However, I see this orphan to be sprung from so goodly a house, thank God, and bearing so strong a resemblance to his father, that without any other

[3] Heppe, 229, 230.

testimony he will make himself not only very agreeable, but also very honourable in the eyes of all that shall see it. For this reason I purpose not to recommend it by any testimony of my own—what need of it?—but rather to lament with it the death of him who has been a common father both to it and to me. For I neither can nor ought I to esteem him less my father because of what God has taught me through him, than should this book and so many other books for having been written by him. I shall therefore bewail my loss, but this shall not be without consolation. For, as regards him of whom I speak, I should have loved him too little while alive here below, if the blessedness into which he is now admitted did not change my personal sadness into rejoicing because of his gain. And I should have derived little profit from his teaching so holy and admirable, from his life so good and upright, from his death so happy and Christian, had I not been instructed by all these means to submit myself to the Providence of God with all satisfaction and content.'[4]

A full year had not passed since Calvin's death when Beza gave to the world, in 1565, the most notable of his contributions to Biblical science. This was an edition of the Greek text of the New Testament, accompanied in parallel columns by two translations into Latin, the one being the text of the Vulgate, the other an original translation of his own. This latter translation he had published as far back as in 1556. This was the reason that the present work bore the misleading designation of a *second* edition, although it was in reality the *first* edition of the Greek text. There

[4] Life of Calvin in French, prefixed to *Com. on Joshua*. Republished in *Œuvres Françises de Calvin* (ed. by Paul L. Jacob), p. 3.

were added annotations which Beza had also previously published, but which on this occasion he greatly enriched and enlarged.

In the preparation of this edition of the Greek text, but much more in the preparation of the second edition of that text which he brought out seventeen years later (in 1582), Beza might have availed himself of the help of a valuable manuscript of great antiquity which the fortunes of war threw into his hands. The uncial now known to the literary world as the 'Codex Bezæ,' and briefly referred to by the letter D, had apparently long rested in the library of the Monastery of Saint Irenæus at Lyons. It was a copy of the New Testament made in the middle of the sixth century, and comprised the Gospels and the Acts of the Apostles both in Greek and Latin. In the iconoclasm and pillage to which Lyons was subjected by Huguenot soldiers in the first civil war, this precious monument of antiquity was happily saved, and passed into the possession of Beza. The great Hellenist undoubtedly recognised its value, but startled, it is said, by the singularity of some of its readings, made little use of it in the preparation of his editions. When, after a score of years, the decline of his powers warned him of the near approach of the close of his period of studious productiveness, he presented the manuscript to the University of Cambridge, where it may still be seen among the choice possessions of that seat of learning. In a similar way, Beza had the advantage of access, for the latter part of the New Testament, to the text of a second manuscript containing only that portion of the Sacred Scriptures, and dating from but a little later in the same sixth century. From the circumstance that it had been found by Beza in Clermont, this manuscript, which is now in the National Library at Paris, is known as the 'Codex Claromontanus.'[5]

It was not, however, to these sources that Beza was chiefly indebted, but rather to the previous edition of the eminent Robert Stephens (1550), itself based in great measure upon one of the later editions (the fourth or fifth, it is said) of Erasmus.

'In order to produce this entire work,' says Beza himself, in his preface, 'I have compared with the remarks of a Valla, Peter Stapulensis, and Erasmus, the most learned writings both of the Greeks and the Romans, as well as the moderns, and I acknowledge that I have often been essentially supported by these, even though I have not made myself so dependent on either these or those as not to remain true to my own judgment. To all this there was added a copy from the library of our Stephens which had been most carefully collated by his son, Henry Stephens (who has inherited his father's indefatigability), with some five and twenty manuscripts and almost all the printed editions.'[6]

The result of Beza's labours was a new edition of the text of the New Testament which, especially in the improved form in which it appeared in 1582 and thereafter, has a recognised place of great influence in the history of Biblical study. That the learned author succeeded in making all the use of his material, limited as it was, which a modern

[5] On the 'Codex Bezæ' see vol. ii, No. 1, of *Texts and Studies. Study of Codex Bezæ*, by J. Rendel Harris, Cambridge University Press 1893. A photographic facsimile has been issued by the same press in 1898, I understand, which I have not seen.

[6] See Heppe, 362.

scholar trained in the rigid system now practised might have derived even from such inadequate apparatus, cannot be affirmed. The rules of textual criticism were of the crudest kind, and Beza himself would seem at times to have adhered with less consistency than at others to the canons which he himself had laid down. But at least there was progress; and Beza's labours in this direction were exceedingly helpful to those that came after. The same thing may be asserted with equal truth of Beza's Latin version and of the copious notes with which it was accompanied. The former is said to have been published over a hundred times. Both were composed with the purpose of conveying a more exact notion of the sense than could be derived from the Vulgate. Both bear in every verse marks of the keen insight, close discrimination, well-trained linguistic skill of a scholar who had made himself by an unusually comprehensive study of profane as well as sacred literature almost as familiar with the idioms of the Greek as with those of the Latin tongue. The apparently unprofitable years spent at Paris in reading the works of the ancients, with no present object in view other than the gratification of personal literary tastes, now bore abundant fruit in an unexpected direction. The Biblical exegete, not less than the elegant orator at Poissy, drew upon a treasury of classic lore stored up in the years of leisure when the chief end of the elegant youth from Vézelay seemed to be above everything else to avoid compulsion to wear life away in the dull and repulsive practice of the law. The merits of his work have been variously estimated; for indeed it possessed along with its conspicuous excellences some peculiarities regarded by adverse critics as undeniable defects. Of these the chief has been found by some to consist in the preponderating influence exercised upon the interpretation of Scripture by the author's view of the doctrine of Predestination. However this may be, there is no question that Beza added much both by his version and by his notes to a clearer understanding of the New Testament. He was no servile follower of the Vulgate, and while he was not always felicitous, either from the standpoint of style or from that of interpretation, in his departures from the rendering of the Vulgate, it is quite certain, as we might expect to be the case in the serious work of so earnest a student, that he introduced no changes for change's sake.[7]

[7] See Heppe, 364-368.

CHAPTER 14

BEZA'S BROAD SYMPATHIES—SYNOD OF LA ROCHELLE—MASSACRE OF SAINT BARTHOLOMEW'S DAY—THE ENGLISH REFORMATION

1566–1574

With Calvin's responsibilities Theodore Beza had also inherited Calvin's broad sympathies and his insatiable avidity to learn everything occurring in any part of the world that bore upon the progress of the kingdom of Christ. This occupied his thoughts almost to the exclusion of matters of purely secular importance. This filled a great part of his correspondence, especially with men likeminded but less favourably situated for the receipt of intelligence from abroad. In particular, his letters to Bullinger, throughout a long series of years, contain what may properly be styled the current history of Christendom. A few sentences of a letter to the Zurich Reformer, written from Geneva, June 6, 1566, may serve as a specimen of this correspondence, while giving a glimpse of the state of Europe two years after Calvin's death. It has never been published.

'We are enjoying our peace, through the singular and incredible kindness of God. For it is clear to us that never have our enemies been more animated than they now are against this little church and this school. But hitherto God has frustrated all the efforts of the wicked. It is probable that were we to stand aloof and hold our peace [the Duke of] Savoy would easily secure everything against that slave of all iniquity, Geneva, wherein reigns that notable robber Beza. We shall live, however, so long as it shall seem good to the Lord. Doubtless you have learned fully all that has been done at Augsburg, and how those thunderbolts of theirs have vanished in empty sound. I hope that the Lord will dissipate the rest of the tempests that are imminent. …

'For the rest, so far as appertains to the French Churches themselves, they are happily growing in the sight of their adversaries. But it is certain that the latter are only watching to obtain an opportunity for overwhelming the chief men and subsequently ruining the rest. Of this our friends have no doubt, and meanwhile look to God [for help]. Among the Piedmontese [Waldenses] after the departure of Mr. Junius, the same thing occurred to our brethren that befell the Israelites when Pharaoh was wonderfully exasperated at the first appeal of Moses. What will happen, God only knows. In England, everything is gradually tending to a manifest contempt of all religion; good men, indeed, groan, but only too few. In Scotland after the slaying of Secretary David [Rizzio] the queen is said to have become so insane as even to have his bones interred in the sepulchre of her fathers. Hence fresh disturbances have arisen. But in short it is represented that all matters are now settled on conditions that are not unequal, if only they be sufficiently stable. Thus much I have to write. Farewell, my father, and continue, as you do, to commend us to God. Two days ago we counted up two thousand students at the promotions of our school.

Pray that the Lord may bless these beginnings, while Satan impotently gnashes his teeth.'[1]

The attempt to make of Geneva a model to Christendom for the purity of its morals, enforced by a legislation of unexampled strictness, was not suspended at Calvin's death, but found in Theodore Beza as decided an advocate as it possessed in his predecessor. Calvin had not been in his grave two years when a signal proof of this fact was afforded.

The number of bishops that were converted to Protestantism and resigned their sees, in the early days of the French Reformation, was larger than one might suppose. Among them was Jacques Paul Spifame, Seigneur de Passy, Bishop of Nevers, who, in 1559, forsook the kingdom and took refuge in Geneva. Here, as a nobleman, he was readily admitted to citizenship, as well as to the ministry. Subsequently he served as pastor at Issoudun. Calvin urged him, in a letter still extant, to return to Nevers and take charge of the newly established Protestant church, showing the people of his former diocese that if he had formerly been their bishop only in name, it was his purpose now to be a bishop in deed.[2] But unfortunately Spifame was not of the stuff of which good pastors are made. The inconsistencies that appeared in his life both when the Prince of Condé selected him for some diplomatic work in Germany, and when he sojourned at the court of the Queen of Navarre, led to investigation, and investigation disclosed crime. In the end he was arrested and tried for adultery at Geneva,

[1] Letter of June 6, 1566. Copy in Baum Coll. MSS., Lib. of Fr. Prot. Hist. Soc.

[2] Letter of January 24, 1562. Bonnet, *Lett. Fran.*, ii, 453, etc.

and being found guilty was sentenced to death. Despite his tardy confession and the contrition for his sins which he testified on the scaffold, by an address to the people that was accepted as satisfactory proof of repentance, he was publicly put to death on March 23, 1566.

It need scarcely be said that so severe a punishment for a crime of which in the neighbouring kingdom the courts of justice were not wont to take cognisance, created a profound sensation and drew down upon the little republic of Geneva, and upon the ministers that approved the republic's course, almost universal condemnation. But the government did not flinch in the determination to uphold the law, nor did Beza fail to espouse its defence. Writing to the eminent Pithou, of Troyes, in Champagne, less than a month after the event, he says, in a letter which, I believe, is inedited:[3]

'I know well that everybody will pass his own judgment, and that Satan will not spare us. But I hope that the wise will call to mind the Lord's warning that bids us not to judge rashly of our brethren, and therefore, with still greater reason, not to think ill of an entire Christian Seigniory and Church. … As to the others, who will judge as they please, it is God's province to stop their mouths, and to him we appeal from all foolish judgments passed in so many places against us.'

While every part of Christendom where the truth was struggling for existence claimed and secured Beza's attention and prayers, it was, next to Geneva and its schools the

[3] Manuscript letter of Beza, of April 22, 1566, now in the possession of Mr Ferdinand J. Dreer, of Philadelphia, to whose kindness I am indebted for a facsimile.

work in France that lay nearest to his heart. In that kingdom the interval of quiet was short. Then two more civil wars rudely disturbed the delusive dream of steady progress in which the Protestants had indulged. The disasters of Jarnac and Moncontour at first seemed fatal blows from which the Huguenot cause would be slow to recover, if ever it should recover from them at all. But the marvellous ability developed by Admiral Coligny, in turning a flight before the enemy into a successful advance that carried war almost to the gates of the capital, raised the hopes of the despondent and wrested from unwilling hands the concession of a peace on favourable terms.

So long as it lasted, the French war brought new cares and anxieties for Beza. Fugitives poured into Geneva in an almost incessant stream, and these fugitives were for the time to be provided with food and shelter. At such crises it was to Beza that all eyes looked for advice and direction. Never did he fail to secure the needy material aid. Furnished with strong letters of recommendation, envoys sent from Geneva at his suggestion laid the pitiable condition of the destitute Huguenot refugees before the charitable Swiss cantons, while by direct appeals the Reformer reached those that were like-minded in the Low Countries and beyond the English Channel.

Meanwhile, although the period was indeed one of deep solicitude, it was relieved, for Beza, from time to time, by some rays of encouragement and hope. The Church of Geneva was steadily growing, the theological school received a constant and indeed a swelling stream of students. In 1569 Beza was able to write to John Knox that the University had so greatly increased the number of its students that he believed that there were few institutions of the kind in Christendom that were better attended. Colladon and he taught theology upon alternate weeks, and there had now come a third professor, Gallasius by name, driven into this haven, as had an almost countless crowd been driven thither, by the tempests of France. Yet were there two circumstances that prevented the Reformer from taking such solid joy as he might otherwise have experienced from these tokens of prosperity: the one was that if the church was growing in a marvellous fashion, it was growing because of the ruin of other churches; the second, that the *plague* which had sorely vexed the little city on Lake Leman a year back had within about a month entered upon a new course of destruction.[4] The state of things was worse, instead of better, three years later, a few months before the news came of the Parisian massacre.

'While you off yonder,' he wrote to the same correspondent, alluding to the intestine commotions and to the deeds of violence that were enacted in Scotland, 'are exercised by tragedies such as not even Greece entire celebrated in her theatres, we have meantime been contending for a full period of six years with the plague, nor are we yet altogether through with this combat, which has certainly carried off not fewer than twelve thousand persons in this little town.'

In fact, he informed Knox, Geneva was no longer the place he had seen years before, for War and Plague had severely handled her, and the forms of the school, once

[4] Letter to John Knox, June 5, 1569. *Tract. Theol.*, iii, 287.

ANCIENT PORTAL OF THE CHURCH OF SAINT PIERRE, GENEVA, TORN DOWN IN MIDDLE OF 18TH CENTURY

crowded with pupils, were now empty.[5] When the Peace of Saint Germain, in 1570, closed the deadliest war to which the Protestants had as yet been exposed, the ardour of Beza's interest in the affairs of his native land did not flag. A few months later there was held, in the month of April, 1571, and within the walls of La Rochelle, most Protestant perhaps of all the cities of France, the seventh in order of the national synods of the Reformed Churches, and one of the most impressive of all these historical assemblies. Not only did Theodore Beza come all the way from Geneva to preside as moderator over this body representative of all the adherents of the Protestant faith, but there was a brilliant representation at its sessions of that large class of princes and nobles that stood at the head of the Huguenot party and had lately been foremost in maintaining its rights on the field of battle. Their enthusiasm had never run higher. Jeanne d'Albret, Queen of Navarre, was there. With her were the two princes in whom centred the hopes of the Protestants— Henry of Navarre, who, it was hoped, would make good the damage wrought by the defection of his father, and Henry of Condé, whom popular expectation regarded as destined to replace his father Louis, slain at Jarnac. There, too, were Admiral Coligny, Count Louis of Nassau, brother of William the Silent, Prince of Orange, and others scarcely less distinguished. The national synods were purely religious bodies, unlike in this the 'political assemblies' which were occasionally convened for more secular purposes. But the present synod seemed almost to be a joint convention of everything most highly revered in

[5] Letter to the same, April 12, 1572. *Ibid.*, iii, 290.

Church and State. The most august moment was when three copies of the Confession of Faith of the Protestant Churches having been carefully engrossed on parchment, each copy was signed, in accordance with a solemn resolution adopted on the first day of the sessions, not only by all the ministers and elders, but also by Queen Jeanne d'Albret and by all the princes and noblemen in the company. The first copy was to be preserved in La Rochelle; the second, in a city of the district of Béarn; the third was sent for safe keeping to Geneva. It was not a mere form in which the delegates engaged when giving to the Confession of Faith which the French Churches had adopted and presented to Francis II twelve years before, their renewed and solemn adhesion. It was not merely to honour Theodore Beza that the Queen of Navarre and her wise counsellors, disregarding his first refusal, had insisted, in a reiterated appeal, that he should come to preside over the synod. Nor was it an accident that the very first subject to be considered was that of the Confession of Faith, to be followed immediately by the Ecclesiastical Discipline or Form of Government. The very existence of the churches under their present constitution was in question, and it had to be decided firmly, explicitly, and once for all, that the structure whose foundations had been so firmly laid, but whose order and symmetry the years of war and confusion through which the Protestants had been passing had seriously menaced, should be reared according to its original design. There were those who wished to disturb the representative system with its successive courts, rising from the session or consistory of the individual church, through the classis or presbytery and the provincial synod, to the national synod of the entire kingdom, and, in place of securing to the faithful a purely independent existence, to subordinate the Church to the State, and make the pastor, instead of the free choice of the Christian community, the appointee of the civil magistrate. 'The civil magistrate,' someone had lately written, 'is the head of the Church, and what the ministers are undertaking to exercise is a pure tyranny.' Theodore Beza was requested by the national synod to reply to the attacks made upon the Confession and Government of the churches.[6] It was not the first nor the last of such important charges which were placed in his hands by the Protestants of France assembled in their highest ecclesiastical councils.

The year following beheld the occurrence of an event which changed the whole face of French history—the Massacre of Saint Bartholomew's Day—of the tragic story of which we may not in this place even attempt to give an outline.[7] The butchery of the Huguenots that began in the city of Paris on the morning of Sunday, August 24, 1572, afforded a fresh opportunity to Beza, and to the little republic of which he was now avowedly the leading statesman, to display their charity toward the persecuted Protestants of France. Several days would have been required in the midst of profound peace for the tidings to pass from the capital to the borders of Switzerland; the news was purposely retarded in the turmoil into which the kingdom was thrown by the dastardly crime that inaugurated the carnage. Not until Saturday, the 30th, did the first information reach

[6] Aymon, *Tous les Synodes*, i, 99.

[7] See a full account in the *Rise of the Huguenots*, chapters xviii, and xix.

Geneva, brought by merchants from Lyons. These were the advance-guard of a great host of fugitives soon to be expected. Startling as was the horrible announcement to the majority of the citizens, it can scarcely be said to have surprised Beza, a keen observer of contemporaneous history, whom acquaintance with the main actors in French affairs and careful study of their characters had prepared even for so tragic a scene as that now presented to the eye in his native land. Least of all did the fate of the magnanimous and unsuspicious Admiral Coligny astonish him; for he had foreseen the catastrophe and attempted to set the victim on his guard. 'Never,' he wrote to a friend in Heidelberg, 'has so much perfidy, so much atrocity, been seen. How many times did I predict the thing to him [Coligny]! How many times did I forewarn him!' Yet Beza's apprehensions had probably been rather for the life of the great Huguenot leader, and could scarcely have embraced the lives of so many thousands, especially of more obscure men, women, and children whose blood drenched the ground in almost every part of the country. In the midst of the deep affliction into which the tidings cast him, the faithlessness of the young king and the ineffable meanness of the afterthought by which it was attempted to make culprits of the innocent, especially raised his indignant protest. 'The king at first laid everything to the account of the Guises,' Beza wrote to a friend in the letter just quoted; 'now he writes that all was done by his own orders. He dares to accuse of a conspiracy those men whom he caused to be assassinated at Paris in their beds, men of whom the world was not worthy.' Most of all did his sympathies go out toward the region nearest

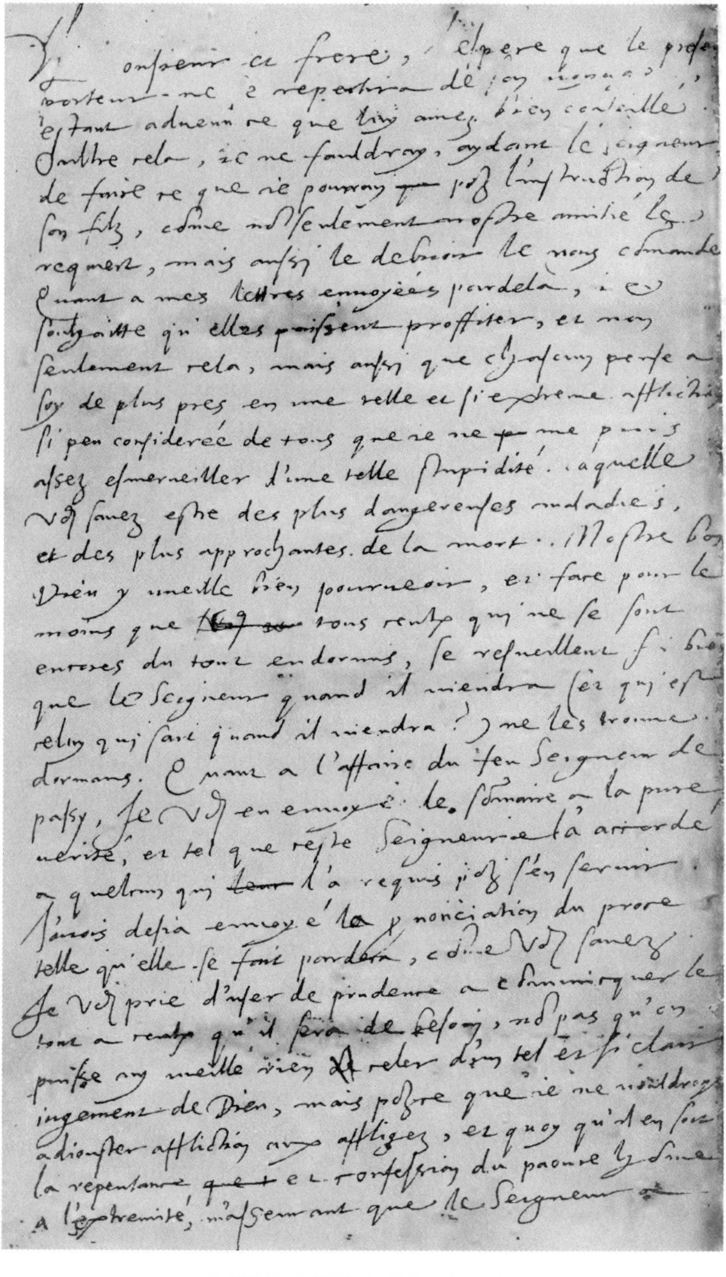

… ensuivir ce frere, j'espere que le present
porteur ne se repentira de son voyage,
estant advenu ce que vous avez bien entendu.
Oultre cela, je ne fauldray, aydant le Seigneur,
de faire ce que je pourray pour l'instruction de
son filz, comme non seulement nostre amitie le
requiert, mais aussi le debvoir le nous commande.
Quant a mes lettres envoyées par dela, je
souhaitte qu'elles puissent proffiter, et non
seulement cela, mais aussi que chascun pense a
soy de plus pres en une telle et si extreme affliction
si peu considerée de tous que je ne me puis
assez esmerveiller d'une telle stupidité, laquelle
vous savez estre des plus dangereuses maladies,
et des plus approchantes de la mort. Nostre bon
Dieu y vueille bien pourveoir, et faire pour le
moins que tous ceux qui ne se sont
encores du tout endormis, se resveillent si bien
que le Seigneur quand il viendra (et qui est
celuy qui sait quand il viendra?) ne les trouve
dormans. Quant a l'affaire du feu Seigneur de
Passy, je vous en envoye le sommaire a la pure
verité, et tel que ceste Seigneurie l'a accordé
a quelcun qui l'a requis pour s'en servir.
J'avois desja envoyé la prononciation du proces
telle qu'elle se fait par dela, comme vous savez.
Je vous prie d'user de prudence a communiquer le
tout a ceux qu'il sera de besoin, non pas qu'on
puisse ny vueille rien celer d'un tel et si clair
jugement de Dieu, mais pource que je ne vouldroys
adiouster affliction aux affligez, et quoy qu'il en soit
la repentance et confession du paovre homme
a l'extremité, m'asseurant que le Seigneur …

FACSIMILE LETTER OF BEZA TO PITHOU, 1566

a commettre ses fautes, me faict desirer que ~~[illegible]~~ l'examen
en soit aussi cogneu devant les hommes, autant qu'il
est expedient pour la gloire du Seigneur. Je say
bien que chascun en donnera sa sentence, et que
Satan ne nous y espargnera. Mais i'espere que
les sages se souviendront de l'advertissement du
Seigneur nous defendant de juger temerairement
de noz freres, et a plus forte raison, de mal estimer
de toute une Seigneurie et eglise Chrestienne,
oultre ce qu'~~ils pouvoyent estre~~ a mon advis maintenant
~~et~~ les plus difficiles auront de quoy estre satisfaicts.
Quant aux autres, qui en jugeront comme il leur
plaist, c'est a Dieu de leur fermer la bouche,
auquel aussi nous appellons de toutes folles sentences
données en tant de lieux contre nous. Au
reste, graces a Dieu, nous suyvons nostre
petit train, heureusement et paisiblement
jusques a present. Les bruicts continuent,
et nous sans apparence. Mais le Seigneur
auquel nous esperons, pourvoyra a tout, s'il luy
plaist. Ce sera l'endroict ou je prieray
nostre bon Dieu et pere qu'en nous multipliant
ses graces, il vous maintiene tous en sa sainte
et digne garde, apres m'estre bien fort
recommandé a voz bonnes prieres. De
Geneve, ce 12 d'avril 1566

Vostre entier frere et
amy Th. de Besze

to Geneva, from which came the majority of those who safely reached its hospitable refuge.

'At Lyons, all, excepting a small number of persons saved by the cupidity of the soldiers, presented themselves of their own accord to be shut up in the prisons; then themselves offered their necks [to the knife]. Not one drew a sword, not one murmured, not one was questioned. All were butchered like sheep at the shambles, and meanwhile the pretext was raised of a conspiracy. O Lord, thou hast seen these things, and thou wilt judge! Pray for us too, who may expect the same fate. Our government is doing its duty, but it is in God that we must put our hope.'[8]

During the weeks that followed, Beza found no lack of employment in encouraging and stimulating the Genevese, whose resources were taxed to the utmost by the sudden addition to their numbers of a multitude of once prosperous but now homeless and destitute refugees, only too glad to have escaped from France with their lives. Not that the citizens themselves needed to be reminded of the claims of common humanity and a common faith. They could boast, in after days, of the fact that as fast as the fugitives arrived, they were carried off to private homes, one citizen contending with another as to which should have the honour of entertaining and caring for those that bore the marks of having endured the greatest hardships or received the most wounds. In fact, so fully did individual liberality provide for immediate wants, that, at first, no public help was called for. Only after the lapse of a month was the need felt of lightening the burden assumed by the citizens. Then a collection

[8] Beza to T. Tilius, September 10, 1572. *Bulletin*, vii, 16.

of funds was made, in which the wealthy councillors and the pastors took, we are told, the largest part. It was Beza who, conscious that, in the danger that threatened Geneva, regarded by the fanatics both of Italy and of France as the very 'mine of heresy,' his own peril was the most imminent, turned his own mind and the minds of others to the certainty of the divine protection. 'My thoughts,' he wrote to Bullinger, 'are more occupied with death than with life.'[9] It was he who, on the day set apart for solemn fasting and prayer to Almighty God, preached in the pulpit of the old church which Calvin had so often filled in former years. His words inculcated firm and unshaken reliance on the goodness of God. 'The hand of the Lord is not shortened,' he said. 'He will not suffer a hair of our heads to fall to the ground without his will. Let us not be affrighted because of the plot of those who have unjustly devised to put us all to death with our wives and our children. Let us rather be assured that, if the Lord has ordained to deliver all or any of us, none shall be able to resist him. If it shall please him that we all die, let us not fear; for it is our Father's good pleasure to give us another home, which is the heavenly kingdom, where there is no change, no poverty, no want, where there are no tears, no crying, no mourning, no sorrow, but, on the contrary, everlasting joy and blessedness. It is far better to dwell with the beggar Lazarus in Abraham's bosom, than in hell with the rich man, with Cain, with Saul, with Herod, or with Judas. Meanwhile, we must drink of the cup which the Lord has prepared for us, each according to his portion. We must not be ashamed of the Cross of Christ,

[9] Moerikofer, *Histoire des Réfugiés de la Réforme en Suisse*, 101.

nor be loth to drink the gall of which he has first drunk: knowing that our sorrow shall be turned into joy, and that we shall laugh in our turn when the wicked shall weep and gnash their teeth.'[10]

Fully twenty Protestant pastors had found their way to Geneva. These shepherds driven from their flocks were the special objects of Beza's fraternal solicitude. The perils to which they had found themselves exposed did not discourage others from entering upon the studies that would qualify them to embrace the same dangerous vocation. Beza's hands were full with providing for the relief of their extreme want. 'Our school,' he wrote at the beginning of winter, 'is full, almost too full; but the greater part of our students have come to us in a state of utter destitution.' At that very time—such was the Reformer's untiring literary activity—he could write that the second volume of his theological works, a ponderous folio, was in press, in which, he added, 'he contemplated the insertion of several new pieces, especially some theological letters, should God grant him leisure.'[11]

The Parisian massacre, great as was the disappointment of cherished hopes which it created, did not permanently dishearten Theodore Beza and those that, like Beza, had looked for the speedy conversion of France to the Gospel. Much less did it chill his affection and dampen his interest in his native land. After it not less than before it, he remained the advocate and counsellor of French Protestantism. The emergency might be purely ecclesiastical, or

[10] Gaberel, in *Rise of the Huguenots*, ii, 555, 556.

[11] Beza to T. Tilius, December 3, 1572. *Bulletin*, vii, 17.

might have reference to the political relations of his fellow-believers; but whatever it was, the Huguenots regarded themselves as entitled to the services of a man equally at home in religion and in diplomacy. Prince Henry of Condé felt that he could not do without this prudent adviser; and so often did he invite the Genevese to make him a 'loan' of their leading theologian, that at length, becoming impatient of the inconvenience to which they were repeatedly put, they politely informed his Highness that he would do well henceforth to depend on the letters, in lieu of the visits, of Beza.[12] Nor was the latter less a tried friend and adviser of Henry of Navarre, who rarely failed to communicate to the Reformer his conclusions on all matters of prime importance, and attempt to justify his course in the Reformer's eyes, in case he seemed to have acted precipitately or ill-advisedly. This does not mean that the wayward prince was much disposed to follow Beza's recommendations, save where these coincided with his own predilections. But he professed to value them highly and not to reject Beza's 'holy admonitions,' even when not profiting by them.

'I beg you to love me always,' was the postscript of one of his letters, 'assuring you that you could not give a share of your friendship to any prince that would be less ungrateful for it, and to continue your good reproof as if you were my father.'[13]

Others were equally anxious to obtain Beza's views and more certain to be influenced by them. The records of the national synods of the French Reformed Churches prove

[1] *The Huguenots and Henry of Navarre*, i, 15.

[13] Letter of February 1, 1581. *Lettres Missives de Henri IV*, i, 351.

that at perplexing points it was customary to rely much upon Geneva, and that Geneva's wise leader was consulted whether, for example, it was deemed opportune to draw up a statement of the reasons for which the Decrees of the Council of Trent were held to be null and void by the Protestant world, or to frame an answer to antitrinitarian books. No action of importance indeed seemed complete which had not been communicated to Theodore Beza.[14]

There was probably no country in which Protestantism had taken any root that did not claim a share of Beza's attention, and with which he did not at some time or other enter into relations by his singularly extended correspondence. Most interesting to us is his part in the reformatory movement in Great Britain, and especially in England.

It is scarcely necessary to remind the reader of the bitter disappointment which upon their return to England, in 1558, and later, awaited the exiles who had fled to the Continent to avoid the persecution reigning in England during the five years of the reign of Queen Mary Tudor. Whereas they had looked for a still more perfect reformation than under Edward VI, they found a retrograde movement tending to the reintroduction of theories and practices long since discarded. In place of greater liberty, they met with more determined repression. In nothing were they more deceived than in the attitude of the new queen. Elizabeth, upon whose sincere Protestantism they had built their hopes during the weary years intervening between her brother's death and that of her elder sister, proved to be far less ardent a friend than they had anticipated. With

[14] See Aymon, *Tous les Synodes*, i, 47, 99, 122, 125, 183, 206.

Geneva and Genevan theologians she had a grievance of her own. It was from Geneva that had issued the unfortunate treatise entitled *The First Blast against the Monstrous Regiment and Empire of Women*. John Knox, who wrote it, was at the time one of the corps of preachers, being pastor of the English church of the city of Geneva. In vain could it be shown that his brethren in the ministry had no part in the composition of the treatise, that they disapproved of it, that Calvin expressed his displeasure to Knox and to Beza, and was only deterred from publicly condemning it by the consideration that it was too late for the application of such a remedy to do any good. Queen Elizabeth's secretary, William Cecil, was apparently satisfied with the explanation, but Elizabeth herself would not be reconciled to the Genevese, whom she regarded as over-severe and precise.[15]

The new queen was peculiarly fond of pompous ceremonial, more fond, in fact, than the very bishops whom she selected to take the places of the prelates of Mary's time who had been removed by death or whom she had deprived. One of their number, John Jewel, writing apparently just before his own nomination to the see of Salisbury, but giving some of the names of his future colleagues, states his 'hope that it has been arranged, under good auspices, that religion shall be restored to the same state as it was in under Edward.' But he adds in the same breath: 'The scenic apparatus of divine worship is now under agitation, and those very things which you and I have so often laughed at are now seriously and solemnly entertained by certain persons (for

[15] Calvin to Cecil (May, or earlier), 1559, in *Calvini Op.*, xvii, 490, and in *Zurich Letters*, 76, etc.

we are not consulted), as if the Christian religion could not exist without something tawdry. Our minds indeed are not sufficiently disengaged to make these fooleries of much importance.'[16]

Bishop Grindal, of London, reverting in mind to this period, wrote six or seven years later: 'We, who are now bishops, on our first return, and before we entered on our ministry, contended long and earnestly for the removal of those things that have occasioned the present dispute; but as we were unable to prevail, either with the queen or the parliament, we judged it best, after a consultation on the subject, not to desert our churches for the sake of a few ceremonies, and those not unlawful in themselves, especially since the pure doctrine of the Gospel remained in all its integrity and freedom.'[17]

There were others, however, and these among the most sincere and pious of the ministers recently returned from the Continent, who honestly regarded the vestments which the queen and her advisers were determined to reintroduce as more of consequence than even the excellent bishops esteemed them, and refused to don them; who viewed the use of the sign of the cross in baptism as no indifferent matter, but as a relic of popery; who declined to kneel at the administration of the Lord's Supper, because to them it seemed to be a plain act of worship and marked a belief in the real corporeal presence of Christ in his sacrament. The neglect or refusal of these men to obey the new prescriptions

[16] J. Jewel to Peter Martyr, not dated, but written before his consecration, January 21, 1560. *Zurich Letters*, 33.

[17] Bp. Grindal to Bullinger, August 27, 1566. *Zurich Letters*, 243.

was visited with harsh measures on the part of the government. The most sincere of Christians and the most devoted of pastors were deprived of their places for no other reason than their scruples of conscience. Particulars of the course of events during these most mournful and disastrous years of English ecclesiastical history must be sought elsewhere. We have no room for them here, save as bearing upon the position taken by the Reformers of Geneva and Zurich. For to Zurich and Geneva the unfortunate clergymen of England naturally turned for sympathy and advice. In those cities many of them had sojourned during their exile. All of them had formed relations of friendship with the leading men of the churches of one or both of the cities. The bishops themselves were on terms of intimacy with Beza, in the one, and with Bullinger and Rudolph Gualter, Zwingli's son-in-law, and Bullinger's younger colleague and subsequently his successor, in the other. In fact, Bishop Parkhurst, of Norwich, had during four years been a guest in Gualter's house at Zurich. Theirs was an ancient friendship begun as far back as when Gualter was studying at Oxford.[18]

Between the ministers returned from the Continent that protested strenuously against the innovations and the reintroduction of practices abolished in the time of King Edward VI, on the one hand, and the new bishops who, after a period of active resistance, acquiesced more or less completely in the measures dictated by Queen Elizabeth, on the other, the position of the Swiss Reformers, consulted now by the former and now by the latter, was of a delicate nature and by no means free from difficulties. The Zurich

[18] Gualter to Cox, Bp. of Ely, June 9, 1572. *Zurich Letters*, 406.

pastors were less happy than Beza at Geneva in meeting these difficulties.

At first, when the trouble seemed to turn chiefly upon the question of vestments, or, at least, was so understood by them, the attitude of Beza and that of Bullinger and Gualter were the same. Beza was at one with his Zurich friends in treating the matter of ecclesiastical habiliments, however absurd and unsuitable these might seem to him to be, as too insignificant to warrant him in countenancing any disposition on the part of aggrieved ministers to abandon the established church. But a divergence of sentiment developed itself later, when the queen demanded a slavish submission and the bishops acquiesced in the demand. The Zurich theologians, having once given their confidence to the bishops, saw no reason to withdraw it, believing them men of piety and integrity. More than all, they were determined not to be involved in a conflict in which the feelings of the contestants had become so exasperated that each side was now to blame, and hardly any remedy could be discovered for the mischief. They disclaimed any power to dictate to the bishops, and therefore refused positively to take part against them when they were pleading their own cause. They equally abstained from attempting to dissuade their opponents from presenting to the elector palatine a petition drawn up by George Withers, one of their number, with the view of inducing that prince to use his influence with Queen Elizabeth to complete the reformation of the Church, or, if this boon could not be obtained, to secure 'for those that abominated the relics of antichrist the liberty of not being obliged to adopt them against their conscience, or to relinquish the ministry.'[19] Bullinger and Gualter wrote to Beza at length that it was now their decided resolution to have nothing more to do with anyone in this controversy, whether in conversation or by letter. 'And if any other parties think of coming hither,' they added, 'let them know that they will come to no purpose.'[20]

Meanwhile they remained on such terms of friendship with the prelates to whom Withers bade the elector palatine transfer all the blame from the queen, as to be frequent recipients of presents, especially of cloth, doubtless very welcome to them in their self-denying and slenderly paid labours, until Bullinger found himself compelled to beg Bishop Sandys and Grindal, now become Archbishop of Canterbury, to desist from sending more. Their enemies were asserting that the bishops sent presents to learned men to draw them to their side. 'I had rather,' said the aged Bullinger, 'that men who are so ready to speak evil and calumniate, should not have the least occasion of detracting from me and my ministry.'[21]

Beza, on the other hand, although still remaining unmoved in his love and respect for Bullinger, as his copious extant correspondence abundantly proves, and although after Bullinger's death, in 1575, continuing his close relations with Zurich by a frequent interchange of letters with Rudolph Gualter, was much more outspoken in his condemnation of the course of the queen and in expressions of sympathy with the distressed ministers who

[19] Petition in *Zurich Letters*, 298-305.

[20] See their letter of August 3, 1567. *Ibid.*, 297.

[21] See the two letters, both written on September 10, 1574, in *Zurich Letters*, 459, 463.

suffered for their conscientious refusal to conform to her arbitrary demands. The letter which Beza wrote to Bishop Grindal (June 27, 1566) is a very long and striking document, intended to stimulate that excellent prelate to put forth strenuous exertion to terminate the distressing state of affairs in England. I shall not even recapitulate the arguments employed to exhibit the dangers of the course upon which the queen had launched the ecclesiastical establishment. He subordinated the question of *ritual* to *doctrine*, conceding that, while the latter, as it has come down to us from the apostles, is perfect, admitting neither addition nor diminution, the forms of worship were not fixed by the apostles themselves for all times and all places. But he deplored the retention of practices either absurd in themselves or injurious in their tendencies. He condemned still more strongly the reintroduction of objectionable practices after they had been discontinued for a considerable space of time—practices in defence of which it could not therefore be truthfully urged that they were followed through fear lest the weak might be offended. He charged the responsibility for schism, if schism should arise, not so much to the account of such brethren as might forsake the Church, as to the account of those who virtually expelled them.

'Relying upon your sense of equity,' said he, 'I shall not fear to say this: If those men sin who, rather than have things of the kind forced upon them contrary to their consciences, prefer to leave the Church, much greater guilt in the sight of God and the angels is incurred by men, if such there be, who allow flocks to be deprived of their shepherds and pastors, and thus permit the beginnings of a horrible dissipation, rather than see ministers in all other respects blameless [officiate] clad in this rather than that garb, and prefer that no Supper be offered anywhere to the starving sheep, rather than that kneeling be omitted. If this be the result,' he adds, 'which I can scarcely believe, it will be the beginning of much greater calamities. And if it be true, as is everywhere asserted, though I do not yet credit it, that private baptism [as in the Romish Church] by women is permitted, I cannot see what it is to return from the goal to the starting-point, unless it be this. Whence has this foulest of errors emanated, save from dense ignorance as to the nature of the sacraments? Whoever is not sprinkled with water (say those that uphold this profanation of baptism) is damned. If this be so, the salvation of infants will arise not from God's covenant (which, however, is clearly the foundation of our salvation), but from the very seal of the covenant that is affixed, and this not that it may be rendered more certain in itself, but rather that we should be made more certain of it. What would be more unjust still, the entire salvation of infants would depend upon the diligence or negligence of parents.'

There were other rumours still more incredible—so improbable were they—that the English prelates had reintroduced abuses than which the antichristian church had none that were more intolerable—the plurality of benefices, licenses for non-residence, permits to contract marriage, and for the use of meats, and other things of that sort. If the story was true, these were not a corruption of the Christian religion, they were a clear defection from Christ. Those consequently were not to be condemned that opposed such attempts; they were rather to be commended.

The letter ended with some stinging words of rebuke for those who wished to force the ministers to pledge themselves to obey whatever the queen and the bishops might hereafter prescribe in matters of ecclesiastical ritual.

'I have yet to learn,' wrote Beza, 'by what right, whether you look at the word of God or at the ancient canons, the civil magistrate is authorised to introduce new rites in churches that have been constituted or to abrogate old ones; what right bishops have, without the advice and consent of their body of elders, to ordain anything novel. For I see that these two curses [arising from] the base and ambitious adulation of superior bishops addressed to their princes, partly abusing their virtues, partly even ministering to their vices, have ruined the Christian Church ; until it has come to such a pass that the most powerful of the Metropolitans of the West, by the just judgment of God punishing both magistrates and bishops, has snatched up for himself all rights, human and divine. Yet I confess that my whole nature shudders as often as I reflect on these things and looking forward see that the same and yet more bitter punishments threaten most of the peoples which so eagerly embraced the Gospel at the beginning, but now are gradually departing from it. Nor do I doubt that the same groans of all the good are everywhere arising. Oh that the Lord may answer them, and for the sake of Jesus Christ, his Son, give to kings and princes a truly pious and religious mind, and good and courageous counsellors. May he bestow his Holy Spirit upon the leaders of his Church, imparting to them, first of all, in abundant measure, both knowledge and zeal; and may he increase, and preserve the peoples that have already professed the true faith, in purity of doctrine and rites and in holiness of life. Farewell, and in turn continue to love me together with this entire Church and school, and to assist us with your prayers.'[22]

Meanwhile Beza, as he informs us, was consulted again and again by those brethren in the English churches who found themselves in the utmost perplexity respecting their duty, in view of the novelties thrust upon them. To their inquiries he states that he long avoided replying, and this for three reasons: First, he was unwilling to believe that such men as the bishops could do things alien to the duty of their office; secondly, he was reluctant to pronounce an opinion based upon *ex parte* statements; thirdly, he feared that he might do more harm than good. Compelled at length to notice the points laid before him, he addressed himself first to the most important of all:

'Can you approve the irregularity of a call to the ministry when a crowd of candidates are enrolled, without the legitimate vote of the body of presbyters, or the assignment of any parish, and after a very slight examination into their life and morals; upon whom subsequently, at the mere good pleasure of the bishop, authority is conferred to preach the word of God for a certain time, or simply to recite the liturgy?'

'We reply,' says Beza, 'that calls and ordinations of such a kind by no means appear to us to be lawful, whether we

[22] *Tract. Theol.*, iii, 209-213.

look at the express word of God or the more pure among the canons. Yet we know that it is better to have something than nothing. We pray God with all our hearts that he may grant to England a more legitimate call to the ministry, in default of which the blessing of the teaching of the truth will surely be lost to her or maintained only in some extraordinary and truly heavenly way. We must beg the queen to attend in earnest to this reform, and her council and the bishops to further it. But, meantime, what? Certainly, as for ourselves, we cannot accept the function of the ministry, even if offered, in this fashion, much less seek it. Yet those to whom the Lord has in this manner opened an avenue to the propagation of the glory of his kingdom, we exhort to persevere courageously in the fear of God; on this added condition, however, that they be permitted to discharge their entire ministry holily and religiously, and consequently to propose and urge, according to the measure of their office, such things as tend to the amelioration of the condition of affairs. For otherwise, if this liberty be taken away, and they be ordered so to connive at a manifest abuse, as even to approve of what clearly should be corrected, what other advice shall we give but that they prefer rather to be private individuals than contrary to their conscience to favour an evil which will necessarily soon bring with it the utter ruin of the churches?'

On another point about which he had been consulted, namely, whether they might not continue to discharge their office contrary to the will of the queen and the bishops, Beza replied that he shuddered at the thought, for reasons which needed not to be explained.

The subject of the vestments naturally received attention and condemnation at Beza's hands. Yet, after a long discussion of their nature and tendencies, when the question recurred, 'What shall those do upon whom these things are thrust?' He could not but reply that they did not seem to him to be of such moment as that, on their account, either ministers should desert their ministry rather than wear them, or the flocks lose their spiritual nourishment rather than listen to ministers thus arrayed. 'But if the order is issued to the ministers, not only to endure these things, but approve them as right by their signatures, or favour them by their silence, what other counsel can we give than that, after testifying their innocence and trying every remedy in God's fear, they yield to open violence?' Such in sum was the advice given by the Genevese Reformer, not indeed without a strong feeling of discouragement, yet also with the hope, which he expressed before concluding, that better things might be in store for a kingdom whose reformation had been sealed by the blood of so many excellent martyrs.[23]

The fortunes of Puritanism in England were watched by Beza with interest that did not diminish as time went on. Less solicitous with regard to details of ritual than with regard to the integrity of the discipline of the Church, he lent his full sympathy to the Presbyterian movement. He honoured and estimated at his true worth Thomas Cartwright, that prince of theologians, of whom on one occasion he wrote: 'The sun, I think, does not see a more learned man.'[24] When Cartwright, for his sturdy maintenance of

[23] Letter of October 24, 1567. *Tract. Theol.*, iii, 218-221.

[24] *Zurich Letters*, 479, note.

A FRENCH NATIONAL SYNOD IN THE 17TH CENTURY

his views, was deprived of his chair as Margaret Professor of Divinity at Cambridge University and of his fellowship in Trinity College, and forbidden to preach or teach, he crossed the Channel, and at Geneva was welcomed by Beza and his colleagues. Strengthened by conference with them and other Reformers of the Continent, he returned later to his native land in time to support by his voice and vigorous pen the 'Admonition to Parliament for the Reformation of Church Discipline,' which so infuriated the opposite party, that its authors, Field and Wilcox, were consigned to prison for their audacity. The Genevese Reformer was held responsible for a great share of the changes which it was sought to introduce into the government of the Church of England. Bishop Sandys wrote to Gualter at Zurich (August 9, 1574):

'Our innovators, who have been striving to strike out for us a new form of a church, are not doing us much harm; nor is this new fabric of theirs making such progress as they expected. Our nobility are at last sensible of the object to which this novel fabrication is tending. The author of these novelties, and after Beza the first inventor, is a young Englishman, by name Thomas Cartwright, who they say is sojourning at Heidelberg.'[25]

Unlike Beza, Bullinger's associate, Gualter, had little sympathy with a movement whose ulterior results he suspected, and had written to Bishop Cox a few months earlier, March 16, 1574: 'I greatly fear there is lying concealed under the presbytery an affectation of oligarchy, which may at length degenerate into monarchy, or even into open tyranny.'[26]

[25] *Zurich Letters*, 478, 479.

[26] *Ibid.*, 466.

CHAPTER 15

CONTROVERSIES AND CONTROVERSIAL WRITINGS

WE see, in his autobiographical letter to Wolmar, that Beza claims for himself, as a theologian, little or no originality. And, although this letter was written in 1560, that is, very early in his literary career, and he lived and studied for not much less than a half-century longer, he would, doubtless, have taken no very different view at the end of the period. His theology was essentially the theology of his great master, John Calvin. Accordingly the leading doctrines of the system of Calvin were also most prominent and fundamental in that of Beza. If there was any difference, these doctrines were more strongly accentuated by Beza and more rigidly carried out to their legitimate consequences. Most of the controversies in which the disciple became involved arose therefore in connection with the doctrines of the divine sovereignty and election, and with the Reformed view of the Lord's Supper.

It would manifestly be impossible, within the compass of the present volume, to speak in detail of all the numerous theological disputes in which Beza took part in the course of his long life, and of the works from his pen to which they gave rise. The greater number of the latter may be read in the three large volumes of his *Theological Treatises* (*Tractationes Theologicæ*), revised and republished by the author himself in 1582. Since his opponents were wont to reply, as best they could, to his arguments, Beza, unwilling to leave the last word to them, usually rejoined with a defence of his first position. Thus we not infrequently find two or even three treatises bearing upon the same point and pursuing the same lines of thought, addressed to the same antagonist.

It will be remembered that Beza informs us that the important work to which he prefixed the letter to Wolmar was his *Confession of the Christian Faith*,[1] composed primarily with the hope of gaining over his aged father, by clearing away the calumnies which the enemies of the truth had circulated respecting it. Subsequently given to the world, this *Confession* took a classical position and was recognised, both by friend and by foe, as an authoritative exposition of the Reformed belief. The former bought and read it, especially in the French language, and circulated it in many successive editions. There are said to have been six French editions printed in Geneva alone, within three years of the original publication. It was translated into English and Italian. That it met with the animadversion of the Roman Catholic Church is not surprising: the reading of any theological writing of Beza is strictly forbidden by the official Index of Prohibited Books down to our own times. But it is certainly significant of the influence which the *Confession* continued to exercise, long after the death of its author, that about a century and a quarter from its first appearance—that is, in 1685, the very year that Louis XIV

[1] *Confessio Christianæ Fidei, et ejusdem Collatio cum Papisticis Hæresibus.* In *Tract. Theol.*, i., 1-79. Letter translated in Appendix of this volume.

recalled the Edict of Nantes—it was still so widely read, and esteemed by the clergy of France so dangerous a book, that it called forth from the Archbishop of Paris a distinct condemnation in a special circular-letter.[2] What rendered the *Confession* specially odious in the eyes of the prelate was the circumstance that, not content with setting forth the Protestant views on such important points as the Trinity, the Church and its Government, and the Final Judgment, the author gave up the last third of the book to a 'Brief Contrast between the Papacy and Christianity,' of a particularly exasperating character. The amenities of discussion were rarely made of much account by disputants in the sixteenth century. The very first position which Beza undertakes to establish is that 'Papists, in place of the true God, worship a fictitious and imaginary divinity that is neither perfectly just nor perfectly merciful,' for 'that cannot be a perfect justice which approves of human acts of satisfaction, nor that a perfect mercy which only supplies the deficiency in man's merit.' To the same class of general treatises belongs *A Summary of the Whole of Christianity*, with the alternative title, *A Description and Distribution of the Causes of the Salvation of the Elect and the Destruction of the Reprobate, Collected from the Sacred Scriptures.*[3] At the head stands a table or diagram, occupying a single page, wherein the author's conception of the whole scheme of God's dealings with the human race is presented to the eye. This is followed by a 'Brief Explanation of the Foregoing Table,' covering thirty-five pages chiefly taken up with proof-texts derived

[2] Baum, *Theodor Beza*, ii, 83.

[3] *Summa totius Christianismi*, etc. *Tract. Theol.*, i, 170-205.

from Holy Writ, but introduced by sundry citations from Saint Augustine, indicating that the question about Predestination is not a question of mere curiosity or of little profit for the Church of God. This treatise is, if we except the defence of the right of the magistrate to punish heretics, which we have considered in a separate chapter, the first of Beza's writings on religious topics, having been written and published in 1555, during his professorate at Lausanne. It is almost needless to remark that it closely reflects the influence of Calvin.

Ten years after the *Confession* and fifteen years after the *Summary* appeared (1570) another systematic treatise from Beza's pen, entitled *A Little Book of Christian Questions and Answers, in which the Chief Heads of the Christian Religion are Epitomised* (*Quæstionum et Responsionum Christianarum Libellus*, etc.).[4] It was subsequently enlarged and accompanied by a *Compendious Catechism*.[5] For clearness of exposition this third treatise, the fruit of Beza's later thought, surpasses its predecessors. The three treatises together comprise the best results of a long study of systematic theology, and the last, in particular, will repay a careful perusal.

On the subject of Predestination, Beza crossed swords, as early as 1558, with Sebastian Castalio, in defending Calvin's doctrine from the accusation of being contrary to natural affection on the part of God, as the Father of mankind, and from other similar accusations.[6]

[4] *Tract. Theol.*, i, 654-688.

[5] *Catechismus Compendiarius. Ibid.*, i, 689-694.

[6] The original title, *Ad Sycophantarum calumnias*, etc., was changed in the collected works to *Ad Sebastiani Castellionis calumnias ... Responsio. Ibid.*, i, 337-424.

What Beza believed on the subject of the Lord's Supper we learn well enough from his own utterances respecting it, both in his great speech before Charles IX at the Colloquy of Poissy, and on other occasions. While denying that the elements of bread and wine are in the Communion transformed into the substance of the body and blood of Christ, according to the Roman Catholic view, or that the body and blood of Christ are present in, with, and under the bread and wine, according to the Lutheran view, he declined, on the other hand, to assert that the elements are mere signs and that the act of partaking is a mere commemoration, as was the Zwinglian view held in German Switzerland, but, with Calvin, believed that the worthy partaker, not in any carnal sense, but none the less truly, by faith feeds upon the body of Christ. He repudiated the notion that he would divorce Christ from the feast he had instituted.

But not even so did Calvin or Beza escape attack from the more ardent advocates of the doctrine of Consubstantiation, and the scholar felt himself compelled to appear in his master's defence as well as his own. To the scurrilous assault made by Joachim Westphal, at Hamburg, he wrote a careful and, on the whole, a more temperate reply than could have been expected in the circumstances. It was entitled *A Plain and Clear Treatise Respecting the Lord's Supper, in which the Calumnies of Joachim Westphal are Refuted* (1559).[7] As Westphal, not content with discussing the main question, had raised a hue and cry against the rejection by the Reformed of so many ancient usages, Beza answered in

[7] '*De cœna Domini plana et perspicua tractatio*' etc. *Tract. Theol.*, i, 211-258.

defence of their position that while themselves dropping the practices which they disapproved, they carefully refrained from condemning their brethren who continued to observe such practices when these related to things indifferent. But Beza waxes angry with a holy indignation when he comes to advert to the gross and vituperative language used by Westphal as to the witnesses for the faith, members of the Reformed Churches of France, burned at the stake, whose ashes were even yet smoking.

'For the insults which you have not been ashamed to vomit forth against the holy martyrs of the Lord, whom Popish tyranny is daily snatching from our assemblies, you will yourself see to it how you shall answer at the Lord's judgment-seat. Their writings survive and will hand down their blessed memory, whether you approve of it or not, to a grateful posterity. In the name of all Christian Churches, I am ashamed that in any Church there could be found a man so insolently wanton as to utter sharp words against those, even when dead, whom their very executioners revered while they were dying. Certainly the Lord will not suffer to go. unavenged this more than inhuman and barbarous cruelty. To him we commend the cause of his martyrs.'[8]

Nor does Beza leave unnoticed the abuse which Westphal, at the very same time that he complains of Calvin's severity, heaps on Calvin's devoted head, not only accusing him of gluttony and winebibbing, but hinting that the Reformer's language, being fit only for the ears of courtesans, he had possibly learned from his mother, the concubine of a parish priest. We can well excuse the

[8] *Tract. Theol.*, i, 257.

outburst of indignant remonstrance to which Beza gives vent, when he stigmatises, with deserved contempt, the man who, in order to crush a theological opponent, accuses the most abstemious of men of excess, and exhumes from the grave a respected matron of an honourable and noble family in Noyon, long since dead, that he may without proof besmirch her unspotted memory.[9]

To Westphal succeeded, in 1561, Tilemann Hesshus, as a defender of the Lutheran phase of doctrine, and as an assailant of the Genevese church and its theologians. That Beza regarded him as a stupid adversary was no sufficient excuse for the open contempt and rudeness with which he treated him, even if we give all the weight possible to the somewhat frivolous plea that the exacerbation of his temper was due to a particularly annoying attack of catarrhal fever with which he was afflicted when he wrote.[10]

These were discussions of the earlier part of Beza's course, anterior to the Colloquy of Poissy, and before the Reformer assumed a place among the disputants most widely known throughout Christendom. After that event, and after the death of Calvin coming so close upon it, Beza fell heir to new controversies, carried on by him, not as Calvin's younger adjutant, but as Calvin's legitimate successor, partly in the same general direction, partly on new lines.

Some of these, doubtless, were not only needlessly bitter, but altogether unnecessary. Such, perhaps, was the controversy that arose from the attempt of Castalio, in his translation of the Scriptures, to modernise his version and

[9] See *Tract Theol.*, i, 257, 258.

[10] See Heppe, 91.

replace the Hebraisms of the Vulgate with good Ciceronian phrases. Yet Beza was right in his position that fidelity to the text had not in a few instances been sacrificed by Castalio to the supposed exigencies of a flawless Latinity.

In the case of the aged and respected Italian scholar, Bernardino Ochino, of Siena, there was much to regret in the attitude taken by Beza and by other Reformers. Ochino was not only a man of great ability, but a Christian that had sacrificed everything for his faith. Before his adoption of Protestantism he had enjoyed wonderful popularity in his native land as a pulpit orator. At the age of fifty he was the prince of Lenten preachers. The praise lavished upon him by the learned was surpassed only by the plaudits of the multitudes that flocked to hear him whenever it was announced that he would speak. If Cardinal Bembo, a leading scholar of the period, wrote to Colonna, in March, 1539, that he had never discoursed with a person of greater sanctity, and that he intended 'not to miss a single one of his beautiful, solemn, and edifying discourses,' the next month he was informing the same correspondent that, at Venice, from which he wrote, Ochino was 'literally adored,' 'there was no one that did not praise him to the skies.'[11] Twice was he elected Vicar General of the Capuchin Order, and so well did he stand with the Holy See that his nomination was cheerfully confirmed by the Pope. But Ochino was becoming more and more evangelical in his preaching, as the Roman Church became more and more pronounced in its opposition to any form of reformation. The inevitable logic of his recognition of the doctrine of Justification by

[11] Karl Benrath, *Bernardino Ochino* (Eng. trans.), 16.

Faith led him out of the establishment in which he held so high and influential a position, to the lands beyond the Alps where he could give free expression to his new convictions. He did not hesitate to take a step which involved the loss of all things that men prize highest—rank, ease, the esteem of the multitude. He fled first to Switzerland. The autumn of the year 1542 found him in Geneva, 'an old man of venerable appearance,' according to Calvin, and one who 'was greatly respected in his own country.' He was warmly welcomed by the Genevan Reformers, and he, in his turn, delighted with the order, purity, and simple worship which he witnessed, poured out an encomium upon the city and its usages which I should be glad, were there space here, to reproduce.[12] From this time forth he lived an exemplary and useful life as a Protestant and a Protestant minister. When he left Geneva, at the end of three years, he went provided with a letter of 'special recommendation' from Calvin. He was well received by Bucer at Strassburg. At Augsburg he became by public appointment Italian preacher to his compatriots residing in that city. Compelled to flee, in 1547, on the approach of the Emperor Charles V, one of the first of whose demands was that the city should surrender to him the person of Bernardino Ochino, he was that same year invited to England by Cranmer, shortly after the accession of Edward VI. The six years of that estimable prince's reign were spent by Ochino in labours for his countrymen sojourning in London whether for mercantile purposes or as exiles for religion's sake. Meanwhile he was made non-resident prebendary of Canterbury. When Mary

[12] Translated from his sermons in Benrath, 148.

came to the throne, Ochino hastily retired to the Continent, and for ten years (1553–1563), or until within about a year of his death, he lived in Switzerland, first at Geneva, and afterwards at Basel and Zurich. At Zurich he accepted the office of minister to Italian Protestants from Locarno. Unfortunately, in this period of his life, Ochino developed a tendency to indulge in curious speculations, for a full discussion of which the reader must look elsewhere. Suffice it to say here that, in a book which he wrote, not so much by direct assertion as by inference, the soundness of the aged author was brought into suspicion. If, for the most part, he seemed in the dialogue himself to assume the defence of the current belief and left the attack to another, yet, with an impartiality carried to the extreme of complaisance, he lent such cogency to the arguments of his opponents as to lay himself open to the charge of a virtual surrender of principles and beliefs that should have been dear to him. Thus his belief in the divinity of Jesus Christ and his equality with the Father naturally becomes in the judgment of the reader more than doubtful. The great problems affecting man and his destiny, divine grace and human ability, and all the views and theories that have troubled the ages, are presented in so antithetical a manner, and the arguments in favour and in opposition are marshalled in such a formidable array, that the decision is veiled in uncertainty. Of such contests the natural issue is in doubt, if not in positive despair of the attainment of certainty in matters of religion. Nor indeed in matters of faith alone. Ochino exhibited the same method in the treatment of moral questions. In setting forth the reasons in favour of polygamy and in condemnation of it, he left the final decision in such suspense that the answer to the question whether, in certain cases, an individual man might or should marry a second wife during the lifetime of a first wife was referred to that man's own decision acting under the inspiration of God. If, after prayer to the Almighty for the grace of continence, the gift is not received, Ochino's ultimate counsel to him is to do whatever God prompts him to do, if only he knows for certain that God is prompting him; for whatever is done by divine inspiration cannot be sin.[13]

That the Swiss Reformers, Bullinger, Beza, and all the others, should have been shocked, amazed, indignant, at the promulgation of such views by a professed adherent of the Reformation, is not surprising. Nor is it surprising that Beza regarded the last matter mentioned as of such vital importance that he published, in refutation of Ochino's views, his two treatises *On Polygamy* and *On Repudiation and Divorce*, extracted from his lectures on the First Epistle to the Corinthians.[14] That Beza styled him 'an impure apostate' may be explained, if it may not be excused, by the fact that the whole trend of Ochino's disputations was directly to that 'academic uncertainty' respecting all truth which the Reformers regarded as more pernicious than any single error of doctrine, since it sapped the foundations of all religion. But it was certainly not to the credit of the Protestant Reformers, especially those of Zurich and Basel, that in their detestation of the utterances of their misguided brother, long their associate in Christian work and the

[13] Benrath, 268, foll.

[14] *Tract. Theol.*, ii, 1-109.

object of their Christian affection, they forgot the past too completely, and sanctioned, if they did not urge, the severe punishment—which the magistrates dealt out to Ochino, without allowing him to be heard in his own defence, or in explanation of books written, not in the vernacular for circulation among the people, but in a foreign tongue for the consideration of the learned and curious. The circumstance that Sebastian Castalio had acted as his translator aggravated the resentment of the indignant Zurichers at having ignorantly harboured for so long a time in their city a disloyal Protestant, in one whom they had known only as a brother in the faith. Old and infirm—he was in the seventy-sixth or seventy-seventh year of his age,—the venerable man whom all had so lately united in honouring for his past services was in midwinter bidden to depart from the city and jurisdiction of Zurich, in company with his four children, within a term of a fortnight or, at furthest, three weeks. Basel would not long receive him, Mülhausen refused him a refuge, Nuremberg consented only to his passing the winter there. From Poland he was expelled with all foreigners not Roman Catholics. He died of the plague at Schlackau in Moravia, in the latter part of the year 1564.[15]

Respecting the bodily presence of our Lord in the Eucharist, Beza continued to be drawn into controversies, reaching through many years, partly with Roman Catholics, partly with fellow-Protestants. Among the former the most prominent was the white friar, Claude de Sainctes, whom he had encountered at the third session of the Colloquy of Poissy. It was Claude who had on that occasion made the

[15] Benrath, 297.

astounding assertion that tradition stands on more stable foundation than do the Holy Scriptures themselves, inasmuch as the latter can be dragged hither and thither by a variety of interpretations.[16] He showed no more wit in the treatise which he brought out, five or six years later, under the title, *An Examination of the Calvinistic and Bezæan Doctrine of the Lord's Supper*. The author's crudity would seem to have warranted Beza's somewhat contemptuous designation of him as a 'theologaster.' De Sainctes had aimed at currying favour with his patron, the Cardinal of Lorraine, by reinforcing the prelate's peculiar attempt to confound or win over Beza and his companions at the great colloquy. The cardinal's strength did not lie in the breadth or depth of his theological acquisitions; but he certainly had no lack of cunning. If, he thought, the Calvinists could not be silenced by argument, at least their cause would be prejudiced if, in any way, they could be set by the ears with their fellow-Protestants from beyond the Rhine.

In his written attack, Claude de Sainctes, reviving his patron's tactics, endeavoured to establish that a difference of theological views separated Geneva from the neighbouring cantons of Switzerland, while there was a fundamental contradiction, amounting to real enmity, between the Calvinists and the Lutherans. Whereupon Beza reminded the friar that his contention did not possess even the merit of novelty.

'Have you forgotten, Claude,' he said, 'the answer I gave to your cardinal, in that more absurd than serious skirmish of his, at a time when he was devising the very same

[16] Jean de Serres, *Com. de Statu Rel. et Reip.*, i, 315.

assault that you are now making? Drawing from his bosom a paper which he at first pretended to be the Confession of Augsburg, but which was in reality, as subsequently appeared, a copy of a private confession of a certain one of the Wittenberg theologians, recently brought to him by one Rascalo, his spy, without their knowledge, the cardinal inquired of me whether we would give our assent to it. In turn, I asked him to tell me whether he himself assented to it. Startled by my unexpected reply, he frankly admitted that he could not do so. Thereupon I retorted: 'What affair is it, then, of yours whether we agree with them or no, since you dissent from us both? And yet, lest you should suppose that I am seeking to evade the question, I will tell you that we regard those whom you call "Protestants" as our very dear brethren—that we disagree with the Augsburg Confession on only a very few points—and that these very points themselves, suitably interpreted, could easily be reconciled, did not the unreasonableness of certain persons stand in the way.' This is what I said on that occasion. I do not imagine that you have forgotten my words. For this reason I should be the more astonished that you have now undertaken the same plan, were it not that the whole world has come to understand what is your sense of shame, what your conscience.'[17]

Into the systematic refutation of the Roman Catholic doctrine of Transubstantiation and the Real Presence, occupying in particular the whole of Beza's third and last answer to Claude de Sainctes, there is no need of our entering. Let it be enough to say that it was careful, comprehensive,

[17] *Tract. Theol.*, ii, 289.

cogent.[18] To us, however, the chief interest attaching to the whole controversy is the personal element which the friar introduced into the matter in his first attack upon Calvin and upon Beza himself. The circumstance that he had not neglected a single opportunity to calumniate them, that he had not omitted a single incident of their lives that could be misinterpreted or wrested to their disadvantage, makes De Sainctes's accusations with Beza's replies uncommonly interesting reading, and invests them with a certain historical importance. Witness, for example, the triumphant retort of Beza to the monk's scurrilous slanders respecting the alleged impurity of his early life at Paris and his compulsory and clandestine flight to Geneva in order to avoid condign punishment for his vices. 'Had I been seized with the love of lewd women,' said he, 'should I have betaken myself to that city which is almost the only one where licentious living is punished by public ignominy and by no insignificant fines, and adultery by death?'[19]

More lamentable than any controversies with the Roman Catholics, because more unnecessary and more productive of evil and discord within the bosom of Protestantism itself, were the controversies with representatives of the dominant phase of the theology of Germany. I am glad that the scope of this work is such that I am not compelled to rehearse in detail the mournful story of the manner in which the divergence of views already subsisting became more and more pronounced, and a mere difference of theory led to a separation, a schism, almost to a positive hatred, between men who should have loved and respected each other as

[18] *Tract. Theol.*, iii, 1-53.

[19] *Ibid.*, ii, 360.

members of one Christian host arrayed against one common enemy.

What were Beza's feelings toward the Lutherans we have already seen. What he said to the Cardinal of Lorraine at the Colloquy of Poissy was the sincere sentiment of his heart,—they were his very dear brethren in Christ. That there were differences between their views on the mode of Christ's presence in the Sacrament and respecting the alleged ubiquity of his human body, he did not affect to deny. But he was disposed, instead of magnifying these differences, to reduce them to the smallest possible dimensions. His manly honesty did not allow him, indeed, to abstain from strenuously maintaining the truth, as he conceived it to be, against every successive opponent, but this loyalty to principle did not prevent him from sincerely desiring, what was also the sincere desire of Philip Melanchthon, especially in his later years, that a cordial and charitable union might be effected between the two great branches of the Church of the Reformation. But that friend of concord was no more, and the loss to Christendom by his removal by death was in Beza's view irreparable. Scarcely had five years elapsed when the latter wrote to the brethren of Bern and Zurich that the enemy were now hoping to effect their designs with much greater ease than hitherto because now, as never before, they would have the Papists as allies in the condemnation of the Reformed, and because 'no Melanchthon survived to restrain them by his great authority.'[20] It is a thousandfold to be deplored that his advances toward conciliation were not responded to with a corresponding cordiality, but

[20] Inedited letter of Beza to the Bernese and Zurichois, Dec. 14, 1565. Copy in Baum Collection, Lib, Fr. Prot. Hist. Soc., Paris.

met with coldness when they did not call forth an absolute denial of the fraternal bond. The latter was the case at the conclusion of the conference held at Montbéliard, in March, 1586. The excellent Count Frederick of Würtemberg, under whose auspices the gathering of theologians was held, was an ardent lover of peace and leaned to the Reformed views. Beza, now an old man, had not, in his zeal for union, hesitated to come in person and endeavour to find the common ground upon which he was convinced that Calvinists and Lutherans could honourably stand without sacrifice of dignity or principle. But the attitude of Andreæ, the chief representative of the other side, was unconciliatory, and, at the end of the discussion, the two parties were farther apart than they were at its commencement. In vain had it been made clear to every impartial man that the two great wings of the Protestant Church were practically in complete accord as against the Church of Rome. When, the conference over, Beza offered his right hand in token of love and confidence to the man with whom the argument had been chiefly sustained, Andreæ declined to take it. He could as little see, he said, how Beza was able to esteem him and the other Würtemberg theologians, to whom he had imputed all sorts of errors, as brethren, as he himself could recognise fraternal communion with Beza, who had shown that he held the imaginations of men above the word of God. But while he could not greet him as a brother, Andreæ was pleased to offer him his hand as a fellow-man. Beza, however, promptly rejected the ostentatious mark of condescension.[21]

[21] *The Huguenots and Henry of Navarre*, i, 401.

CHAPTER 16

BEZA AND THE HUGUENOT PSALTER

It has frequently been said that to Beza the world is indebted, if not for the whole of the Huguenot liturgy for the Lord's Day service, at least for the beautiful confession of sins and prayer that constitute its most striking feature. It has been asserted that this simple but grand formula was taken from the extemporaneous words used by the Reformer at the beginning of his historical defence of the Reformed Churches and their doctrine at the Colloquy of Poissy, without doubt the most picturesque and impressive scene not only in the life of Beza himself, but in the early period of the French Reformation. We have seen, however, that the story is a pleasing fiction, and that the confession of sins, so far from being uttered for the first time before the august assembly that met in the nuns' refectory of Poissy, had before then been repeatedly on the lips of martyrs at the stake, nay, that for nearly twenty years it had been a component part of Protestant worship, both when secretly and when openly celebrated, at Strassburg, at Geneva, and in a multitude of places in France. Composed and used for several years before Theodore Beza fully broke with the Church of Rome, that liturgy had for its author not the young student from Vézelay, but John Calvin himself.

But Beza rendered to Huguenot devotion a service not less notable in another direction. The worship of God's house could have been conducted in an orderly and impressive manner and with undiminished fervour without Calvin's liturgy at all; but deprived of the metrical psalms the worship would have lost its most characteristic feature. Without those psalms, too, the very history of the Huguenots, civil as well as religious, would have been robbed of a great part of its individuality. In the long conflict that arose out of the effort to crush the Protestant doctrines and their professors in France, from the first outbreak of civil war in the middle of the sixteenth century down to the Revocation of the Edict of Nantes in the seventeenth, and indeed far beyond that time, when the Reformed faith was supposed to have been annihilated, the psalms were the badge by which the Huguenots were recognised by friend and foe alike, they were the stimulus of the brave, the battle-cry of the combatant, the last consolatory words whispered in the ears of the dying.

Now the French psalms were peculiarly the work of Theodore Beza.

True, indeed, it is that the collection bears and has always borne the joint names of Clément Marot and Théodore de Béze, and that it was the success of the brilliant and versatile poet of the Renaissance in his attempts to turn the psalms of David into French verse that led Beza to follow his example. But what had been approached by the former, it would seem, mainly as a literary task, aiming first of all at the gratification of the reader, was with the latter a labour of love and an attempt to achieve for the cause to which

CLÉMONT MAROT

he had devoted his life the most noble of works. For it can hardly be denied that efforts which give to pious thought the most appropriate vehicle for its expression fall short of no other human ambitions in usefulness and dignity.

It may be admitted from the start that in native poetical genius Beza falls distinctly below Marot. The verdict of the literary world on this point is not likely to be reversed. In any production of a kind demanding the exercise of a lively imagination, on any subject where the light touch of a master in the graceful expression of thought is of the first importance, there can be no question that his countrymen would give the palm to the poet whose days were spent in the court and in the frivolous circles of the great. Yet it is not unreasonable to look for a more adequate treatment of religious themes at the hands of a writer in full and lasting sympathy with their high truths than at the hands of a poet whose religious feelings are either shallow or evanescent. As Beza could enter more easily than Marot into the devotional spirit of the Hebrew original, so there are psalms or parts of psalms which have been rendered by him with a dignity approaching to grandeur, with a dignity which the most prejudiced critic must confess is unsurpassed in anything from the pen of Marot. Among these psalms stands prominent the sixty-eighth, of which the initial stanza of twelve lines deserves, more than any other passage, to be regarded as the choicest jewel of the entire collection—a worthy introduction to the psalm which stands unchallenged as, above all the rest, the Huguenot battle-song. Sung at the charge at many an encounter of the period when the Huguenots were at their strongest, it is no less associated in every line with those humbler but scarcely less glorious and equally heroic conflicts when, in the Camisard war of the eighteenth century, the 'Children of God,' as they styled themselves, having survived the supposed overthrow of their religion, dared defy the arms of Louis XIV.

It was in the year 1533, apparently, that the first of Clément Marot's translated psalms appeared in print, appended to the former part of that curious work of the Duchess of Alençon, only sister of Francis I, entitled *Miroir de tres chrestienne princesse Marguerite de France*. This was the sixth psalm of David, whose plaintive cry was admirably reproduced in the opening verses, 'Ne vueilles pas, O Sire,' etc.[1] Six years later came out at Strassburg what has been styled the first edition of the Protestant psalter, containing twelve new psalms translated by Marot, but strangely enough omitting the sixth, with which the editor or publisher seems not to have been acquainted.[2] Two years more passed, and in 1541 there appeared with the imprint of Anvers (Antwerp) a fuller collection of thirty psalms translated by Marot.[3] Finally, in 1543, there was given to the world by Marot the entire collection of fifty psalms, with which his activity in this direction closed, together with the Song of Simeon and the Ten Commandments, as well as one or two versifications such as the Angelic Salutation, which never found a permanent place in the Protestant psalter.[4]

[1] O. Douen, *Clément Marot et le Psautier huguenot*, ii, 505.

[2] *Ibid.*, i, 302.

[3] *Ibid.*, i, 315.

[4] According to Douen (i, 413), the Angelic Salutation was inserted in some editions of the Huguenot psalter published in France, even after the Venerable Consistory of the Church of Geneva, doubtless jealous

It was to this publication that the poet prefixed the poetical 'Letter Addressed to the Ladies of France' which he had recently written to persuade his fair readers to substitute for the songs of love, always worldly and often foul, with which their abodes resound, songs of quite another strain; yet songs of Love alone, their author very Love, composing them by his supreme wisdom (while vain man has been but the mere writer), and having conferred language and voice to sing his own high praises. Blessed be he, exclaims the poet, that shall live to see that golden age when God alone shall be adored, praised, and sung, and when the labourer at his plough, the teamster on the road, and the artisan in his shop shall lighten their toil by a psalm or hymn; happy he that shall hear the shepherd and the shepherdess in the wood make rocks and lakes echo and repeat after them the holy name of their Creator. The whole was summed up in the closing injunction thus to hasten the coming of the golden age.

The poem, if it does not prove that its author was a true Huguenot at heart, a Protestant by deep conviction, at least furnishes evidence that he was not devoid at times of genuine religious feeling.[5]

Clément Marot died at Turin in the summer of 1544. After a life of singular variety, in which his unconcealed

---

of the worship of the Virgin Mary so intimately associated with the use of the 'Ave Maria' in the Church of Rome, had ordered its removal from the book containing the psalms and ecclesiastical prayers. Marot protested without avail that, the Salutation being a part of Holy Writ, the suppression seemed to place the Consistory's authority above the authority of the word of God.

[5] *Ibid.*, i, 396-398.

aversion to the Roman Catholic Church had exposed him to danger and imprisonment in France, and led him to sojourn at the court of Duchess Renée at Ferrara, and for a time in Venice, he spent a little over a year in Geneva. Not only did he frequently confer with Calvin on the matter of the translation of the psalms, but the great Reformer himself recommended the council of the city to employ him at public expense in completing the work. The council rejected the application, and Marot withdrew from Geneva. That he was compelled to do so, having been found guilty of adultery and escaping only through Calvin's intercession, seems to be a pure fabrication of the royal historiographer Cayet, who, having from Protestant turned Roman Catholic, was not unwilling to circulate stories of the kind against the poet who had attacked his newly espoused faith. For the fact is that no record of any proceedings against Marot has been found on the Genevese registers, while, on the other hand, it is known that the penalty for the crime of adultery had not as yet been fixed at death, and was not so fixed until sixteen years after Marot's death.[6]

At Clément Marot's death the Protestants had an incomplete psalter, consisting of barely one third of the whole number of psalms, and these not continuous, but with certain gaps. A writer uniting the requisites of a faithful translator to those of a poet by nature it was not easy to find. Marot had no rival during his lifetime, nor had he his equal among the poets that survived him ; but it was natural that, under the circumstances, the eyes of Calvin and of others should turn to Beza. The *Juvenilia*, written and published

[6] *Ibid.*, i, 416.

before his conversion, had long since proved him to possess high literary abilities. He was himself anxious to show that these abilities could be employed to better purpose than when the ambition to rival Ovid and Catullus reigned supreme in his breast. Accordingly, within about two years from the date of his reaching Lausanne, that is, in 1551, we find Beza publishing a separate collection of thirty-four psalms. A year later he republished these in connection with forty-nine of those which Marot had translated. With these eighty-three psalms the Protestant psalter was more than half-way on toward completion. It was appropriate that Beza, in imitation of Marot, should now provide it with a poetic letter dedicatory. Marot had dedicated his psalms to his patron, Francis I, and had written to the 'Ladies' of France to incite them to sing these in lieu of worldly songs. Beza addressed the epistle which he placed at the head of his work to 'The Church of our Lord,' the 'little flock' which in its littleness surpasses the greatness of the world, the little flock 'held in contempt by this round globe and yet its only treasure.' The choice of Beza was the better, and he made of his address, regarded by some writers not without reason as his masterpiece, so excellent an introduction to the psalms that for centuries it continued to hold its place even when the circumstances to which it made reference had long since faded from the memory of the majority of the faithful who used the collection in their devotions. The exordium is calm in its quiet strength.

'Petit Troupeau, qui en ta petitesse
Vas surmontant du monde la hautesse;
Petit Troupeau, le mespris de ce monde,

Et seul thresor de la machine ronde;
Tu es celui auquel gist mon courage,
Pour te donner ce mien petit ouvrage:
Petit, je di, en ce qui est du mien.
Mais au surplus si grand, qu'il n'y a rien
Assez exquis en tout cest univers,
Pour esgaler un moindre de ces vers.
Voila pourquoi chose tant excellente
A toi, sur tout excellent, je presente.'

Let kings and princes, clothed in gold and silver, but not in virtues, stand back. With them lying flatterers fill their pages. They are not addressed here. Not that they are not spoken to; but they have neither ears to hear, nor heart to learn the message. The poem is for those other true kings and true princes, worthy to possess realms and provinces, potentates who beneath the shadow of their wings defend the life of many a poor believer. Let them hear the enchanting harp of the great David, and being kings hearken to the voice of a king. Let shepherds listen to a shepherd's pipe which God Himself was pleased to sound. Let the sheep catch the divine music which communicates both joy and healing. Do they mourn? They shall be comforted. Do they hunger? They shall be filled. Do they endure suffering? They shall be relieved.

The poet was writing, as I have said, in 1551, that is, in the midst of the persecutions under Henry II. That very year the monarch published a terrible law against the Protestants of his realm. The Edict of Châteaubriand, of June 27, 1551, we have already seen,[7] sent the new heretics straight to the

[7] *Supra*, 69.

flames on the mere sentence of an ordinary judge, and cut off all right of appeal. Nor was Geneva forgotten by the legislator. As Calvin remarked, that city was honoured with a mention in the ordinance more than ten times. The importation of books of any kind from Geneva, and from other places well known to be in rebellion against the Papacy, was prohibited under severe penalties. So was also the retention by booksellers of any condemned book, as well as clandestine publications in any shape. Every printing establishment was now subjected to a visitation twice a year. The great affairs of Lyons were searched three times a year, because it had been discovered that many suspected books were introduced into France by that channel. In fact all book packages from abroad were to be examined by the clergy, before their contents could be put into circulation. Book-peddling was utterly forbidden, on the ground that peddlers from Geneva smuggled books into France under cover of disposing of other merchandise. It became a punishable offence to be the bearer of a simple letter from Geneva. To have fled thither was sufficient to lead to confiscation of property, and the informer was promised one third of the forfeited goods. So resolved was the king to extinguish Protestantism once for all, that all simple folk were warned not even to discuss matters of faith, the sacraments, and the government of the Church, at table, in the fields, or in the secret meeting.[8] Would it have been surprising, when Geneva was thus singled out for special hostility by the malice of Henry II, had Beza, in his general view of the enemies of the 'little flock,' noticed with peculiar

[8] See *Rise of the Huguenots*, i, 279-281.

execration the king of his native land? Yet, while the Pope naturally comes in for mention, as 'the wolf that wears the triple crown, surrounded by other beasts of his kind,' the poet prefers to call attention among monarchs only to the good King Edward VI, of England, hospitably greeting on the shores of his insular domain the fugitives that have escaped the fires of persecution. For him he prays that, as in his youth he has already surpassed, all other kings, so in his advancing years he may surpass even himself:

'Que Dieu te doint, O Roy qui en enfance
As surmonté des plus grands l'espérance,
Croissans tes ans, si bien croistre en ses graces,
Qu' après tous Rois toi-mesme tu surpasse.'

But the poet's thoughts turned by preference to the victims of persecution with whom the prisons of France were overflowing. To these sufferers, Beza's words were words of encouragement to patience and endurance in the profession of their faith, with the lips, if speech was allowed them, if not, let courage supply a testimony which the tongue was not permitted to give. After which the poet enforces his injunction with a couplet that seems to anticipate by ten years the famous warning which this same Beza made to the recreant King of Navarre, to the effect that the Church of God is indeed an anvil to receive and not strike blows, but an anvil that has worn out many hammers.[9] Let persecutors, he says, tire of murdering God's children sooner than the latter tire of withstanding the assaults of his enemies:

[9] See above, 216.

'Que les tyrans soyent de nous martyrer
Plustost lassez [lassés], que nous de l'endurer.'

The remainder of the 'Epistle to the Church of our Lord' need not detain us long. In order that no one should have an excuse for not singing God's praise, Marot, says Beza, turned into French the psalms once written by David, but, alas! died when he had completed only one third of his task. What was worse, he died leaving no one in the world, no learned poet, to continue his labours. This was the reason that when death snatched him away, with him David also was silent, for all the best minds feared to try their hands at the task which a Marot had undertaken. What, then, someone will say, makes you so brave as to attempt so grave a work? To which question Beza replies by pleading his own consciousness that his powers fall far short of his good-will, and by promising to applaud the efforts of those whom he would incite to enter upon the same office and perform it in a manner more worthy of its great importance. In conclusion, as Clément Marot had begged the 'Ladies' to cease singing of Cupid, 'the winged god of love,' and give themselves to the celebration of the true, the Divine Love, so Beza challenges the poets of his time, those 'minds of heavenly birth,' to turn from the low subjects of their songs to themes of higher merit. Let the time past suffice to have followed such vain inventions, and objects of adoration which shall perish with the works of their adorers. But whatever others may conclude to do, the poet declares that, insignificant as he is, he will celebrate the praises of his God. The mountains and the fields shall be witnesses, the shores of the lake shall repeat, the Alps shall take up the cry in the clouds.

We have seen that in 1551 Beza had added only thirty-four psalms to those translated by Marot, and that the united collection comprised but eighty-three. Eleven years more passed before the Genevese Reformer gave to the world (in 1562) the remaining sixty-seven, and thus completed the psalter.[10] The appearance of this work coincides in time with most striking events in the history of the French Protestants, and itself marks a singular crisis in their fortunes.

Up to this date the psalms in the vernacular had been almost uniformly proscribed by Church and State. The singing of them by the common people was taken as a sure sign of heresy. It is true that there was a short period in the reign of Francis I when they seemed to be in high favour at court. Charmed by the rhythm, or by the music to which they were sung, the monarch and the nobles of his suite were pleased to adopt certain psalms as their favourite melodies, quite regardless of the religious sentiment expressed. According to the account of a contemporary, a gentleman by the name of Villemadon, Francis himself was so much pleased with the thirty psalms translated by Clément Marot and dedicated to the king, that he bade the poet present his work to the Emperor Charles V, who in turn set high store by the translation, rewarding the author with a gift of two hundred doubloons, encouraging him to complete his work, and asking him, in particular, to send him as soon as possible his version of the psalm 'O give thanks unto the Lord, for he is good; for his mercy endureth for ever' (Psa. 107).[11]

[10] Douen, ii, 523.

[11] *Ibid.*, i, 317.

The dauphin, the future Henry II, showed particular fondness for the psalms, and ordinarily went about singing or humming them, to the great satisfaction, we are told, of all good and pious souls. Nothing more was needed to induce the courtiers, and even the king's old mistress, Diana of Poitiers, to pick out each his or her favourite psalm, and beg of the dauphin to let them have it, to his no small perplexity as to which one of them he should thus gratify. For himself, Henry, as yet childless, though he had been married to Catharine de Medici for not far from a score of years, chose Marot's rendering of the one hundred and twenty-eighth psalm—a selection dictated, doubtless, by the wish that he too might be blessed as the man that feared the Lord, his wife being as a fruitful vine by the sides of his house, and his children like olive plants round about his table. It was about the same time, and for a similar reason, that Catharine de Medici declared her preference for the one hundred and forty-second psalm ('I cried unto the Lord with my voice,' etc.).

The short-lived enthusiasm of the court for the singing of the psalms had little or no effect upon legislation. For nearly twenty years after this time the laws against the use of the psalter in the vernacular continued to be as severe and were as persistently executed as ever. It was not, as has been said, until 1562, that a change, induced by political considerations, was effected.

For two years and more France had seemed to be arousing itself from the sleep of ages and clamouring for the word of God. Thus, for instance, in 1558, about a year before the sudden death of the persecuting Henry II, a singular and unlooked-for outbreak of psalm-singing took place in the heart of Paris and on the favourite promenade of the best society, the so-called *Pré aux Clercs*. Here, just across the Seine from the Louvre, it happened one afternoon in May that two or three voices started the tune of one of the proscribed psalms. In an instant other voices joined in, showing that the words and the air were familiar to many, and soon almost the whole body of promenaders—students, gentlemen, ladies among the rest—were unitedly celebrating God's glory. The next day, and the next, the thing was repeated. There were said at last to be five or six thousand engaged in the unlawful act of praising the Almighty in French, among them many notable personages of state, including the King and Queen of Navarre. The irregularity did not escape the notice of the bigots of the neighbouring college of the Sorbonne, the theological faculty of Paris; nor did they rest until the bishop of the city had called the attention of parliament to an incident which was declared to tend to sedition, public commotion, and a disturbance of the public peace.[12]

Other features of the awakening are referred to elsewhere, and need not be recalled here. Let it suffice my present purpose to repeat what Montluc, Bishop of Valence, said in his famous speech in the Assembly of Notables held at Fontainebleau, in August, 1560, while the old laws were still in full force. After begging the young king (Francis II) to have daily preaching in his palace, in order that the mouths of those might be closed who asserted that God was never spoken of among those about his Majesty's person,

[12] See *Rise of the Huguenots*, i, 314, 315.

CATHARINE DE MEDICI

the prelate turned to Catharine de Medici and Mary of Scots, and exclaimed:

'And you, Mesdames the Queens, be pleased to pardon me if I venture to beg you to command that, in place of silly songs, your maids and all your suite shall sing only the psalms of David and the spiritual songs that contain the praises of God. And remember that God's eye searches out all places and all men in this world, but rests nowhere [with favour] save where his name is invoked, praised, and exalted.' 'And hereupon,' he added, addressing himself to the king, 'I cannot abstain from saying that I find extremely strange the view of those who would interdict the singing of the psalms, and who give occasion to the seditious to say that we are no longer fighting against men but against God, for we strive to prevent his praises from being proclaimed and heard by all.'

This he followed by proof which it would have been difficult for his opponents to refute, and which they took good care not to notice.[13]

The Guises kept the good advice of Montluc and others from bearing fruit, but the movement which he represented did not stay its course. At last in September, 1561, the colloquy came. It was no longer a matter of doubt that a considerable body of people in France had espoused the doctrines of the Reformation; although it had not yet been decided definitely how they were to be dealt with. Then it was that a few weeks before the publication of the tolerant 'Edict of January,' Beza secured for the complete psalter translated by Clément Marot and himself a privilege, or

[13] *Recueil des Choses Memorables* (1565), 295, etc.

governmental authorisation and copyright. The date of its issue was December 26, 1561.[14]

And now began a very deluge of editions of the psalter following one another almost without intermission. Such was the new and quickened demand, that it was difficult, almost impossible, to keep up with it. Besides other issues which have undoubtedly escaped notice, we know of twenty-five or twenty-six distinct editions that were put out within the bounds of the single year 1562; that is, a distinct edition on the average for every fortnight. Six different printers or companies of printers published nine editions in the city of Geneva alone for circulation in France. Paris was not far behind with seven editions. Lyons had three. Saint Lô had one. Five editions were without designation of place. There are known fourteen editions of 1563, ten of 1564, thirteen of 1565—in all more than sixty editions in four years.[15] The books were of all sizes. There were diminutive volumes and stately folios. No other book of the period, not the most fascinating of romances, had such a surprising circulation. It was not curiosity that had to be gratified; it was a veritable famine for the word of God that had to be satisfied. The men, women, and children even would sing the psalms, and at any price they must have the books containing the psalms, for use at home, in the shop, especially in over two thousand congregations.

That the Reformed religion gained ground in no slight extent from the stress that was laid upon psalm-singing, is a fact that cannot be ignored; nor can it be denied that

[14] Douen, i, 561.

[15] *Ibid.*, i, 561-563.

the psalms themselves owed much of their power to the suitable and attractive music to which they were set. In the Roman Catholic churches the psalms were indeed repeated, but in a language not understood by the laity, being monotonously chanted by the clergy. The enemies of the Protestants might inveigh against the novelty of permitting every worshipper to take part in what was the priest's prerogative by immemorial usage. They might with Florimond de Ræmond condemn and ridicule as incongruous, if not positively indecorous and profane, the very idea that these holy compositions of David the king should be transferred from the church to the workshops of artisans; that the cobbler as he sewed shoes should sing the divine 'Miserere' (the fifty-first psalm) at his bench, or the blacksmith as he smote upon the anvil, drone the solemn 'De Profundis' (the one hundred and thirtieth psalm), or the baker hum some other psalm at his oven. They might make much of the confusion arising in a great congregation when in one part of the vast building in which they were assembled the singers were engaged in repeating one verse and in a distant part a different one, the leader being unable by use of hands or feet to bring them into unison. They might protest that not without reason had the Catholic Church prohibited the promiscuous, rash, and indiscreet use of those holy and divine hymns dictated to David by the Holy Spirit himself, on the ground that the worship of God is not to be mingled with our ordinary actions, unless with an attention and reverence bred of honour and respect, and that a boy ought not to be permitted to delight himself at his work with the psalms as with a pastime, in the midst of vain and frivolous thoughts. They might question whether when, in the smaller congregations, the maidens raised their sweet voices in song, their hearts were as firmly directed to God as both the hearts and the eyes of the listening youth were riveted upon the fair singers.[16] Whatever the jealous enemies of the Protestants and their worship might affirm or suspect, at least they could not deny that in the popular use of the psalms lay a most attractive feature of the Protestant service.

The celebrity attained by Beza as a translator of the psalms led the national synods of France to look to him for help when the need was felt of enriching the worship of God's house with additional hymns. Late in the century, the thirteenth national synod, meeting at Montauban in 1594, requested him 'to translate into French rhyme the Hymns of the Bible, for the purpose of their being sung in the church together with the Psalms.'[17] Four years later, the fifteenth synod, of Montpellier, inserted in its records a minute to the effect that 'as regards the Hymns of the Bible which have been put in rhyme by Monsieur de Bèze, at the request of several synods, they shall be sung in the families to train the people and incline them to make public use of them in our churches; but this regulation shall have effect only until the next national synod.'[18] The fact, however, seems to be that the Huguenots took less kindly to these later poetical productions of the venerable author than to his early efforts. The hymns, sixteen in number, appeared

[16] Flor. de Ræmond, ii., 555, 625, 626.

[17] Aymon, *Tous les Synodes*, i, 185.

[18] *Ibid.*, 1, 219.

in 1595, but promptly fell into disuse. On the other hand, Marot's and Beza's psalms retained their place in the love of the Huguenots, throughout the checkered existence of French Protestantism, though with many verbal alterations dictated by changes in the French language, down almost to our own times.

CHAPTER 17

BEZA'S CONTRIBUTIONS TO HISTORY

THEODORE BEZA's direct contributions to historical science were few. He was a scholar and a teacher first, and by preference; afterwards a man of action through the strength of his convictions and the force of providential circumstances. As a teacher he wrote to inform and convince others, and readily passed from the field of calm and quiet instruction into the field of controversy, that he might refute and silence those who held different views from his, and who undertook to maintain these views by argument. As the man of action he was chiefly concerned with the future of the great cause to which he had deliberately sacrificed every prospect of wealth and promotion in his native country. Present duties left him little time to look backward, had his tastes inclined him so to do. The nearest approach that Beza ever made to entering upon the writing of history was a sketch dashed off on the spur of the moment and with a distinct bearing upon present controversies. I have already had occasion to refer to the *Life of Calvin*, as a tribute of filial love and respect to one whom he held above all others to be entitled to the appellation of father. Melchior Wolmar alone could have disputed with John Calvin the claim to be Beza's intellectual and spiritual parent. But great as was Beza's indebtedness to him who had emancipated his higher powers from the slavery of ignorance and superstition, and implanted a thirst for the truth, it was to the wonderful hold that Calvin took upon him that was due the mysterious change that made of Beza a true Reformer qualified to take up the onerous work of leader of the Church of Geneva and preëminently the counsellor of French Protestantism.

The Life of Calvin breathes in every line the deep affection and unbounded reverence in which his biographer holds him. It is no blind panegyric, but a eulogy based on firm conviction. The writer's contention is contained in two or three sentences:

'It can be affirmed (and all those that have known him will be good and sufficient witnesses to the truth of this), that never has Calvin had an enemy who, in assailing him, has not waged war against God. For from the time that God introduced His champion into the lists, it may well be said that Satan has selected him, as though having forgotten all the other challengers, for the object of his assault, and has sought to bring him, if possible, to the ground. On the other hand, God has shown him this favour, that he has conferred on him as many trophies as he has had enemies opposed to him. If therefore an inquiry be instituted into the combats he has sustained from within for doctrine's sake, nothing can make them appear slight but the diligence he has used so as not to give his enemies leisure to recover their breath, and the steadfastness God has conferred on him never to yield, be it ever so little, in the Lord's quarrel.'[1]

[1] *Discours de Theodore de Bèze contenant en bref l'histoire de la vie et mort de maître Jean Calvin.* In *Œuvres Françoises de Calvin* (Paris, 1842), 4.

In carrying on these struggles with God's enemies, of whom Beza gives the formidable list, and wherewith he occupies many pages of his treatise, he does not deny that the subject of his biography was vehement and by nature prone to anger, but maintains that that vehemence in God's service assumed a truly prophetic type and invested him with a majesty apparent to all.

'Those who shall read his writings and shall seek the glory of God in uprightness, will there behold the shining of the majesty whereof I speak,' says the admiring writer. 'As for those who at the present time treat religion as they treat political affairs, being colder than ice in regard to the affairs of God, more aflame than fire in what concerns themselves, and call anger everything that is more frankly said than pleases them; as he never tried to please that kind of people, I also shall make it a matter of conscience not to amuse myself with answering them. What then would these wise men say, these men so moderate (provided that God alone be in question), if they had had experience of such anger from closer at hand? I feel confident that they would have been as much displeased as I myself esteem, and shall all my life long esteem, myself happy to have been the hearer of so great and rare an excellence, both in public and in private.'[2]

To Theodore Beza has been commonly ascribed the authorship of an extensive work that appeared in three volumes at Antwerp in 1580. The title in translation reads: *Ecclesiastical History of the Reformed Churches in the Kingdom of France; wherein are truthfully described their revival*

[2] *Ibid.*, 18.

and growth from the year 1521 until the year 1563, their laws or discipline, synods, persecutions both general and particular, the names and labours of those who have happily toiled, the cities and places where they were established, with the account of the first troubles or civil wars.

Of the value of this history too much cannot be said. It is the earliest, as it is the fullest, account of the first forty years of the Reformation in France. It is accurate, thorough, authentic. There is no pretence of anything like fine writing, the author being quite content with the simple statement of events as they occurred. This being its object, its author has not hesitated to incorporate into his narrative extensive passages in which the phraseology agrees word for word with passages in other contemporary Huguenot writings, such as the *Histoire de l'Estat de France sous le Règne de François II*, attributed to Regnier de la Planche, the *Commentaires* of Pierre de la Place, the *Martyrology* of Jean Crespin, and others. Documents of importance are inserted without change or abridgment. The stories of the growth and development of individual churches are reproduced apparently in the very words of the local accounts forwarded to Geneva or Paris. In short, it is a compilation laboriously and judiciously made, the general trustworthiness of which has been established beyond controversy by a comparison with information derived from other sources, and, within our own days, more than once corroborated by the unexpected discovery of official documents long hidden from the knowledge of men. Who the true author was will perhaps never be known. It was certainly not Beza, although he was a friend of Beza and doubtless received much help from Beza in the collection of materials for the composition of the work. This is evident from a mere inspection of the book itself. The writer speaks of Beza uniformly in the third person. He is prevented by no feeling of modesty from praising Beza's great speech at Poissy, asserting that it was delivered in a manner very agreeable to all those who were present, as the most difficult to please subsequently admitted, and that it was listened to with remarkable attention until the orator reached the point in his discourse which the prelates chose to make an occasion for their noisy interruption.[3] He refers to conversations which he had himself held with Beza; as where he says: 'Beza made no answer for the moment because, as I have since heard him say, he was satisfied with replying to the chief point without touching upon what was accessory.'[4] He inserts an address made by Beza to Queen Catharine de Medici in the name of the Protestant ministers in the great council chamber of the castle of Saint Germain, prefacing it with the remark that it was 'as follows, so far as could be gathered.'[5] But the inference drawn from the contents of the work that it was written by someone else than Beza is converted into certainty by a passage in a letter to the Landgrave of Hesse, from the hand of Beza himself, who, in sending a copy of the history, soon after its publication, commends it both for its substance and for the fidelity and absence of all literary embellishment with which it is written, 'although

[3] *Histoire Ecclés.*, i, 578.

[4] *Ibid.*, i, 646.

[5] *Ibid.*, i, 781.

the author has suppressed his name, fearing that truest of sayings, "Truth begets hatred."'[6]

Somewhat more than a mere collection of eulogies, yet decidedly less than a series of unprejudiced biographies, was a book, the genuine work of Beza, that saw the light of day in the same year 1580. It bore the title *Icones* (Images), with a sub-title showing that it consisted of 'True Portraits of the men, illustrious for learning and piety, by whose ministry chiefly, on the one hand, the studies of good letters were restored, and, on the other, true religion was renewed in various regions of the Christian world within our memory and that of our fathers; with the addition of descriptions of their life and works.' It was a veritable gallery wherein the reader seemed to pass successively in front of not far from one hundred picture-frames, intended to be filled by correct representations of the most famous characters of the modern religious world. The desire of the author had indeed outrun his ability. Over one half of the places were unoccupied, and the descriptions confronted blank spaces which the reader was exhorted, if possible, to supply with the necessary canvases. None the less were the rude delineations of the more fortunate subjects calculated to deepen in the reader's mind the impression made by those heroic characters that had played a prominent part in the religious affairs of the century. A few representatives of earlier centuries were there in their appropriate places—the forerunners or advance-guard in the great procession,—Wyclif, Hus, Jerome of Prague, and Savonarola; but the majority were men of contemporary times,

[6] Heppe, 382, 383.

or, at least, of times within the memory of men still alive. To anyone that remembers the close connection which the Reformers always recognised as existing between the progress of letters and the advance of pure religion, 'it will not be startling to find occupying no inconspicuous place not only the great humanist Erasmus, of Rotterdam, in company with his rival Reuchlin, but Francis I, of France, as the patron of learning and of the Renaissance, with the corps of literary men with whom he and his sister surrounded themselves—Budé, Vatabie, and Toussain—while Michel de l'Hospital, Scaliger, and the great printer Robert Étienne, or Stephens, were not far off. Clément Marot, the translator of one third of the psalter, had his own place as a reward for 'the extreme usefulness to the Churches of the work which he had accomplished, a work deserving eternal remembrance'; despite the fact, recorded by his appreciative continuator, that the poet had never, even to the last days of his life, amended his bad morals, acquired during a protracted residence at court, that worst of teachers of piety and honourable deportment. Apart from the pictorial illustrations, the *Icones*, notwithstanding the brevity of the sketches, constitute an important source of trustworthy information, to which we willingly admit our indebtedness on more than one occasion. For if the spirit of high appreciation pervades the work, the words of panegyric are, for the most part, reserved for the epigrams that are interspersed—a species of composition to which Beza was much addicted even down to his latest years.

No more convenient place than this may occur to make a passing reference to the circumstance that Beza interested himself in the matter of the correct pronunciation both of the Latin and Greek languages and of the French, and published short treatises on the subject of the first two in the years 1580 and 1587, and of the third in 1584. This last treatise, of which copies have now become so extremely scarce as to be practically unobtainable, possesses a real value as a historical discussion of the fluctuations of Beza's native tongue.

CHAPTER 18

BEZA THE PATRIOTIC PREACHER—BEZA AND HENRY IV'S APOSTASY

1590–1593

The patriotism which Beza had always exhibited in behalf of the little commonwealth which he chose to be his adopted country, had a fresh opportunity to display itself in the new dangers that menaced Geneva in the years from 1590 to 1592. The peril came from the persistent efforts of an implacable enemy, the Duke of Savoy. To the exposure to actual warfare were added the discomfort and losses of a state of virtual siege, emphasised from time to time by an approach to a real famine of bread. There was dissension at home. If the greater part of the citizens did not falter in their purpose, there was no lack of faint-hearted men, even among the citizens, men who would have been glad to purchase safety with submission. But in the crisis of the peril the voice of Beza was raised in no irresolute tones proclaiming from the old pulpit of the church of Saint Pierre the same doctrine that he had advocated more than a generation before. The sermons which he preached—he believed they would be his last—were intended to be a testimony and, so to speak, a testament containing a final recapitulation of the teaching of a lifetime. He inculcated, on the one hand, repentance and amendment of life in the sight of God, and, on the other, a bold and unflinching maintenance of the rights and the liberties of the republic. The war was unavoidable. It was also just, because waged in self-defence. Seldom has an orator of threescore years and ten more vigorously or more eloquently set forth the motives for a hearty and hopeful prosecution of an honourable struggle. Let me give a single passage which has deservedly called forth the admiration of an acute writer of recent times,[1] who, referring to its construction formed altogether on classical models, well observes that we might almost fancy that we were listening in Athens itself to the voice of Pericles exhorting his fellow-citizens to persevere in carrying on the Peloponnesian War.

'Humanly speaking,' says Beza, 'common sense of itself teaches us to lay down life for the salvation of our country and for a just freedom. And, before going any farther, people of Geneva, how often, in conflict against the same enemies, have your fathers, when reduced to the last extremity, maintained very bravely that liberty which they have left you—a liberty which I also hope and dare assure myself that, with the Lord's help, you will preserve to the very end! And this for a reason still more just than that which all your predecessors had. For, not to mention the yoke of a miserable slavery which men would impose upon us, it is God's glory and truth, it is our souls, our conscience, our eternal salvation that are now at stake, whatever colour or pretext may be alleged to the contrary. As for all the fine promises that may be made to you on this point, have you not made

[1] A. Sayous, *Études Littéraires sur les Écrivains Français de la Réformation*, i, 306.

proof enough of what the good faith and the honesty of those with whom you have to do amount to? And as to us, gathered here from so many different places, who have found here not an Egypt, but all gentleness and kindness, can it be that there should be found one in the midst of us that would consent, in so cowardly a manner and with such base ingratitude, to leave the home under the shelter of which we have been received, rather than show by our deeds, and until the last breath of life, that it was zeal for the glory of God alone, and the desire to be fed with his holy word, and to serve him purely, that made us renounce all the advantages of this world in order to obtain that pearl of great price which we have found and which illuminates us in this place? I do not believe it, nor is it this that leads me to speak. I speak solely for the purpose of persuading those that may be in doubt, and confirming those that may in any way be wavering.

'But let us consider whether the difficulties are such and so great as they are represented to be. If it be a question of provisions, it cannot be said that there is a lack as yet. If in this circumstance we do not recognise the great and extraordinary kindness of God, experienced more than once within a few years, when not only war, but famine, from far and near, threatened to be immediately upon us, shall we not deserve by our ingratitude that what we fear and still worse may befall us? I ask, upon his conscience, if there is a person in this assembly who, had he thought that this war would last three months only, would have dared to promise himself that there would be a market for the purchase of the necessaries of life in Geneva? Yet God has brought this to pass and still continues it, after the loss of harvest and vintage, after so many fires and the devastation of the whole region. And what shall make us distrustful respecting the future, if it be not forgetfulness of the past? What! shall those miserable Parisians and other conspirators against their king go so far as to eat their horses and asses, instead of renouncing what they have so miserably undertaken, and can it be that we should lose courage so soon in so just and necessary a defence of our property, our lives, and our souls?

'Our money has given out. Perhaps our enemy is not in less perplexity than we are. But, however that may be, he that has provided for us hitherto is not dead, he will never die. And were those to fail us who serve us only for money's sake, let us boldly say that we should have lost nothing whereon we ought to have leaned. A single man armed with faith toward God, with zeal for his glory, and with love of his country, will be worth a thousand hirelings. The chief captains are confined to their beds in consequence of disease or wounds. So be it; God will raise them up again when it shall please him, and when they shall be needed. We shall then have learned from experience more than once, to the great astonishment of the captains themselves, that the arm of the God of hosts is not dependent upon either the prudence and experience of captains or the valour of soldiers to such a degree that he cannot do his work all by himself, when it so pleases him. And when will it please him? When those who fear him and trust in him have need.

'We have been twice beaten with rods within a few days; but let not our enemies boast. It is neither their courage nor their strength that has done this, but our fault and rashness. To go back to the source of this disaster, it is our too great and long-continued errors that God has determined to chastise very lightly and for our great good, if he be pleased to grant us grace to amend our ways. The ten tribes of Israel in the very just and necessary war against Benjamin lost forty thousand men in two battles; yet they did not desist and happily accomplished what they had justly begun. And, I pray you, ought this sortie, which met with poor success in consequence of our great mistake, to have more power to astonish us and lead us to adopt disorderly plans than over six stout and stiff encounters against a larger force of our adversary shall have to encourage us when we have God before us and with us? If the Lord demands our lives as a sacrifice for his glory, what greater happiness could we desire than to pass from this life into life everlasting in so just a defence of the cause of the Lord and of our country together? And those who, by reason of a lack of the true and holy steadfastness of which we speak, may be disposed through cowardice to abandon our standard, whereon the name of Jesus Christ is inscribed, whither shall they flee to escape from his hands?

'Now this is not spoken, my brethren, for the purpose of trumpeting the war, to which may our good God and Father be pleased to put a good and happy end. But in order that we may reach it, let us not take counsel of distrust or of an inordinate apprehension of the difficulties that offer. But knowing how we entered upon the war, let us commit ourselves to him who is the safe refuge of the oppressed and who requites the proud and ambitious. Let us acknowledge and correct the faults because of which what had been well and holily resolved upon has not always been carried out in like manner. Let us ask him for the increase of zeal unto his glory, and of the faith needed in the midst of such tempests, that we be not swallowed up of them, but reach the haven through all these winds and storms. Let us not join his arm to the arm of flesh; but commit ourselves to him with such prudence as it may please him to give us, as well respecting the means as respecting the time of our deliverance. Let us keep bound and close, first to him, the strongest of the strong, and then to one another, by a true mutual love, so as at last to say with David: "I waited patiently for the Lord, and he inclined unto me." So doing, what have we to fear, since God is for us, and death itself is made for us the entrance into the true life? Otherwise, we must needs come to what was published in the camp of God's people in the matter of war: "What man is there that is fearful and fainthearted? let him go and return unto his house, lest his brethren's heart melt as well as his heart." But I dare to hope that none such shall be found, and that rather the great God of hosts will show us his great wonders. Amen.'[2]

It is a somewhat singular circumstance that so staunch a Protestant, so fearless an advocate of the principles of the Reformation as Theodore Beza should have been misrepresented as actually approving, if not applauding, the act of apostasy by which Henry IV secured undisputed possession of the crown of France at the price of the denial of his conscientious convictions. Still more strange is it that it is not a Roman Catholic, but a Protestant biographer of

[2] Sayous, i, 308-314.

the Reformer and a writer of no mean repute, Friedrich Christoph Schlosser, who makes the paradoxical assertion, maintaining that Beza gave a signal proof that he was far removed from a blind fanaticism, in that, instead of lamenting the king's defection, he regarded that defection as a necessary step to heal the wounds of a country rent asunder by religious dissension.[3]

In point of fact, so far from acquiescing in Henry's defection, Beza opposed it with all his might. Using the freedom of an old friend, he wrote earnestly in advance to dissuade the king from showing any weakness. His letter has been brought to light and shows that Beza, at seventy-four years of age, had lost none of his old-time vigour. Apprehending the increasing severity of the attacks to which Henry would certainly be exposed in the conference with the Roman Catholic prelates for which the time of meeting was already determined upon, the Reformer tells the monarch that the prayers of his fellow-believers continually rise to heaven that by his steadfastness he may win in the sight of God and man a crown far more precious than the two earthly crowns (of France and Navarre) which were already divinely conferred upon him, although as yet he had not come into complete possession of them. He therefore begs him to see to it that, in the coming conference for instruction, the truth shall be provided with good and sufficient advocates as against the teachers of falsehood, and that only such arms shall be allowed as ought to be employed in this spiritual combat. Let not the king permit himself to be dazzled by the glitter of alleged antiquity and of Fathers

[3] *Leben des Theodor de Beza* (Heidelberg, 1809), 272.

and Councils of the Church, but insist on an appeal to the Holy Scriptures alone, all additions thereto of whatever kind having first been removed. Then let the world know that he enters into this conference, not because he is in doubt or irresolute respecting a religion in which he has been nurtured from his infancy, but because he would have all men know that he is a lover of truth, and neither a heretic nor a relapsed person, as there are some that dare to affirm. Let Henry make it understood that he cannot and will not suffer violence to be done to his own conscience, as he will never use violence toward the conscience of others. Let him therefore humble himself and from the bottom of his heart pray for a truly contrite spirit, to the end that having obtained pardon for everything wherein he has offended, being a man as he is, God may not take away from him His Holy Spirit, without whom it were far better to have been only a simple private person rather than a king or prince, yea, never to have been born at all rather than live and draw upon himself a condemnation so much more severe as he has received more favours from the Creator. As to the difficulties of his position, let Henry ask himself whether he has not by the grace of God encountered and overcome greater perils from his childhood up. Has he never been accompanied by fewer friends? Has he never been more destitute of human help?

Here Beza could scarcely have been more frank and insistent.

'Have not your most faithful servants been massacred, as it were, in your very arms? And how many times has your life been at the mercy of your enemies, in thousands and thousands of ways? Thereupon, what has become of the enemies of God and your enemies, against whom he has stretched forth his powerful arm, yea, often when you could not have imagined it? Have not those enemies that remain still to do with the same Judge and for the same cause? Has that great God changed in his power against his hardened enemies, or in his will to maintain and raise up his own servants, when and in such manner as it shall please him? The issue can never be other than very good and very happy for those that follow him without straying from the path by which he leads them. … Moreover, Sire, we are assured that, over and above what we have said, and all that could be said on this point, you have not forgotten and never will forget that precious sentiment of which, as we have learned, you were so expressly reminded by the late queen, your mother of immortal and most blessed memory, in her last will and testament, namely, that "God knows them that honour him and casts dishonour on them that dishonour him." Nor also, as we believe, have you forgotten that excellent speech which God put into your heart and into your mouth to utter in the midst of alarms, as it has been reported to us: "If it be my God's will that I reign, I shall reign, despite any attempt to prevent me; and if it be not his will, neither is it mine." They were words worthy of a king Most Christian both in name and in fact. Such God grant that you may always be, for his glory and for the establishment of your France, and may your Majesty remember the firmness of the poor city of Geneva, for religion's sake reduced to great straits,—Geneva that is little in power, but very sincere in its attachment to your service.'

The letter closed with a reference to the instructive example of King David, rescued from a thousand deaths, miraculously carried to the throne, and, after exposure for years to civil war, finally placed in full possession of his regal rights; and with a prayer that Henry might surpass even David, by avoiding David's faults and imitating David's virtues.[4]

The author of so sturdy a plea for manly perseverance amid temptations to weakness would have been slow to approve the pusillanimous surrender of principle made by Henry IV, on July 25, 1593, at the abbey of Saint Denis. He would have been the last man on earth to applaud the Abjuration as a necessary step to heal the wounds of his unfortunate kingdom, or, to use a more modern phrase, as a disinterested sacrifice of personal preferences upon the altar of patriotism.

[4] Beza to Henry IV, June, 1593, in *Bulletin*, i, 41-46. *The Huguenots and Henry of Navarre*, ii, 334.

CHAPTER 19

BEZA'S LAST YEARS IN GENEVA

THE last twenty or twenty-five years of Beza's life at Geneva were years of diminishing activity, but not of idleness. Burdens too heavy for his impaired health were gradually thrown off, but there remained a wide range of labours useful to Church and Republic.

His property did not, we may believe, place him among. the wealthy citizens of Geneva. It sufficed for his wants and not only made him independent of others, but permitted him to gratify his well-known hospitality and liberality. Thus it was that, on occasion, when the University lost its professors whom it had no means of paying, Beza was glad to carry on the work of instruction at his own charges, until the advent of better times.

With the same gratitude to Heaven with which in his autobiography he chronicles the fact that he was born of a noble Burgundian family, he alludes in his later years to the comparative ease of his pecuniary circumstances. He was no indigent refugee. In dedicating the first edition of his collected theological works to Sir Thomas Mildmay (in February, 1570), he stated it as his chief reason for so doing, that the English knight had in times of great calamity generously relieved the necessities of the poor exiles who had forsaken their native land for the Gospel's sake.

'Since then,' he adds, 'I also am one of their number—by no means indeed needy, by God's kindness, but nevertheless so united with them by the same spirit in Christ, that whatever things befall them I regard as my own,—I have believed that I could not escape the vice of ingratitude, unless I gave expression to the respect in which I hold you, by proffering these volumes as a pledge. The time is most opportune; since I had them in my hands at the very moment when the announcement reached me of your benevolence toward our poor students.'

Evidently the Rector of the University of Geneva was not dependent upon the scanty emolument, irregularly paid, of his office, but had retained or recovered no insignificant part of the family inheritance.[1] If the sight of the honourable position attained by Beza, the professor at Lausanne, had affected deeply his father and brothers, who had learned of his departure from France with great displeasure, the admiration of the survivors knew no bounds when, at the

[1] M. Charles Borgeaud refers (*Bulletin*, xlviii [1899], 64) to the fact that a number of Beza's scholars lived under his roof and ate at his table, and adds: 'This great man, who was the counsellor of so many kings and princes, the incontestable head of a powerful party, and the spiritual director of a republic, was throughout his whole life obliged, in view of the slenderness of his resources, to have boarders in his home. To one of these last, George Sigismond of Zastrisell, he sold his library (for six hundred gold crowns).' The, truth seems to be that while Beza's means were ample for his personal wants, he was so liberal in his gifts to every good work, including the University, and to every deserving applicant for his assistance, that he could put to good account every little addition to his income. He was childless, and his house could accommodate without inconvenience additional guests. He and his wife were of a social disposition, and were not averse to having the companionship of young people, if of congenial tastes.

court of France, about the time of the Colloquy of Poissy, their kinsman gained such distinction as he could not possibly have acquired through the favour and patronage of his Roman Catholic connections. One circumstance, a result of Beza's voluntary withdrawal from France in 1548, has not been noticed. A year or more had elapsed since he reached Geneva, when the 'procureur general,' or king's attorney, attached to the Parliament of Paris took cognisance of the fact. As an absentee Beza was summoned to appear before the court within the space of three days, and, having failed to present himself, was, on the last day of May, 1550, condemned to be executed in effigy, all his property being declared forfeited to the king. The sentence was never published or executed. Fourteen years later, both Henry II and Francis II being now dead, the Reformer obtained from Charles IX (August 1, 1564) a formal annulment under the great seal of France and accompanied by honourable expressions. It was the king's will, moreover, that Beza should enjoy, in company with all his other subjects, the full benefits of the edict of pacification.[2] The document was a complete refutation of the malignant accusations of Beza's enemies.

This was three years after the Colloquy of Poissy. To the period of the colloquy itself belongs a touching incident of family history. The Reformer was unexpectedly visited at court, probably at Saint Germain, by his brother Nicholas, toward the end of September, or at the beginning of October, 1561. The brother brought the intelligence that the aged

[2] Baum, i, 67, inserts a part of the document, which is in the great collection of the late Col. Henri Tronchin, at Geneva.

father—he was seventy-six years old—was fast declining in health, and was anxious to see his son Theodore at Vézelay before he died.[3] The latter dutifully promised to go there on his return to Geneva. But, as we have seen, the return was long deferred. The colloquy was followed by private conferences, the conferences by the Assembly of Notables, and there was no one whom the queen-mother and the royal council regarded it more important for the peace of France to detain at court than Beza. With the passage of time, Pierre de Bèze became more urgent. In a letter written to his son in French, which Beza translated and inserted in his own letter of November 25, 1561, to Calvin, he said:

'That you have not yet come, my son, I forgive, because you have wisely placed public affairs before private. But see to it that you remember also what you owe a parent, and that you do this as soon as possible, when you shall be permitted. I desire that your brother also, who is there, should come with his wife, and that you should summon your wife also when you come. For I have resolved in the presence of you all, my children, to make my will, and, if so it please God, to die. Consequently you will do me a grateful service if you should be able to bring also from her monastery your sister, who is now my only daughter.'[4]

It was an unfortunate conclusion to the matter that Beza and his father after all did not meet again. The civil war broke out. It became impossible for Beza to traverse Burgundian territory, and the long-looked-for opportunity never came to reach Vézelay before his father's death.

[3] *Ibid.*, ii, 458.

[4] Text in Baum, ii, documents, 136.

I have said that Beza's burdens were somewhat lessened as the years passed on. Let it not be supposed, however, that they were, until the very last, what most men would call light. In a letter to Melanchthon's son-in-law, Gaspard Peucer, written in 1594, we find a few lines telling us what he could and did accomplish at seventy-five years of age. 'With the exception of a trembling of the hand that almost prevents my tracing a line, I am well enough, thank God! to preach every Sunday and to deliver every fortnight my three theological lectures. The auditorium is pretty well filled for these trying times. I am overwhelmed with occupations of different sorts and infinite in number—not those which depend on my office and to which I am accustomed by virtue of it, but occupations that come every instant from without, difficulties that must absolutely be met and solved, of which you can easily imagine the multitude and importance in this whirlwind of war that drags us along. Thus it is that in the midst of agitations, I struggle and am nearing the end of my course, with my spirit as much as possible on high.'[5]

Meanwhile Beza found time to give a careful and final revision to the French version of the Bible in common use among Protestants. This was essentially the translation made by Robert Olivetanus, a cousin of John Calvin, regarding which the most interesting circumstance was that the Waldenses of Piedmont, out of their deep poverty, had collected the sum, enormous for them, of fifteen hundred

[5] I find this quotation in Charles Borgeaud's valuable monograph on 'Theodore Beza and the Academy of Geneva' (*Bulletin*, xlviii [1899], 64), to which I am indebted for a number of interesting particulars.

gold crowns, to pay the expenses of the printing, in 1535, by Paul de Wingle, in the village of Serrières, near Neufchâtel.[6] Calvin and others had laboured to perfect it. Now Beza and his colleagues—especially Corneille Bertram, who held the chair of Hebrew—gave it a further revision. Thus was developed the famous 'Bible of the Pastors and Professors of Geneva,' which, from 1588 on to almost our own times, has passed through a multitude of editions and exercised a vast influence on successive generations of readers. The remarkable preface was written by Beza at the request of the Venerable Company of Pastors.[7] The Library of Geneva still boasts among its many objects of interest a richly bound copy of this Bible, bearing the arms of France and Navarre, which the Council of the city had had prepared for presentation to Henry IV. Its companion volume, similarly prepared for his sister, Catharine of Bourbon, was graciously accepted by her. But Henry, when his copy reached the court, was about to abjure, and the presentation, which would at the time have led to embarrassing complications, was deferred until some favourable juncture might arise, and the Bible ultimately returned to Geneva.[8]

Of all the lectures in the University, those of Beza were naturally the best attended. The students of all the faculties made it a point to be present at them, no matter what part of the Bible he happened to be commenting upon. It was the Epistle of Paul to the Romans when young Louis Iselin, in 1581, wrote a letter to his uncle which has come down to

[6] For a fuller account, see *Rise of the Huguenots*, i, 233; and for a copy of the title-page, *Bulletin*, i, 82.

[7] *Bulletin*, xlviii, 65-67.

[8] *Ibid.*, *ubi supra*. Baedeker, *Switzerland*, 204.

us. Beza's lecture hour alone was announced by the ringing of the bell of the cathedral of Saint Pierre, as if calling to a religious function, and precisely as it used to ring for the lectures of John Calvin before the University was instituted.[9]

Nor was this strange. Beza was the first citizen of Geneva, the man who was always at his post, however it might be with others, the one man whom everybody went to see on arriving, and again before his departure. No student was well satisfied with himself unless he took away a letter of commendation from the old patriarch, or, at the very least, an album in which was inscribed his characteristic signature with some verses kindly composed for the occasion.[10] In the estimation of the University and of the burgesses, and not less in that of the outside world, Beza stood for both School and State. Every appeal to foreign princes or foreign commonwealths for one or the other either originated from him or was urged under his patronage. It was the authority of his great name, the memory of his great services in the past in behalf of Protestantism, that secured the great results which flowed from the appeals, the abundant funds which saved both the school and the commonwealth from a destruction which otherwise might have overtaken both almost at any moment in a long succession of years. So long as he lived, such was his high standing, such were his relations with the Protestant sovereigns of Europe, that they made of him, as it were, a permanent minister of foreign affairs.[11]

[9] *Bulletin*, xlviii, 63, 64.

[10] An example of such an inscription by Beza in a student's album is reproduced in facsimile in *Bulletin*, xxxvi, 82.

[11] Borgeaud, *ubi supra*, 75 *et passim*.

In the year 1588 Beza's wife died of the plague after a married life of forty-four years. She was the Claude or Claudine Desnoz whom he had espoused secretly, but before witnesses, three or four years before leaving France, afterwards confirming and ratifying his engagements in the presence of the church, immediately upon his arrival at Geneva. The union, although childless, had otherwise proved a source of unmingled happiness. The wife, whom he had married for love and in an irregular manner, was devoted, affectionate, and helpful. Her husband celebrated her virtues and his own grief in a long consolatory poem addressed to the eminent Jacques Lect, a member of the Council of Geneva, who, not long after the death of Beza's wife, had been called to pass through a similar affliction.[12]

Not many months, apparently, after Claudine's sudden death, Beza married a second wife, Geneviève del Piano, the widow of a Genoese refugee. Being now in his seventieth year, and somewhat of a victim to rheumatism, he had been urged to this step by his friends, who wished to provide him with a companion in his loneliness. As the expressions of his joy over his new union were moderate, so the results were satisfactory to the full measure of his wishes and prayers.

'Here again, esteemed friend and very dear brother,' he wrote to Pastor Grynæus, of Basel, August 20, 1588, 'here again, by the advice of friends, and led by the very many inevitable ills of old age to seek for the help of another, I have returned to matrimony. I have taken to wife a widow approaching her fiftieth year, so adorned, according to the testimony of all good people, with piety and every matronal

[12] Schlosser has inserted it in his *Leben des Theodor de Beza*, 290.

virtue, that a wife more suitable and more to my mind could not fall to my lot. Regarding this blessing of God toward me, I wish you to render thanks to him with me, and to join your prayers to mine that the sequel may correspond to this commencement.'[13]

Beza had no children by either of his wives.

The even tenor of the aged Reformer's later years was interrupted by a curious attempt at conversion. A young ecclesiastic of noble family, born at Sales, a castle belonging to his family in the neighbourhood of Annecy, was at this time engaged in a brilliant work of proselytism which was to render the name of Francis of Sales famous throughout Christendom. It has been the boast of his friends and admirers, that by his instrumentality no fewer than seventy thousand Protestants, constituting almost the entire population of the district of Chablais, east and south of the Lake of Geneva, were brought into the bosom of the Roman Catholic Church. His methods have been represented as purely spiritual, inspired by love and carried out in gentleness. In reality they were an appeal to worldly considerations, backed by a display of military force and characterised by cruelties such as have rarely been exceeded in the history of religious intolerance. The conversion of Chablais was a foretaste of the Revocation of the Edict of Nantes; for the Dragonnades of the Duke of Savoy were only the counterpart, on a smaller scale, of the 'booted missions' organised under Louvois and executed by Foucault and the other servile intendants of Louis XIV. The future

[13] Inedited letter of August 20, 1588. Copy in Baum Collection, MSS., French Prot. Society.

FRANCIS OF SALES

Saint Francis of Sales was the prototype of the prelates of that monarch's court.[14]

It was while engaged in the reduction of the Protestants of Chablais that a suggestion was made to Francis of Sales that he should try his skill in bringing over to Roman Catholicism Theodore Beza, the hero of many an intellectual contest and the famous Protestant champion. Beza was born in 1519, early in the century. Sales was born in 1567, when two thirds of the sixteenth century had elapsed. In 1597, the former was consequently almost an octogenarian, the latter was barely thirty years old. What a triumph would it be if the experienced Goliath of the heretics were to be overthrown by a well-directed pebble from the sling of the youthful David!

Francis of Sales was moved to make the attempt by a papal brief of which his nephew has given us a translation:

'Dear and well-beloved son: We have been informed of the piety that is in you and the zeal you have for the honour of God, a thing that has been agreeable to us. The messenger will intimate to you in our name certain matters which concern the glory of God and which we have much at heart. You will employ herein all the diligence which we promise ourselves from your prudence and affection to the Holy See. At Rome, October 1, 1596.'

All accounts agree that Francis of Sales made several visits to Beza at his home in the city of Geneva, and that he was met with kindness. Beza was, says Auguste de Sales, the future saint's nephew and biographer, 'a handsome old man of about seventy years, who affected an appearance

[14] See *The Huguenots and Henry of Navarre*, ii, 472, 473.

of gravity'; and his visitor, 'on entering his abode, did not forget the dictates of civility in saluting him, as also Beza received him very courteously.' According to the same authority, Francis introduced the conversation with a jest, of no great merit certainly, but sufficient to draw a hearty laugh from his indulgent host. It consisted in a play of words, made on the spur of the moment, upon an inscription which had caught the guest's eye below a portrait of Beza's great predecessor. By the slight change of two or three words in the Latin verses, Francis of Sales, without marring the metre, had made Geneva from 'happily' to 'insanely' listening to the words of her great teacher Calvin, and that teacher's writings 'condemned,' in place of 'celebrated,' by the pious throughout the world.

From trivialities the talk turned to things more serious, and Francis of Sales plied Beza with the question so commonly raised in contemporaneous controversy with Protestants, whether a man could not be saved in the Roman Catholic Church. To this Beza promptly answered that a man might thus be saved, not, however, by means of that multitude of ordinances and ceremonies with which Christ's teachings had been overlaid. A discussion ensued on the subject of good works which would be immaterial to our purpose, even could we know with certainty what was really said.[15]

Francis did not fail to report this interview to Pope Clement VIII, in words reproduced by his nephew:

[15] *Vie de François de Sales, par son neveu, Auguste de Sales* (1632), 133, in M. Gaberel's article, 'Tentation de Théodore de Bèze par François de Sales,' *Bulletin*, viii, 15, 16.

'I began by entertaining good hopes of the conversion of the first of Calvinistic heretics. With this object in view. I entered Geneva several times, but never had the least opportunity to speak to the man in private; until finally, three days after Easter, I found him alone and did my very best. But his heart was not moved. He is altogether stony, being inveterate in his hardness, as the result of a long series of years miserably spent. Perhaps I shall bring him back to the fold; but what is to be done?'

To which the pontiff replied in his letter of May 29, 1597:

'Your zeal is worthy of a servant of God. We approve what you have done until now, in the matter of bringing back the lost sheep. We passionately seek this divine work. Prosecute therefore, with the help of the grace of God, what you have begun.'[16]

Thus encouraged, Francis repeated his visit and entered upon new discussions, involving the question of good works and the authority of the Holy See. In the course of the conversation, as he reported, Theodore Beza made the remark: 'As for myself, if I am not in the right way I pray to God every day that He will lead me into it.' The words, for some reason or other, gave his visitor fresh hope, possibly because they were accompanied by a sigh. In a third interview he returned to the charge. His panegyrists regard it as a signal proof of his courage that he thrice exposed himself to the peril of entering Geneva and encountering enemies enraged at him by his previous visits; though certain it is that never was he safer in his life than he was within its walls. It was on this occasion

[16] *Ibid.*, 136, in *Bulletin*, viii, 17.

that, approaching Beza, as his nephew tells us, De Sales made an extraordinary speech:

'Sir, you are doubtless agitated by many thoughts, and since you recognise the truth of the Catholic religion, I do not doubt that you have the wish to return to her. She calls you to enter her pale. But it may be that you fear lest, should you return to her, the comforts of life may fail you. Ah! sir, if that be all, according to the assurance I have received from His Holiness, I bring you the promise of a pension of four thousand crowns of gold every year. In addition, all your effects will be paid for at double the price at which you value them.'[17]

Up to this point we may believe Francis of Sales's nephew. Another biographer, Marsollier, writing in the present century, in a notice prefixed to the complete works of Saint Francis of Sales, asserts that, convinced of Beza's friendly dispositions toward him and resolved to take advantage of them, Francis informed the Reformer that he had brought with him a pontifical brief, recently received, in which Beza was offered an honourable refuge wherever he might choose to go, a pension of four thousand gold crowns, the payment for his furniture and books at his own valuation, in fine all the security he might judge proper to exact.[18]

Up to this point, I repeat, we can believe narratives possibly the one a reproduction of the other, but both from Roman Catholic sources. It is otherwise, however, when Auguste de Sales makes 'poor Beza remain speechless with his eyes fixed upon the ground, and then confess that the

[17] *Bulletin*, viii, 19.

[18] Marsollier, quoted in *Bulletin*, vii, 227.

Roman Church was the mother Church, but add that he did not despair of being saved in the religion wherein he was.' Whereupon the future saint gave up the case as lost and returned to Thonon. Fortunately there are other accounts that have more verisimilitude and do less violence to our knowledge of Beza's manly dignity, to which his nearly fourscore years had lent a still greater title to respect.

'When,' adds a Genevese manuscript, 'Beza heard these odious words, a severe majesty replaced on his countenance the kindly cordiality with which he had been speaking to the young priest. He pointed to his library shelves empty of books; for these had been sold to defray the expenses of the support of a number of French refugees. Then conducting his visitor to the door, he took leave of him with the words: "*Vade retro, Satanas!*"—"Get thee behind me, Satan!"'

And an oral tradition makes Beza conclude his leave-taking with the trenchant observation: 'Go, sir, I am too old and deaf to be able to give ear to such words!'[19] But whatever may have been the particular form of De Sales's dismissal, this much is certain, that he returned whence he came without having effected his purpose. Unfortunately he or his friends had boasted of his victory before it was won. Therefore the news was spread throughout Europe that De Sales was about to lead his aged convert in triumph to be reconciled to Mother Holy Church at the See of Saint Peter. Crowds waited at Siena and elsewhere on the road to Rome for the edifying spectacle, but waited in vain. Beza never came. Others reported the story differently. The arch-heretic, Calvin's successor, had died, forsooth,

19 Gaberel's article in *Bulletin*, viii, 19.

but, before his death, he had recanted in the presence of the Council of Geneva, had begged them to be reconciled to the Romish Church and to send for the Jesuits, and had himself received absolution by special order from the Pope, at the hands of the (titular) Bishop of Geneva, Francis of Sales. Wherefore, after Beza's death, the city sent to Rome an embassage of submission. It is Sir Edwin Sandys that gives us, in his *Europæ Speculum*, this amusing account of the death-bed conversion of the Reformer, who did not die for a good period of eight years yet, and of the 'ambassadors of Geneva, yet invisible.'[20] The Jesuits took part in the matter by printing a document which Lestoile, in his Journal, says began with the words: 'Geneva, mother and refuse of heresies, now at length that Beza is dead, embraces the Catholic faith.' As for Beza himself, thus quickly blotted out of existence by popular rumour and inimical pamphleteers, it seemed good to him to vindicate both his own existence and his honour, by publishing a letter that very year and over his own name, full of the old sprightliness and setting forth with relentless sarcasm the shameless inventions of the members of the 'company of monks that lyingly assume the name of Jesus.' This and a pungent epigram called out by the same circumstances are among the very last of the products of Beza's pen that have come down to us.[21]

But up to the end of his life the passion for letters continued, and now that the time for sustained labours had clearly passed, it was chiefly in poetry that he continued to divert himself, the epigram which had been the pastime

[20] *Europæ Speculum*, 111. *The Huguenots and Henry of Navarre*, ii, 470, 471.

[21] Heppe, 315.

of his youth thus becoming the solace of his old age. The homeliest circumstance of every-day life afforded subject enough for verses—Latin verses, of course—in which the trivial occurrence was turned to spiritual account and made to bear a higher interpretation. In the freedom of familiar correspondence with his old friend, Grynæus, the pastor of Basel, he jots down, for example, the fact that that very morning of his seventy-sixth birthday, his aged servant had greeted him on awaking with news from the poultry-yard. A hen had been bought a month before and had been lost sight of at once; she just now appears, but not alone; fifteen little chickens, her progeny, follow and crowd about her.

'You see,' he writes to Grynæus, 'by this homely incident how unconventionally I treat you. I gave thanks for this increase of wealth to the Author of all good, and I saw in it—shall I tell you?—without regarding myself in this as being guilty of superstition—the presage of some special favour. I even composed on this subject an epigram, and I send it to you, in order not to leave you a stranger to these light relaxations of my mind.'

The eight verses enclosed were of faultless Latinity, but need not be transcribed here. The thought was simple but pious. The hen bought but a month ago rewards her purchaser, who expended for her but ten sous, with a whole brood of young. 'And I, O Christ full of benignity, what fruits have I returned to thee in the seventy-six years that I have lived until now?'[22]

It was five years later (1600) that a nobleman from Guyenne, happening to pass through Geneva on his way back

[22] Ad. Schaeffer, *Les Huguenots du 16e Siècle*, 150. *Bulletin*, iii, 146.

from Rome in company with the physician of the King of Morocco, as Florimond de Ræmond relates, called upon Beza. The patriarch, now past fourscore, received his visitors with all his old-time dignity, courtesy, and affability. He was clad in a long tunic that came down almost to his feet and girt with a leathern belt held by a large buckle in front. His beard was long and grey. His hair reached his well-turned shoulders. Upon his head was a broad hat of generous dimensions. Altogether the sketch drawn by Ræmond's pen is a counterpart of the famous portrait that still hangs in the Public Library of Geneva.

Beza had been writing, and still held in his hand some leaves of paper on which his visitors could see verses written and re-written with many erasures, and when he looked up and greeted them at their coming in, he remarked as he called their attention to the lines, 'This is the way that I beguile my time!' It is a pleasant view to which the historian introduces us, of a man of magnificent natural endowments and magnificent achievements in Church and State, placidly occupying the enforced leisure of old age, and striving to forget the ailments of a suffering body, by the composition of unpretending stanzas, for the amusement of himself or the chance friend that might drop in. Not so in the opinion of his suspicious visitor. We hardly know whether we should rather be diverted by the silliness or be disgusted by the malignant suggestions of the 'nobleman from Guyenne.' He could not read the verses Beza had been scribbling, and therefore used to say that he was in doubt whether they were of an amatory character or not; but, at any rate, he sighed and said to himself: 'Alas! Does this holy man, with one foot already in Charon's bark, so spend his old age! Is this the sort of meditations with which a theologian occupies himself!'[23]

Meanwhile, though apparently retired from active participation in affairs whether of Church or of State, Beza did not fail to exert himself to good purpose where anything could be done by him either for the advantage of the cause of religion or for the good of the republic of Geneva. Henry IV, in particular, entertained for him a reverence and accorded to him a consideration which even the events of the unfortunate Abjuration, and Beza's manly frankness in rebuking that Abjuration, had been unable to disturb. Nominal Roman Catholic that he was, the tone of his correspondence was unaltered.

'Monsieur de Bèze,' he writes, February 9, 1599, 'I have heard with much satisfaction of your continued good-will towards me, and that you lose no opportunity to exercise it for the advantage of my affairs. This increases still more the favour which I have always borne you, and while waiting to display it in deeds, I have been desirous to assure you anew by this message, that you could not seek for its manifestation for yourself or for others in any matter in which you will not find me greatly disposed to gratify you. Meantime I pray God to have you, Monsieur de Bèze, in his holy guard. This ninth of February, at Gandelu.'[24]

Nor were these empty words, as the event proved. In 1600, Henry, when starting out upon his Italian campaign, passed near Geneva, and encamped, at the distance of two

[23] Florimond de Ræmond, ii, 635, 636.

[24] *Bulletin*, xxxvi, 77.

leagues from that city, before the fort known as Sainte-Catherine. This fort, originally erected by the Duke of Savoy, had been a source of great annoyance and anxiety to the Genevese, ever suspicious, and not without good reason, of their neighbour and enemy. When the syndic and deputies of the city went out to congratulate the monarch, the latter inquired very kindly regarding the health of Theodore Beza and expressed a desire to see him. Despite his years, the Reformer promptly hastened to pay Henry his respects, and greeted him with a short address in the name of the pastors, which could not have been better received.

'My father,' Henry replied, addressing the Protestant patriarch in the hearing of all, 'your few words signify much, being worthy of the reputation for eloquence which M. de Bèze has gained. I take them very kindly and with all the tender feelings they deserve.'

And then upon the very spot he granted to the Genevese what Beza and his fellow-citizens had asked.

'I want to do for you,' he said, 'all that may be to your convenience. Fort Sainte-Catherine shall be torn down, and here,' pointing to the Duke of Sully, who stood by, 'is a man in whom you may trust with good reason, and to whom I now issue my commands.'[25]

The speech was the more remarkable as a testimony of affection and esteem because Henry had styled Beza 'father,' a title which, as Benoist observes, is little used by Protestants in addressing their pastors, but upon which the monks pride themselves and which they have, as it were,

[25] *Bulletin*, xxxvi, 72, based on Spon.

appropriated to themselves among the Roman Catholics.[26] They were consequently scarcely less indignant when the king applied it to Beza than they were a year later, when, before restoring Fort Sainte-Catherine to the Duke of Savoy, according to the terms of the treaty of peace, he secretly allowed the inhabitants of Geneva to destroy the walls with their own hands, a permission of which they availed themselves so gladly that, when the moment arrived for turning the fort over to their hereditary enemy, there was not one stone upon another where the walls had lately stood.[27]

The perils to which Geneva was exposed were not dissipated by the overthrow of Fort Sainte-Catherine, for Charles Emmanuel was an implacable foe whose treacherous attempts upon the republic ended only with his life. He made little account of compacts or of treaties of peace. Scarcely had two years elapsed since Henry's visit when a new and more formidable conspiracy was set on foot. The Savoyard frontier at that time ran closer to Geneva than the French frontier does at present; the canton having gained a considerable accession of territory and population in the nineteenth century. An army secretly massed on the border could traverse the intervening space and reach the walls by a few minutes' march. This is what occurred on the night of December 21, 1602, one of the longest, as it is apt to be one of the darkest, nights of the year. There were eight thousand soldiers in the force that stealthily approached the fortifications, preceded by their four generals and a picked body of troops. It is said that as the ladders were raised and

[26] Benoist, *Histoire de l'Édit de Nantes*, i, 358.

[27] See *Huguenots and Henry of Navarre*, ii, 469.

the advance-guard began to climb in the most profound silence, the Savoyards were encouraged by the whispers of the Jesuit missionaries in attendance, who said: 'Climb boldly; every round is a step heavenward!' The project had almost proved a complete success, for no one on the inside had perceived them, when a sentinel on guard gave the alarm by discharging his musket. Two hundred men had already scaled the walls and stood on the ramparts. A few soldiers had actually entered the city. The main body was approaching the gate which a traitor had agreed to open to them. But a Vaudois, Mercier by name, thwarted the plot by his presence of mind and let the portcullis fall. The citizens, awakened from their sleep, rushed to meet such of the enemy as had penetrated into the streets, and slew to the number of three hundred of the assailants. The survivors were put to flight, and retired to Savoy. Sixty-seven that were taken prisoners were afterwards ruthlessly beheaded. Of the Genevese there were but seventeen killed.

The conflict over, the people flocked to the church of Saint Pierre to render thanks to Almighty God for his wonderful interposition in their behalf. In the religious services Theodore Beza, notwithstanding his advanced age and bodily feebleness, took the most prominent part. At his bidding the worshippers with one accord chanted the words of the one hundred and twenty-fourth psalm, turned into verse by the Reformer himself a half-century before, than which no jubilant words more appropriate to the occasion could have been found in a collection that lends itself wonderfully to the expression of every phase of human experience.

'If it had not been the Lord who was on our side,
Now may Israel say;
If it had not been the Lord who was on our side,
When men rose up against us;
Then they had swallowed us up quick,
When their wrath was kindled against us.

'Blessed be the Lord, who hath not given us
As a prey to their teeth.
Our soul is escaped as a bird out of the snare
  of the fowlers;
The snare is broken and we are escaped.
Our help is in the name of the Lord,
Who made heaven and earth.'

On every recurring anniversary of 'The Escalade,' from that day to this, the same psalm is joyfully sung in Saint Pierre at the commemorative services; and the visitor sees upon one of the bas-reliefs of a fountain erected in 1857, on the Rue des Allemands, and known as 'The Monument of the Escalade,' a representation of Theodore Beza in the act of returning thanks to God.[28]

[28] Daguet, *Hist. de la Confédération Suisse*, 356. Baedeker, *Switzerland*, 201.

CHAPTER 20

CLOSING DAYS
1605

HONOURED for his long years of service, revered for his signal piety and the virtues that had characterised his entire life, held in special veneration as the sole survivor of the group of Reformers that glorified the first half of the sixteenth century, and now by his very aspect recalling an age long since passed, Theodore Beza spent the remnant of his earthly existence in placid contentment and with a happy anticipation of the rewards of the heavenly. As his infirmities increased, so also multiplied the sedulous attentions of his devoted friends and of his colleagues in Church and University. A touching evidence of affection and solicitude was given in the resolution adopted by his brethren of the ministry, a few months before the end, to the effect that at least two of their number should visit him daily, to inquire respecting his health, and to minister such comfort as they might be able. Thus as the flame of life flickered in the socket before quite going out, there were always friendly eyes that watched with mingled hope and fear. When for a brief moment he seemed to be snatched from the borders of the grave, there sat by his side those from whose lips the precious assurances of the Gospel were doubly precious, because recalled by friends with whom he had enjoyed sweet communion in the past. On Saturday, October 12, 1605, he listened with folded hands and with evident joy, as his colleague La Faye recited the words of Saint Paul, 'Therefore, being justified by faith, we have peace with God through our Lord Jesus Christ,' and discoursed respecting God's grace to the called according to his purpose, whom he has justified and glorified. On the morrow, the last day of his life, he awoke feeling so much relieved of suffering that he rose, allowed himself to be dressed, offered his morning prayer, took a few steps, and ate a little food. It was characteristic that his last thoughts before the end came were directed to his beloved Geneva, which for its own sake, and as the representative of the cause of the truth, had long been dearer to him than life itself. 'Is the city in full safety and quiet?' he asked. Then, on receiving an affirmative answer, he suddenly sank down, losing strength and consciousness at once, and in a few minutes passed peacefully away, while sorrowing friends prayed about his bedside.[1]

A great man, indeed, had fallen, over whose mortal remains all that was highest and best in Church or State in Geneva did well to weep, deploring the loss that both State and Church had sustained.

There is still in existence, saved by one of those strange freaks of fortune which occasionally preserve the most fragile of shells through the midst of the storms that dash to pieces the most strongly built frigate, a copy of the simple notice that summoned the friends to attend the last rites in Beza's honour. It runs thus in translation:

[1] Heppe, 316, 317.

Quod nauigantibus est portus, hoc migratio in aliam vitam iis, quorum pretiosa mors in oculis Domini. Quum igitur, hesternâ die, magnum illud Ecclesiæ lumen, R. vir D. Theodorus Beza, annis confectus, ex hac momentanea & ærumnosa vita ad illam, in qua est, sine perturbatione, æterna felicitas, placidè translatus sit, hodie verò sepulturæ mandandus, rogantur, Pastorum ac Professorum nomine, Illustres ac Generosi Domini Comites, Barones, Nobiles, omnes denique litterarum studiosi, qui in hac Academia versantur, vt hodie, horâ duodecimâ, postremum hunc honorem, tanto viro, ac tam piè defuncto, debitum, tribuant, vt funus ipsius prosequantur. Cujus quidem corpus, vt omnium in Christo defunctorum, σπείρεται ἐν φθορᾷ, ἐγερθήσεται ἐν ἀφθαρσίᾳ: ita vt neque mors, neque vita, nos separet ab illa dilectione, qua Deus suos prosequitur in Domino nostro Iesu Christo, qui suos à morte ad vitam transmittit. Obiit XIII. die Octobris, anni CIↃ. IↃC. V.

NOTICE OF BEZA'S DEATH AND INVITATION TO THE FUNERAL

'What the haven is to those that sail, that is the removal into another life to those whose death is precious in the eyes of the Lord. Inasmuch, therefore, as yesterday that great light of the Church, that reverend man, Doctor Theodore Beza, worn out with years, was peacefully translated from this transitory and wretched life to that other life in which there is eternal blessedness free from disquietude, and inasmuch as he is this day to be consigned to burial, the illustrious and generous lords, counts, barons, nobles, all in fine that apply themselves to letters now present in this Academy, are invited, in the name of the Pastors and Professors, today at noon, to pay this last honour due to so great a man and one that has died in so pious a manner, and to attend his funeral. Whose body indeed, like as the bodies of all that die in Christ, is sown in corruption, but shall be raised in incorruption: in such wise that neither death nor life shall separate us from the love which is in Jesus Christ our Lord, who translates his children from death to life. He died on the thirteenth of October, 1605.'[2]

In imitation of his great master, John Calvin, and in accordance with the city ordinances, Theodore Beza, before his death, had expressed a wish that his body should be interred in the public cemetery of Plainpalais, outside the walls. His preference was disregarded, and the magistrates ordered that the place of burial be in the heart of Geneva itself. It was not so much for the sake of conferring superior honour upon the great theologian and leader that

[2] The original of this mortuary notice is in the library of the French Protestant Historical Society in Paris. A facsimile is printed in that Society's *Bulletin*, xxxvi (1887), 81, and is herewith reproduced.

this resolution was reached, as to forestall the possibility of danger to the republic. A watchful enemy was in the neighbourhood, and might take advantage of the moment when all Geneva's best citizens and most valiant soldiers should have gone forth accompanying Beza's remains to the grave, to make a sudden attack upon the defenceless place. Moreover, there were rumours that the enemies of the Reformer intended at a later time to disinter his corpse and, if they exposed it to no other indignity, to carry it off in triumph to Rome. Accordingly, it was to the buildings then known as the cloisters of the cathedral church of Saint Pierre that Beza's body was carried on the shoulders of his former students, and was there laid to rest within a stone's throw of the sacred edifice where he had for so many years lectured and preached. Strange as it may appear, during the course of the eighteenth century the cloisters, having fallen into a ruinous condition, were torn down, and the tomb of Beza shared in the demolition. Whither his remains were taken is unknown. It is as impossible for the visitor to Geneva at the present time to discover the last resting-place of Theodore Beza, the pupil, as to identify the humble and unmarked grave of his master, John Calvin, at Plainpalais.[3]

Church and State pledged themselves to one another over Beza's grave to concord and a union of effort for the welfare of Geneva. Speaking through his successor in the moderator's chair, the Venerable Company recalled to memory the fact that the Reformer had been not only a shining light in the house of the Lord, but a wall of defence to the republic of Geneva, which owed to his prevalent intercession every

[3] Charles Borgeaud, in *Bulletin* (for February, 1899), xlviii, 58, 59.

honour and every favour which it had received at the hands of foreign princes. And the syndic who responded in the name of the magistracy, reciprocated the hope that, for the advantage of the common country, there might ever subsist a good understanding between Church and State. To the accomplishment of this end, he urged that all should walk in the footsteps of those two great men, John Calvin and Theodore Beza, who had so happily served the interests of the commonwealth.'[4]

[4] Gaberel, in Heppe, 316-318. Borgeaud, *ubi supra*, xlviii, 57-76.

APPENDIX

AUTOBIOGRAPHICAL LETTER OF BEZA TO WOLMAR

Prefixed to his 'Confession of the Christian Faith,' and printed in the first volume of the *Tractationes Theologiæ*, second edition, revised by the author [Geneva], 1582.

THEODORE BEZA, of Vézelay, to Melior [Melchior] Wolmar Rufus, his most respected preceptor and parent, grace and peace from the Lord.

As often as I recall my past life (and this I do very frequently as is meet), so often do your numberless acts of kindness to me necessarily come into my thoughts. And although I can in no way make you an adequate return, yet am I resolved to cherish them as becomes a man who is grateful and mindful of benefits received. Since, then, it has. pleased me to call this little book a Confession,—I have decided to join to the profession of my faith the narrative of my previous life, and indeed to commence at the very beginning. For I hope you will suffer me, as it were, to become a boy again in repeating matters the narration of which I trust will not be irksome to you nor useless to myself.

It pleased Almighty God that I should first see the light of this world in the year of our Lord 1519, on the twenty-fourth of June, the day consecrated as the birthday of John the Baptist, and in Vézelay, the ancient city of the Ædui. My parents were Pierre de Besze (Beza) and Marie Bourdelot, both of them, thank God, of noble stock (would that rather they had been imbued with the knowledge of the true God!) and of unblemished reputation. I was educated most tenderly in the paternal home. I had at that period an uncle on my father's side, Nicholas de Besze, a member of the Parliament of Paris, who was indeed himself unmarried, but was so fond of the children of his brother, that is, my father, that he would have been glad to bring them at once to his home, and spared neither expense nor diligence in having them reared in the most honourable manner. Having by chance come from Paris to visit his relatives, he was seized by a certain love for me when I was still but an infant, God even then providing for my salvation, and did not desist until he had obtained from my father the permission that, though I was still a babe at my nurse's breast, I should be taken to Paris. This, as I often remember to have heard, my mother took greatly to heart, as though foreseeing coming disaster; yet, deferring to her husband's authority, she accompanied me when I was but lately weaned, as far as Paris. Thence having returned home, not very long after she fell from a horse and broke one of her thighs, and with her own hands set it. For she was, as I have understood, much inclined, by a natural impulse according to the notions of women, to the study of physiology, and had from infancy exercised herself in such matters. Most willingly, and not without a certain dexterity, was she wont to relieve the poor in various ways of this kind; to such a degree that she was beloved by all as after a fashion their common parent. As for myself,

I account it a singular kindness of God that it was his will that I should be born of such a woman. But, to return to my subject, shortly after this, my mother was seized with a raging fever and died at the age of thirty-two years. It was a great loss to our family. She left seven children, namely, four girls and three boys, of whom I was the youngest, having not yet completed my third year.

Meantime, though I was brought up at Paris with the greatest care, I was rather dying than living; for I was so prostrated by continual languor that it was almost five years before I left the cradle. And scarcely had I left it when unfortunately I contracted a cutaneous disease from an attendant with whom as a child I was playing, ignorant of the danger of contagion. The malady was of itself obstinate, but at that time particularly severe, because the unskilfulness of the physicians, although in a very celebrated city, was such that they used only the strongest and therefore the most cruel drugs to expel the disease. My mind shudders to remember what tortures I underwent at that time, my uncle looking on with pity and trying everything to no purpose. And here, too, I wish to relate a singular example of the Divine kindness to me. Since the surgeon who had undertaken to treat me used to come to our house, and my uncle would on no consideration permit him even to lay his finger on me in his absence (so tenderly and ardently did he love me), this most humane man could no longer be the witness of such great suffering. He therefore ordered his *valet de chambre* to accompany me daily, together with a relation of mine whom he was rearing with me, and who had been attacked by the same complaint, to the house of the surgeon, since he could not even bear the sight of the latter. My uncle resided in that part of the city which is known as the 'University' [the part south of the river Seine]. The surgeon, on the other hand, lived not far from the royal castle called the 'Louvre,' the two quarters being united by a bridge that takes its designation from the Millers [*Pont des Meuniers*]. So, then, we had to cross this bridge to our daily tortures, which were particularly intolerable at that time of life. We would hurry on and the servant followed, as servants are wont to do, without watching us carefully enough. Here I remember (and my mind shudders at the remembrance) my kinsman, who even then breathed a warlike spirit, often urged that we should cast ourselves into the river that flowed below, and thus once for all deliver ourselves from our sufferings. I, being more timid by nature, was at first horrified, but afterwards, compelled by the violence of my suffering and greatly pressed by him, I promised that I would follow his example. So, then, but this one thing remained for Satan to effect our ruin, when the Lord, having compassion on us, brought it to pass that my uncle, chancing to return from court without suspecting anything of the kind, met us and, noticing that the servant followed us afar off, bade us return home and ordered that the surgeon should resume his visits to our house. Thus, then, the Lord rescued us as from the jaws of Satan himself, and put it into the mind of my uncle, as soon as I had been healed of that disease, to have me taught at home by a tutor to distinguish the forms of the letters and to unite syllables. For God was so favourable and kind that my uncle determined to devote me wholly to the study of letters.

Here again God preserved me in a marked and altogether unexpected way. For whereas I was living in that city which heretofore had been esteemed the most flourishing school of the whole inhabited world, it came to pass that, contrary to the advice of all our friends, and on a sudden impulse, rather than by calm judgment, I was sent to Orléans to you, my revered teacher, who at that time had established there a school for the training of a few select youths. Now you yourself were altogether unknown to my uncle, but by the singular providence of God it happened that on one occasion there supped with him a certain one of our kinsmen, a citizen of Orléans and a member of the king's greater council. When this man caught sight of me, he remarked that he had a son of his own of just my age, whom he had placed under the instruction of one Wolmar, a man most learned in the Greek language—a thing that was at that time quite a novelty—and possessed of wonderful skill in the training of youth, according to the judgment of Nicholas Bérauld and Pierre Stella [L'Estoile], most learned men. Thereupon my uncle, doubtless inspired thereto by God, not only welcomed the suggestion, but solemnly promised shortly to send me to Orléans, and asked his guest to be permitted to make me the companion of the latter's son.

Thus it came to pass that I reached you on the nones of December [the fifth of December] of the year of our Lord 1528—a day which I am wont with justice to celebrate not otherwise than as a second birthday. For that day was in my case the beginning of all the good things which I have received from that time forward and which I trust to receive hereafter in my future life. For, from the time when you received me, a mere boy, into your house to train me in company with pupils of great promise already more advanced in their studies, what labour did you not of your own accord undergo in forming me? What trouble did you not take in teaching me, first at Orléans, afterwards at Bourges, when the Queen of Navarre had called you thither by the offer of an honourable salary to profess Greek literature? In fine, what exertions did you not put forth in order not to appear wanting in your duty to me in any direction? For I can truly affirm that there was no famous Greek or Latin writer of whom I did not get a taste in the seven years which I spent with you; that there was no liberal study, not even excepting jurisprudence, whose elements, at least, I did not learn with you as my instructor. You wished indeed to have only a few pupils, but all these you desired so to train, that when you sent them out you might have in them so many witnesses in the family of your unbounded diligence. Nor did this expectation cheat you. A thing happened to you which has happened to very few others: I can scarcely remember that anyone left your school, excepting me alone, who did not attain to notable learning. It was, however, by far the greatest of the benefits I received at your hands, that you so imbued me with the knowledge of true piety sought in the knowledge of the word of God, as in the most limpid fountain, that I should be the most ungrateful and churlish of men did I not cherish and honour you, I say not as an instructor but as a parent. When your wife's father induced you to return from France to Germany, what stone did you and your gentle wife leave unturned to induce my father to permit me to accompany you to Germany? So much did both of you love me and so much in turn did I revere you, that it was only with the greatest reluctance that you left me behind, and only with the greatest sorrow could I tear myself away from you.

That first day of May, therefore, was fixed in my mind and will always remain there, on which I was dragged from you, and you departed toward Lyons, while I in accordance with my father's directions set out for Orléans. I do not remember nor shall I ever remember a day of greater sadness and grief.

Three days later, in the course of the year 1535, I reached Orléans with the purpose of applying myself to the civil law. But there, being strangely averse to this study, which was taught in a barbarous manner and without method, while pursuing it I spent a much greater part of my time in polite literature and in the perusal of the writers of the two [classical] languages. I took wonderful delight in the study of Poetry, to which I felt myself drawn by a certain natural impulse. This led me to have the closest intimacy with all the most learned men of that University, men who at present are enjoying the greatest honours in France. At that time they greatly incited me to join with civil law the study of polite literature and poetical culture. Here therefore before my twentieth year I composed almost all those Poems which, a few years later, I published and dedicated to you. Although there are among them several written with somewhat too great freedom, that is to say, in imitation of Catullus and Ovid, yet I by no means feared at that time, nor do I even now fear, that anybody who then knew what sort of a man I was, would judge of my moral character by these fictitious exercises. But of this hereafter.

Accordingly I thus lived in Orléans, in company with most honourable and learned men, until I was promoted to the grade of licentiate, as it is called. This occurred, I remember, on the second day before the Calends of August [the thirtieth day of July], 1539, when I had entered upon the twentieth year of my life. I then returned to Paris. My uncle and 'Mæcenas' had died some years before, but another uncle was still alive, the Abbé of Froidmont, who loved me just as much. But, good God! how important it is for us that we have friends not only rich and loyal, but also truly pious and religious! Certainly those who were most desirous of being of advantage to me came as nearly as possible to ruining me. When I reached Paris, first of all, I found that many members of Parliament, partly kinsmen and connexions, partly old friends of our family and these personally very friendly to me, had conceived great hopes of me in consequence of the opinions expressed by certain persons. To this fact was added the circumstance that I had been loaded—I a lean youth and moreover, as I testify truthfully, utterly ignorant of such matters, and in my absence—with two fat and rich benefices, the revenues of which amounted annually to seven hundred crowns, more or less. Moreover, my uncle, whose abbacy was valued at not less than five thousand crowns a year, had mentally designated me as his successor. Finally, my eldest brother, whose health was even then so infirm as to be despaired of, held certain other benefices in reserve for me. In short, I found an infinite number of snares laid for me on every side by Satan. As for myself, I shall here confess, as I ought, how matters stood. I had previously determined that as soon as I should be master of myself and should have obtained certain resources, I would leave France and go to you, preferring the freedom of a pure conscience to all other things. I used very often to beg of God with prayers and tears to hearken to me, bound as I was by this vow. But I was young and abundantly provided by my relatives with leisure, with money, with all things, in short, rather than with good counsel, when Satan suddenly threw all these things in my way. I confess that I was so allured by the empty glitter and vain enticements of these things that I suffered myself to be wholly drawn hither and thither. But why should I here relate the infinite perils in which I involved myself, casting knowledge and discretion to the winds? How often at home and abroad did I risk body and soul? Yet while the recollection of all that period cannot but be on many accounts very bitter, on the other hand the singular and incredible kindness of Almighty God to me causes me to be filled, as often as I remember them, with a certain marvellous delight, as I recognise within me the clearest and most distinct exemplifications of the fatherly care with which that best of fathers has promised to attend his elect. For though I had of my own accord strayed from the way, He never suffered me so to wander that I did not very often utter groanings and cling fast to that vow which I had made regarding an entire repudiation of the papal religion. In fine he brought it to pass that I so ordered my life that, by his singular kindness, though I deserved neither the one nor the other distinction, I was held to be in piety not the lowest among the pious, nor in culture altogether rude among the cultivated. Besides those hindrances which I have mentioned, Satan had thrown about me a triple snare, namely, the allurements of pleasure that are so great in that city, the sweets of petty glory which, in the judgment of Marcus Antonius Flaminius, himself a very learned poet and an Italian, I had attained in no small measure by the publication especially of my *Epigrams*, and, lastly, the expectation set before me of the greatest honours, to which some of the leading members of the court called me, while my friends incited me, and my father and uncle did not cease from exhorting me. Yet it was God's will that I who, wretched man that I was, had entered so perilous a path with my eyes open, should escape these dangers also. For, in the first place, that I might not be overcome by those base desires, I espoused a wife, secretly however, I confess it, and with the privity of only two pious friends, partly that I might not scandalise others, partly because I could not as yet bring myself to renounce that accursed money which I derived from priestly benefices, 'as the unclean dog cannot be frightened off from the besmeared leather' [see Horace, *Sat.*, ii, 5, 83]. There was, however, added to the rite of betrothal an express promise that I would at the very first opportunity put all hindrances aside and bring my wife to the Church of God and there publicly ratify my marriage with her, engaging meanwhile to bind myself to none of the popish orders. Both of these engagements at a subsequent time I religiously fulfilled.

Moreover the same most kind Father effected my determined rejection of that paltry glory and the honours held forth to me, to the wonder of my friends and the reprehension of most of them, who jocularly styled me 'the new philosopher.' Meantime I was still plunged in the mire. My friends urged me at length to embrace some kind of life. My uncle placed everything at my disposal. On the one side, conscience pressed me and my spouse called on me to fulfil my promise. On the other, Satan with most placid countenance used his blandishments. My income was made greater by the death of my brother. I lay as it were incapable of coming to a decision in the midst of this mental solicitude. How wonderfully the Lord had compassion upon me, I shall here most cheerfully narrate.

Lo! he inflicts upon me a very severe illness, to such a point that I almost despaired of life. What should I do, wretched man that I was, when I saw before me naught but the terrible judgment of God? What more shall I say? After infinite tortures of mind and body, the Lord, pitying his runaway slave, so consoled me that I entertained no doubts of the concession of his pardon to me. Therefore I renounced myself with tears, I asked for forgiveness, I renewed my vow openly to embrace his true worship—in short, I consecrated myself wholly to him. Thus did it come to pass that the image of death, seriously confronting me, excited in me the desire of the true life that lay dormant and buried, and that disease was for me the beginning of a true soundness. So wonderful is the Lord in that he casts down and raises up, wounds and makes whole again his children by one and the same stroke.

As soon therefore as I could leave my bed, I burst asunder every chain, collected my effects, forsook at once my native land, my kinsmen, my friends, that I might follow after Christ, and, accompanied by my wife, betook myself to Geneva in voluntary exile. Accordingly, on the ninth day before the Calends of November [the twenty-fourth of October], AD 1548, having left Egypt I entered that city, and there found what previously I could not even suspect, although I had heard the commonwealth greatly praised by certain pious men. There I took up my abode. Subsequently while I was revolving in mind what course of life I should pursue, and after I had made a visit to you, my father, at Tübingen, lo! as I anticipated nothing of the sort, the Academy of Lausanne called me thither to be a professor of Greek Literature. The illustrious Council of Bern having ratified this invitation, I was compelled to follow the call of Christ. Accordingly in the following year I came to Lausanne. There, thank God, I believe that I so lived in the society of my colleagues, most learned and excellent men, as not to displease any good person. From that place, after ten years, partly because I was desirous of giving myself altogether to Theology, partly for other reasons which need not here be recorded, I returned again, with the kind permission of the Council, to this city [Geneva] as to a most peaceful haven. It was not so much my own will that brought me, as the judgment of men of the greatest authority that compelled me to come, that I might assume the office of the sacred ministry. May the Lord supply me such strength to sustain this very weighty burden, that I may discharge its duties with some edification of the Church!

You have here, my father, a brief narrative of the entire life of your pupil, nay, rather, of your son who was too unseasonably torn away from you. I have written it, because I am wont gladly to view, and not without very great profit to myself, so many examples of the divine providence for my preservation. Nor do I doubt that you, above all others, are wont to be similarly affected by my success. I wrote this *Confession of my Faith* at first in the French language, for the purpose of satisfying my own father, whom the calumnies of certain persons had alienated from me, as though I had been an impious man and a heretic, and with the further view of winning him, if possible, to Christ in his extreme old age. Subsequently I was urged to publish it, and did not hesitate to do so. I have put it in Latin; if only I am suffered by the learned to call Latin what I have preferred to express in a simple and artless mode of speech, rather than adorn by a far-fetched and abstruse eloquence. These same subjects, I confess, have been happily set forth by many writers, especially in this century of ours, and indeed among the first (for I shall state the case as it is, despite the prattle of envy) by that great John Calvin, my second parent; who has treated of all these matters very copiously in his Institutes, and very briefly but very accurately in his *Catechism* of this Church [of Geneva]. From these books also I profess to have derived the present work. But where there is such a superabundance of viands, nothing forbids that the same feast be repeated with a slight change in the arrangement, to the great enjoyment of those that partake. Moreover, I deem most useful the zeal of those who compose short and perspicuous summaries of these controversies, in order that such persons as apply themselves to the reading of the Sacred Scriptures may have certain heads ready at hand, to each of which they may afterwards refer and accommodate what they read. In fine, I hope that some of my readers may admit that they have received some profit from this labour of mine.

Moreover I have desired to dedicate to you this treatise, whatever it may amount to, partly because it is very just that you should reap some fruit from the field which you first sowed, of such sort as can be gathered from land not over fertile; partly in order that, in place of those books of Epigrams of mine, which you desired me again to publish, you might receive this book which is infinitely better and more holy. For so far as respects them, who is there that has condemned them more than I, their unhappy author, have done, or who today detests them more? Would therefore that they might now at length be buried in a perpetual oblivion! And may the Lord, as I hope may be the case, grant that, since that which has once been done can never be undone, those persons who hereafter read writings of mine very diverse from those poems, shall rather congratulate me upon the greatness of God's goodness to me, than accuse. him who voluntarily confesses and deplores the fault of his youth. Farewell. Geneva, this fourth day before the Ides of March [the twelfth of March], AD 1560.

Monsieur et Frere.—J'espere que le present porteur ne se repentira de son voyage, estant advenu ce que luy auiez [aviéz] bien conseillé. Oultre cela, ie ne fauldroy, aydant le Seigneur, de faire ce que ie pourray pour l'instruction de son filz, comme non seulement nostre amitié le requiert, mais aussi le debvoir le nous commande. Quant a mes lettres envoyées par dela, ie souhaitte qu'elles puissent proffiter, et non seulement cela, mais aussi que chascun pense a soy de plus pres en une telle et si extreme affliction si peu considerée de tous que ie ne me puis assez esmerveiller d'une telle stupidité, laquelle vous sçavez estre des plus dangereuses maladies, et des plus approchantes de la mort. Nostre bon Dieu y vueille bien pourveoir, et face pour le moins que tous ceulx qui ne se sont encores du tout endormis, se resveillent si bien que le Seigneur quand il viendra (et qui est celuy qui sait quand il viendra?) ne les trouve dormans.

Quant a l'affaire du feu Seigneur de passy, Je vous en envoye le sommaire a la pure verité, et tel que ceste Seigneurie l'a accordé a quelcun qui l'a requis pour s'en servir. J'avois desia envoyé la prononciation du proces telle qu'elle se fait pardeça, comme vous savez. Je vous prie d'user de prudence a communicquer le tout a ceulx qu'il sera de besoin, non pas qu'on puisse ny vueille rien celer d'un tel et si clair iugement de Dieu, mais pource que ie ne vouldroye adiouster affliction aux affligez, et quoy qu'il en soit la repentance et confession du paoure homme a l'extremité, m'asseurant que le Seigneur a couvert ses faultes, me faict desirer que l'ignominie en soit aussi abolie devant les hommes, autant qu'il est expedient pour la gloire du Seigneur. Je say bien que chascun en donnera sa sentence, et que Satan ne nous espargnera. Mais i'espere que les sages se souviendront de l'advertissement du Seigneur nous defendant de iuger temerairement de noz freres, et a plus forte raison, de mal estimer de toute une Seigneurie et eglise Chrestienne, oultre ce qu'a mon advis maintenant les plus difficiles auront de quoy estre satisfaicts. Quant aux aultres, qui en iugeront comme il leur plaist, c'est a Dieu de leur fermer la bouche, auquel aussi nous appellons de toutes folles sentences données en tant de lieux contre nous. Au reste, graces a Dieu, nous suyvons nostre petit train, heureusement et paisiblement iusques a present. Les bruicts continuent et non sans apparence. Mais le Seigneur auquel nous esperons, pourvoyra a tout, s'il luy plaist. Ce sera l'endroit ou ie prieray nostre bon Dieu et pere qu'en Vous multipliant ses graces, il vous maintiene touts en sa saincte et digne garde, apres m'estre bien fort recommendé a vos bonnes prieres. De Geneve, ce 22 d'avril, 1566.

Vostre entier frere et amy,
TH. DE BESZE.

A Monsieur,
Monsieur Pithou,
A Troyes.

TRANSLATION

My dear Brother.—I hope that the present bearer will not repent of his journey, that having happened to him of which you gave him good advice. Beyond that I shall not fail, with the Lord's help, to do what I can for the instruction of his son, as not only does our friendship demand but our duty bids us. As to my letters sent to your quarters, I wish that they may be of advantage, and not only that, but also that every man may consider himself more closely in such and so extreme an affliction so little regarded by all that I cannot sufficiently marvel at such insensibility, which you know to be among the most dangerous maladies and most approaching to death. May our good God be pleased to provide well therefor, and grant at least that all those who are not yet altogether asleep, may awake so thoroughly that when the Lord shall come (and who knows when he will come?) he shall not find them sleeping.

As to the affair of the late Lord of Passy, I shall send you the summary according to the pure truth and such as this Seigniory furnished it to a person who applied for it in order to make use of it. I had already sent you the rendering of the sentence as it is practised here as you know. I pray you to use prudence in communicating the whole to those to whom it may be necessary to do so; not that it may be possible or desirable to hide anything in such and so clear a judgment of God, but because I would not add affliction to the afflicted, and, be that as it may, the poor man's repentance and confession at the end giving me the assurance that the Lord has covered his faults, make me desire that its ignominy may also be abolished in the sight of men, so far as is expedient for the glory of the Lord. I know well that everybody will pass his own judgment, and that Satan will not spare us. But I hope that the wise will call to mind the Lord's warning that forbids us to judge rashly of our brethren, and therefore with still greater reason to think ill of an entire Christian Seigniory and Church; beside that in my opinion the most captious will now have grounds for being satisfied. As to the others who will judge as they please, it is God's province to stop their mouths, and to him we appeal from all foolish judgments passed in so many places against us. Meanwhile, thanks to God, we pursue our usual course, happily and peacefully until now. Rumours continue not without colour of probability. But the Lord in whom we hope, will provide for everything, if it be his good pleasure. And hereupon I shall pray our good God and Father that multiplying his favours to you, He may keep you all in his holy and worthy care, and commend myself to your good prayers. From Geneva, this twenty-second of April, 1566.

Your devoted brother and friend,

THEODORE DE BÈZE.

To Mr Pithou,

At Troyes.

BIBLIOGRAPHY

THE CHIEF WORKS QUOTED IN THE PRESENT WORK

I. THE SOURCES AND MS. COLLECTIONS AND REPRINTS OF THE SOURCES.

Aymon, Jean, *Tous les Synodes Nationaux des Eglises Réformées de France*. The Hague, 1710. 2 vols. Contains the minutes of the twenty-nine French Protestant National Synods, 1559–1659. Prefixed to the first volume (pp. 1-283) are fifty letters written from France by the papal nuncio Cardinal Prospero di Santa Croce to Cardinal Borromeo, giving an account of the years 1561–1565, including the Colloquy of Poissy.

Baum, Coll. MSS., as referred to in the footnotes of this volume, designates a collection of many hundred copies of Beza's letters found in the libraries of Geneva, Zurich, etc., intended for use in a continuation of his great biography mentioned below. This manuscript collection is now in the Bibliothèque du Protestantisme Français, in Paris.

Benoist, Élie, *Histoire de l'Édit de Nantes*. Delft, 1693–95. 3 parts in 5 vols.

Beza, Theodore, *Icones, id est, Veræ Imagines Virorum doctrina simul el pietate illustrium*, etc. (for full title and description see page 312). Geneva, 1580.

Beza, Theodore, *Tractationes Theologicæ*. Geneva, 1582. 3 vols., fol. The Reformer's collected theological works.

Bonnet, Jules, *Letters of John Calvin* compiled from the original manuscripts and edited with historical notes. Translated from the original Latin and French. Edinburgh and Philadelphia, s. a. 4 vols.

By the same editor, *Lettres Françaises de Jean Calvin*. Paris, 1854. 2. vols.

Bulletin historique et littéraire de la Société de l'Histoire du Protestantisme Français. Paris, 1853, foil. This monthly, now (1899) in its forty-eighth year, contains a vast number of original documents heretofore unpublished, as well as monographs, etc., and is indispensable as one of the chief sources for the history of the French Reformation and of the Huguenots.

Calendar of State Papers (Foreign Series) preserved in the State Paper Department of H. M. Public Record Office. Reigns of Edward VI, Mary, Elizabeth. Edited successively by Turnbull, Tytler, and Stevenson. London, 1861, foll.

Calvini Opera. Edited by the Strassburg professors, Baum, Cunitz, Reuss, Brunswick, 1863, foll. More than fifty volumes of this accurate and comprehensive work have appeared. The letters to Calvin and other illustrative matter are scarcely less important for history than the Reformer's own letters.

Condé, Mémoires de. London, 1743. 6 vols., 4to. A reproduction of rare tracts, etc., of the sixteenth century, together with some hitherto unedited papers, almost all of great interest and permanent value.

Crespin, Jean (Latinised Crispinus), *Actiones et Monimenta Martyrum*. Geneva, 1560. For full titles of the early French and Latin editions, see p. 36. An accurate republication of the later editions in the French language, was published with notes of Lelievre. 3 vols. Toulouse, 1889.

De Thou, Jacques Auguste (Latinised Thuanus), *Historiarum sui Temporis Libri 138*. Published in French as well as in Latin in many shapes and different number of volumes. The French ed. with the imprint of The Hague, 1746, in 11 vols., has been used.

Haton, Claude, *Mémoires*. Edited by Felix Bourquelot. 2 vols. Paris, 1857. The work forms part of the magnificent 'Collection de Documents Inédits sur l'Histoire de France,' published under the auspices of the Ministry of Public Instruction at the suggestion of Guizot. Haton was a priest, of Meriot, near Provins. His memoirs cover the years 1553–82.

Herminjard, A. L., *Correspondance des Réformateurs dans les Pays de Langue Française*. Geneva and Paris, 1866, foll. 9 vols, have appeared up to 1897, reaching only to 1544.

Histoire Ecclésiastique des Églises Réformées au Royaumè de France. Édition nouvelle avec Commentaire, etc. Edited by Baum and Cunitz. 3 vols. Paris, 1883–89. Best edition of this great history which, was first published at Antwerp in 1580, See p. 310.

Jacob, Paul L., *Œuvres Françoises de Calvin, recueillies pour la première fois, précédées de sa vie, par Theodore de Bèze*. Paris, 1842.

Languet, Hubert, *Epislolæ Secretæ*. Halle, 1699. Collection of despatches of a shrewd, honourable, and well informed statesman.

La Place, Pierre de, *Commentaires de l'Estat de la Religion et Rèpublique sons les rois Henry et François seconds et Charles neufviesme*. Paris, 1865. Reprinted in the 'Panthéon Littéraire,' ed. by J. A. C. Buchon. Paris, 1836. The author, an eminent judge, was murdered at the Massacre of St Bartholomew's Day.

Layard, Sir Henry, *Despatches of Michele Suriano and Marc' Antonio Barbara, Venetian Ambassadors at the Court of France, 1560–1563*. (Publications of the Hug. Soc. of London) Lymington, 1891.

Le Chroniqueur. An historical collection under this name published fortnightly at Lausanne in 1835 and 1836, by L. Vulliemin. Contains a detailed narrative and to a great extent the documentary history of the corresponding years three centuries back.

Le Livre du Recteur. Catalogue of the Students of the Académie of Geneva from 1559–1859. Edited by C. Le Fort, G. Revillot, and E. Fick. Geneva, 1860.

Pasquier, Étienne, *Les Recherches de la France*. Paris, 1621.

Ræmond, Florimond de, *Historia de Ortu, Progressu, et Ruina Hæreseon hujus sæculi*. Cologne, 1614. The author, a counsellor of the Parliament of Toulouse, had from a Protestant become a Roman Catholic, and his book betrays his strong Roman Catholic bias. It is lively and interesting and is full of striking facts.

Recueil des choses mémorables faites et passées pour le faict de la Religion et Estat de ce Royaume, depuis la mort du Roy Henry II jusques an commencement des troubles. S. l. 1565. Subsequently incorporated in the first volume of the *Mémoires de Condé.*

Serres, Jean de (Serranus), *Commentarii de Statu Religiouis et Reipublicæ in regno Gallia.* In five parts or volumes, published in 1571–80, in the first four *sine loco*, the last at Leyden. One of the most faithful and valuable of the histories of the French Protestants from the persecution at Paris in 1557 to the publication of the Edict of 1576. The last volume is exceedingly scarce.

Zurich Letters. Correspondence of several English Bishops with some of the Helvetian Reformers during the reign of Queen Elizabeth. Published by the Parker Society. Cambridge, 1846.

II. BIOGRAPHIES OF BEZA AND OTHER WORKS DRAWN FROM THE SOURCES.

Baum, Johann Wilhelm, *Theodor Beza nach handschriftlichen Quellen dargestellt.* Leipzig, vol. i., 1843, vol. ii., in two parts, 1851, 1852. The most thorough and scholarly life of Beza, but coming down only to 1563. The appendices in this work contain many documents, especially letters of Beza printed from copies made by Prof. Baum in various libraries on the Continent. These are generally referred to in the notes as 'Baum Doc.'

Benrath, Karl, *Bernardino Ochino of Siena.* Translated from the German by H. Zimmern. New York, 1877.

Douen, O., *Clément Marot et le Psautier Huguenot*. Paris, 1878, 1879. 2 vols. A work of wide research published in part at the expense of the French government, and printed by the national printing office. A portion of the second volume is devoted to the melodies of the Psalms. The author's bias is in favour of Marot, whom he regards as a finer type of the reformatory movement than Beza.

Gaberel, J., *Histoire de l'Église de Genève depuis le Commencement de la Réforme jusqu' en 1815*. Geneva, 1855–63, 3 vols.

Haag, Eugène and Émile, *La France Protestante*. An exceedingly valuable biographical work. The first edition, Paris, 1856, foll., 10 vols., is out of print. The second, edited by Henri Bordier, Paris, 1877, foll., projected on a much more extended plan, has been temporarily interrupted at the close of the sixth volume by Mr Bordier's death.

Heppe, Heinrich, Theodor Beza, *Leben und ausgewählte Schriften*. Elberfelt, 1861. The author, a professor at Marburg, contributed this volume to the series ('Leben und ausg. Schriften der Väter und Begründer d. reformirten Kirche') edited by Hagenbach. Less full and detailed than Baum's biography, it possesses the great advantage of covering the entire life of Beza.

Sayous, A., *Études Litiéraires sur les Écrivains Français de la Réformation*. Paris, 1841. 2 vols. Discriminating and scholarly sketches. The sketch of Beza in the first volume covers more than a hundred pages.

Schlosser, F. C, *Leben des Theodor de Beza und des Peter Martyr Vermili*. Heidelberg, 1809. The life of Beza is written fairly but unevenly and with occasional inaccuracy.

Weiss, N., *La Chambre Ardente*. Paris, 1889. A study on religious persecution under Francis I and Henry II, containing about five hundred recently discovered sentences rendered by the Parliament of Paris.

Many other works less frequently used are omitted from this list.

To the above may be added the following three Huguenot histories written by the author, to which frequent reference is made and in which additional authorities are given.

History of the Rise of the Huguenots of France. New York, 1879, London, 1880. 2 vols. Covers the period from 1512 to 1574, including the Massacre of St Bartholomew's Day.

The Huguenots and Henry of Navarre. New York and London, 1886. 2 vols. Covers the period from 1574 to 1610, or to the death of Henry IV, including the Wars of the League, the Abjuration of Henry IV, and the Enactment of the Edict of the Nantes.

The Huguenots and the Revocation of the Edict of Nantes. New York and London, 1895. 2 vols. Covers the period from 1610 to 1802, terminating with the full recognition of Protestantism by Napoleon Bonaparte.

INDEX

The Banner of Truth Trust originated in 1957 in London. The founders believed that much of the best literature of historic Christianity had been allowed to fall into oblivion and that, under God, its recovery could well lead not only to a strengthening of the church, but to true revival.

Interdenominational in vision, this publishing work is now international, and our lists include a number of contemporary authors, together with classics from the past. The translation of these books into many languages is encouraged.

A monthly magazine, *The Banner of Truth*, is also published, and further information about this, and all our other publications, may be found on our website, banneroftruth.org, or by contacting the offices below:

Head Office:
3 Murrayfield Road
Edinburgh
EH12 6EL
United Kingdom

Email: info@banneroftruth.co.uk

North America Office:
PO Box 621
Carlisle, PA 17013
United States of America

Email: info@banneroftruth.org

Geneva